The Weaver's Book of FABRIC DESIGN

The Weaver's Book of FABRIC DESIGN

JANET PHILLIPS

ST. MARTIN'S PRESS, NEW YORK

To Nigel and Alistair

ACKNOWLEDGEMENTS

I would like to thank Liz Humphries for her enthusiastic approach and constant hard work in weaving the many samples I gave her, for her encouragement in the early stages, and for her constructive criticism of the final manuscript.

Another special thank-you must go to Evelyn Tucker for her speed, accuracy and enthusiasm in typing the manuscript many times, and to my husband, Nigel Phillips, for his continuous support in all my weaving activities and for taking all the excellent black and white and colour photographs carefully and patiently.

I would also like to thank the numerous friends and acquaintances who answered queries quickly and fully: Virginia Buxton, Joyce Coleman, J. Piper, Mary Boyle, Rosalind Dorning, Janet de Boer, Savithri Nandaraj and many members of the Oxford Guild of Weavers, Spinners and Dyers.

I should also mention the staff of the Scottish College of Textiles, who 12 years ago introduced me to the wealth of colour, shape and texture that can be found in woven cloth, a world that is still wide open with interest and excitement.

All the fabrics illustrated in the book were designed by the author.

J.P.

Printed in the United Kingdom

THE WEAVER'S BOOK OF FABRIC DESIGN

Library of Congress Catalog Card Number 83-50272

ISBN 0 312 85980 5

First published in Great Britain by B.T. Batsford Ltd
First US edition

10 9 8 7 6 5 4 3 2 1

CONTENTS

COLOUR PLATES

GLOSSARY OF TERMS

BACK—The underside of a fabric.
BEAT-UP—The precise action of hitting a pick, with the reed, into the fell of the cloth with the exact same strength as previous beats.
BOBBIN—A spool for holding weft which fits into a shuttle.
BOBBIN WINDER—Geared spindle used to fill up bobbins with weft evenly and quickly.
CARDING—Brushing wool fibres in order to produce an even web prior to spinning.
CHEESE—A package of yarn wound onto a straight bobbin.
CLEAN CUT JOIN—Joining two weaves so that the warp floats of one weave coincide with the weft floats of the other.
COMBING—A process which ensures that only the longest fibres are presented parallel to the spinning machines in order to produce a smooth and even worsted yarn.
CONE—A package of weaving yarn wound into a conical shape.
COUNT—A number denoting the thickness of a yarn in relation to its length and weight.
COUNTERBALANCE—A loom shedding mechanism which allows the shafts to balance against each other.
COUNTERMARCHE—A loom shedding mechanism which allows each shaft to move independently, either up or down.
CRABBING—The stabilising of a wool fabric by means of heat and steam.
CRAZING—An ugly distorting pattern which often results after a plain weave fabric is washed.
CREEL—A frame for holding yarn packages ready for warping.
CRIMP—The natural waviness inherent in wool fibres.
DENT—The space between each reed wire.
DOUP—A half heddle which causes ends to cross over each other during weaving.
DRAW—Threading the warp ends through the heddle eyes on the shafts.
DRESSING THE LOOM—The several processes of transferring a warp onto a loom, threading it up through the shafts and the reed, and preparing the loom for weaving.
END—One thread of the warp.
FACE—The top side of a cloth.
FANCY YARNS—Yarns spun to produce textured effects.
FELL—The edge of a cloth formed by the last pick that has been beaten-up into it by the reed during weaving.
FILLING—*See* Weft.
FLOAT—The length, that an end or pick extends across the face of a cloth before it intersects and runs along the back.
FOLD—To loosely twist two or more yarns together.
GROUND CLOTH—A stable fabric on top of which can be woven simultaneously an interesting pattern effect.
HARNESS—*See* Shaft
HEDDLE (HEALD)—String or wire cords suspended on the shafts, with a hole at their centre through which ends can be threaded.
HEDDLING—The process of threading (drawing) the ends through the heddle eyes.
INTERSECT—The point on the weave where an end or pick stops floating on the face of a cloth and moves onto the back, and vice versa.
JACK LOOM—A loom mechanism which uses two pivoting levers positioned underneath each shaft, and pedals to lift the appropriate shafts.
JACKS—Pairs of wooden levers pivoting above the shafts on countermarche looms.
KEMPS—Coarse wool fibres which resist the take-up of dyes.
LAM (LAMM)—Narrow wooden bars found on counterbalance, countermarche and jack looms, which produce the intermediary action between the shafts and the pedals.
MILLING—Subjecting a woollen cloth to heat, moisture and agitation in order to allow the fibres to expand and felt up, thus giving a cloth bulk and a fibrous handle.

PEDAL (TREADLE)—Pivoted levers used to activate the lams and shafts of foot powered looms.
PICK (SHOT)—One weft thread.
PIRN—A conical shaped bobbin that fits into a shuttle and unwinds from the narrow end.
PLY—To twist together two or more single threads to make a plied yarn.
POINT PAPER—Graph paper divided into $\frac{1}{8}$″; $\frac{1}{2}$″; 1″ sections, used to interpret weave interlacings and drafting and lifting plans.
RAISING—A finishing process given to woollen fabrics, which brushes the face and gives it a fluffy surface.
REED—A coarse closed comb which spaces the warp out evenly and parallel, and also beats each pick into the fell of the cloth.
ROVING—A wool sliver that has been reduced in diameter to make it suitable to be spun into yarn.
SCOUR—Washing a cloth in hot soapy water to remove oil and dirt.
SELVAGE—A firmly woven closed edge on either side of a cloth.
SETT—The correct number of ends and picks per cm/inch that must be put into a cloth to produce the desired appearance, weight and handle, when using a particular weave and yarn.
SHAFT (HARNESS)—A pair of flat sticks, or a metal or wooden frame, which is suspended inside the loom, and which carries the heddles.
SHED—The opening formed by the shafts rising and/or falling, through which the shuttle, holding weft, can pass.
SHOT—*See* Pick.
SHUTTLE—A tool which allows the weft to pass quickly and smoothly through the shed.
SINGLES YARN—A yarn produced from spinning raw fibres, that is not plied.
SKEIN—A hank of yarn.
SLEY (SLEYING)—Threading ends through the dents of a reed.
SLIVER—A twistless rope-like form of fibres produced by carding.
SQUARE SETT—When the number of ends per cm/inch equals the picks per cm/inch.
STRETCHER—*See* Temple.
SWIFT—A tool for holding different sizes of skein.
TAKE-UP—The decrease in the length and width of a warp due to the ends and picks bending around each other as they interlace.
TEMPLE (STRETCHER)—A device to hold the fell of the cloth wide during weaving.
TENTERHOOKS—Pins used to hold the cloth wide and parallel on the tenter.
THRUM—Yarn wastage produced because the last metre of warp cannot pass the shafts, and therefore cannot be woven.
TWIST—The means of giving staple fibres strength and cohesion.
WADDING—A thick end or pick used to increase the prominence of a cord.
WARP—The group of parallel threads that stretch between the back beam and front beam of a loom, and run along the length of a woven cloth.
WARPING FRAME and WARPING MILL—Devices which enable a warp to be made with all the ends of the same length and of even tension.
WEFT (FILLING)—The group of parallel threads that stretch across the width of a cloth.
WORSTED—Wool fibres which have been combed prior to spinning to produce a smooth and strong yarn.

INTRODUCTION

This book is concerned with the designing of woven fabrics on four-shaft and multi-shaft handlooms. I have limited it to those cloths which can be woven using the basic mechanisms of a loom, without having to resort to loom or thread manipulation.

To me, designing a woven fabric means thinking about the many factors which together create the fabric I want; the weight, the feel, the look, the size. Time spent thinking before starting production is vital as well as being stimulating; it is worth more than the many hours that will be needed actually to produce the cloth, enjoyable though these hours will be.

In fact thinking, and thus designing, should take place all the time. I am subconsciously looking at my surroundings and noting shapes, colours and textures in natural and man-made things, which I then try to relate to weave patterns and textures that I know. Quite often I note them down in a sketch book, which can be referred to later when needing ideas to begin designing a cloth.

I have devoted a chapter to each of the different factors which go to make up a cloth: the fibres, the yarns, their colour, weight and texture, the numerous weaves that can be employed and the finishes to be given to a cloth after it is woven. I believe that only with a thorough knowledge of these aspects can handweavers begin to make a constructive decision about the components of their fabrics and thus become designers as well.

A large part of the book covers the construction on paper of the many traditional weaves that are at the disposal of the modern handweaver to use. Where possible a photograph of the basic woven effect accompanies each weave diagram, allowing the reader to visualise a weave pattern in cloth form before actually weaving a sample themselves. I hope that with careful study of the weave diagrams and the photographs, and by following the design ideas suggested, the weaver can understand and experiment with the basic weaves, on and off the loom, and that this will lead on to the individual interpretation of traditional patterns and, I hope, the development of innovative designs.

The ability to understand weave diagrams and thus to design off the loom is crucial to enabling a weaver to become a designer as well. All too often the shaft-controlled loom seems to become the decision maker in regard to the patterns that can be woven. Many books reinforce this idea by describing patterns and their developments in terms of shaft drafting plans and shaft lifting or treadling plans. The shafts and treadles, though, do not create the pattern, the ends and picks do. These can be made to interlace in any order to create shapes and textures. The weave is, therefore, the tool to use when designing, and whereas one must be aware of the loom's mechanical limitations, the loom is in fact merely the means to produce the actual fabric that you have already designed.

I have for this reason only illustrated weave diagrams, and have not normally given their drafting and lifting plans. I have, however, given precise instructions as to how these plans can be simply and quickly obtained from a weave diagram, and it should only require a beginner to follow the procedure through a few times, before it becomes a quick and easy routine to be adhered to whenever a weave has been constructed.

All decisions concerning the choice of the fibre, yarn, weave and finishes, however, must be regarded in conjunction with the purpose to which a cloth will be put after it is woven. Clothing fabrics need to be of a material that is comfortable to wear and easy to launder. Any weave that is used should be stable enough to maintain the shape of the garment, but not be so stiff as to produce an inflexible boardy cloth. The surface pattern must be designed in proportion to the size and shape of the person that will be wearing the garment. On the other hand, a close sett with a tightly interlacing weave is an important factor for an upholstery fabric, as is a fibre and yarn that is hardwearing. Textured yarns made up of slubs or loops would not be as practical as a more tightly twisted yarn.

Upholstery and furnishing fabrics can also usually cope with bold surface patterns as large areas are being covered. Blankets, in contrast, should be soft and flexible, as must shawls and scarves.

It is this concept of producing functional fabrics that is so challenging to the modern handweaver. Fabrics are an essential part of living, certainly in the western world, as they appear in the home, and in work and leisure places. It should be the aim of all textile designers, whether they are weaving for pleasure or working in industry, to ensure that the fabrics they design are imaginative and fashionable, yet practical, thus enabling everyone to live in more pleasant surroundings. I hope this book gives some help to reaching this end. It is aimed at those weavers who already have a basic knowledge of dressing their loom and of making their loom operate smoothly. I hope it will be of value to the beginner, building up essential knowledge and confidence in designing, to the student looking for excitement in functional fabric design, and to the more experienced amateur or professional who needs to see another designer's view of a situation in order to stimulate new ideas.

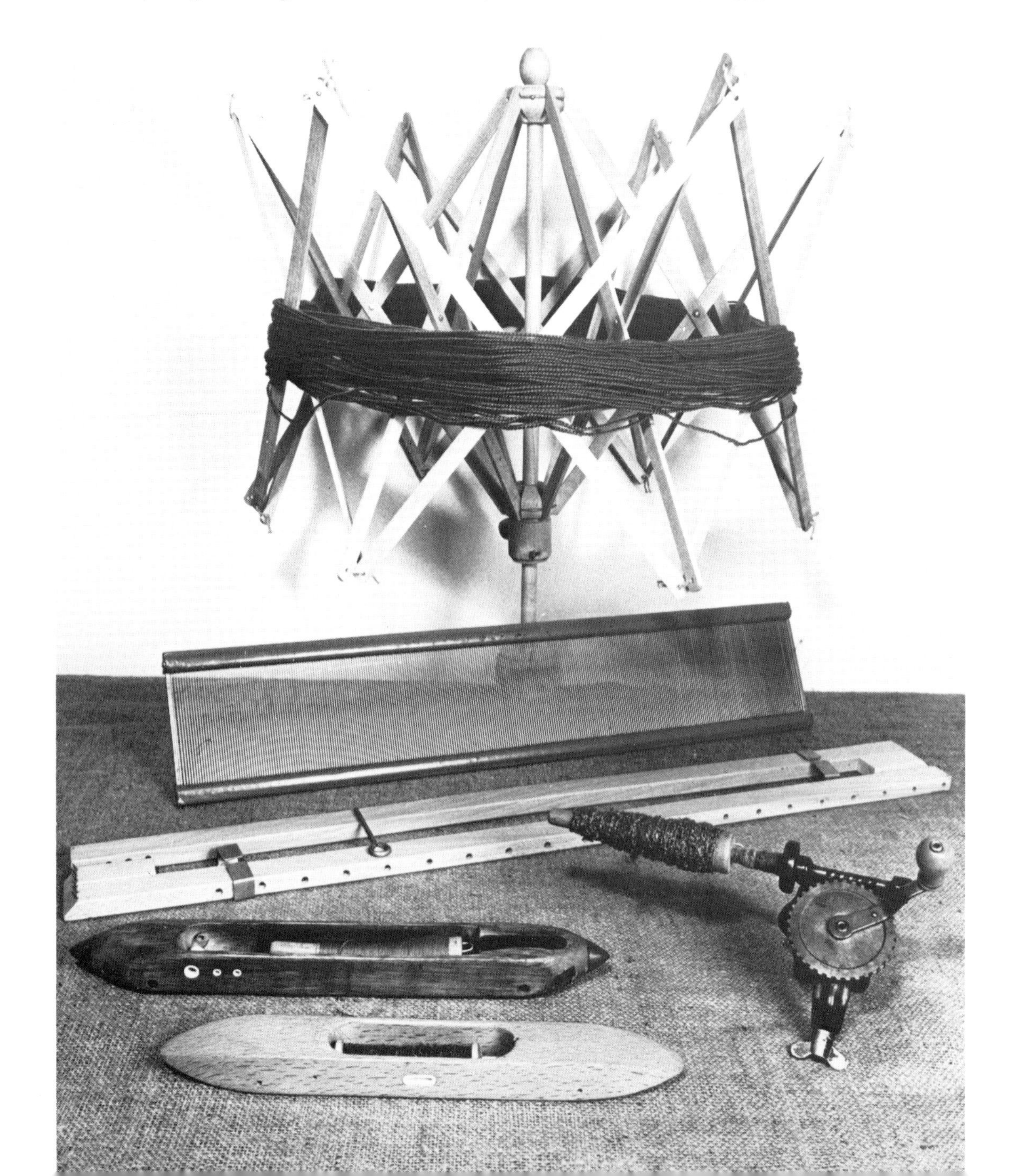

TOOLS AND EQUIPMENT

There are numerous pieces of equipment which can be owned by the weaver. Some are so basic that to be without them would make weaving very slow and difficult. These include a well-built and smoothly-working loom with a selection of reeds to fit, a sturdy warping frame or mill on which to make a long and even warp, and a few shuttles with bobbins or pirns to fit for sending the weft across the warp. Other items are useful additions to the weaving studio which help to speed up the weaving process, or improve the appearance of the finished cloth. A bobbin winder quickly fills a bobbin full of weft, a swift neatly holds a hank of yarn for ease of unwinding and a yarn creel conveniently holds many yarn packages ready for warping and winding. A temple will help to keep a cloth at the correct width during weaving and ensure a neat selvage (Figures 1, 2 and 3).

Only two pieces of equipment, however, have a precise influence over the design of the cloth. These are the loom and the reed.

The Shaft-controlled Loom (Figure 4)

The function of a loom is to hold the lengthwise threads (*the warp*) taut during weaving. All shaft-controlled looms achieve this by having a back beam and a front beam between which the warp is stretched. All additional parts of the loom have been designed to facilitate good tension control over the warp and to speed up the weaving process.

The shaft-controlled loom uses the shafts which are fitted with heddles to lift and lower each warp thread (*an end*), to create a passage (*shed*) through which the crossing threads (*the weft*) pass. The loom is designed to allow each weft thread (*a pick*) to traverse directly from one side of the loom to the other. As handweavers, we can deviate from this regime and lift certain ends by hand or bring the weft up to the face of the cloth at different places if necessary, but if the loom is to be used as intended, the shafts in fact impose considerable design limitations on the weaver, for the benefit of speed and efficiency.

Fig 1 Weaving equipment
From top to bottom: swift, reed, temple, bobbin winder with pirn, fly shuttle, boat shuttle.

SHAFTS

The shafts are either wood or metal frames suspended in the loom. Each frame holds numerous string or wire heddles. These heddles have an eye or hole in their centre through which the ends are threaded (Figure 5).

The majority of handlooms accommodate four shafts. The variety of different patterns and textures which can be woven with four shafts are numerous. However, looms which can accommodate 8, 12, 16 or even 24 shafts allow, progressively, a greater variety of weaves and patterns to be woven, giving the weaver greater freedom for design. These larger looms usually have the facility of removing some of the shafts, so that any number of shafts can be used at one time depending on the pattern requirements. Weaving, however, becomes slightly slower and harder work as the shaft numbers increase. Eight shafts are an acceptable number, being still light to work with, like a four-shaft loom, but considerably increasing the design scope for the weaver. An understanding of designing with four shafts is useful before attempting to design with more shafts, although the design procedure for working out a pattern is exactly the same.

The Reed

The reed is an essential piece of equipment and is required in addition to the loom. Its purpose is to space the warp ends parallel, in a predetermined order and with a predetermined number of ends per cm or inch, known as the sett. In addition, it has to beat the picks evenly into the fell of the cloth after each shuttle has traversed the shed.

It is a coarse closed comb between 7–11 cm (3″ to $4\frac{1}{2}$″) in height (Figure 1). The length varies

OPPOSITE PAGE **Fig 2** Warping frame

Fig 3 Yarn creel

Fig 4 Table loom
(a) Front (cloth) beam, (b) Breast bar,
(c) Batten, (d) Reed, (e) Loom frame,
(f) Shafts, (g) Levers, (h) Back (warp) beam,
(i) back bar.

Fig 5 Shafts with heddles

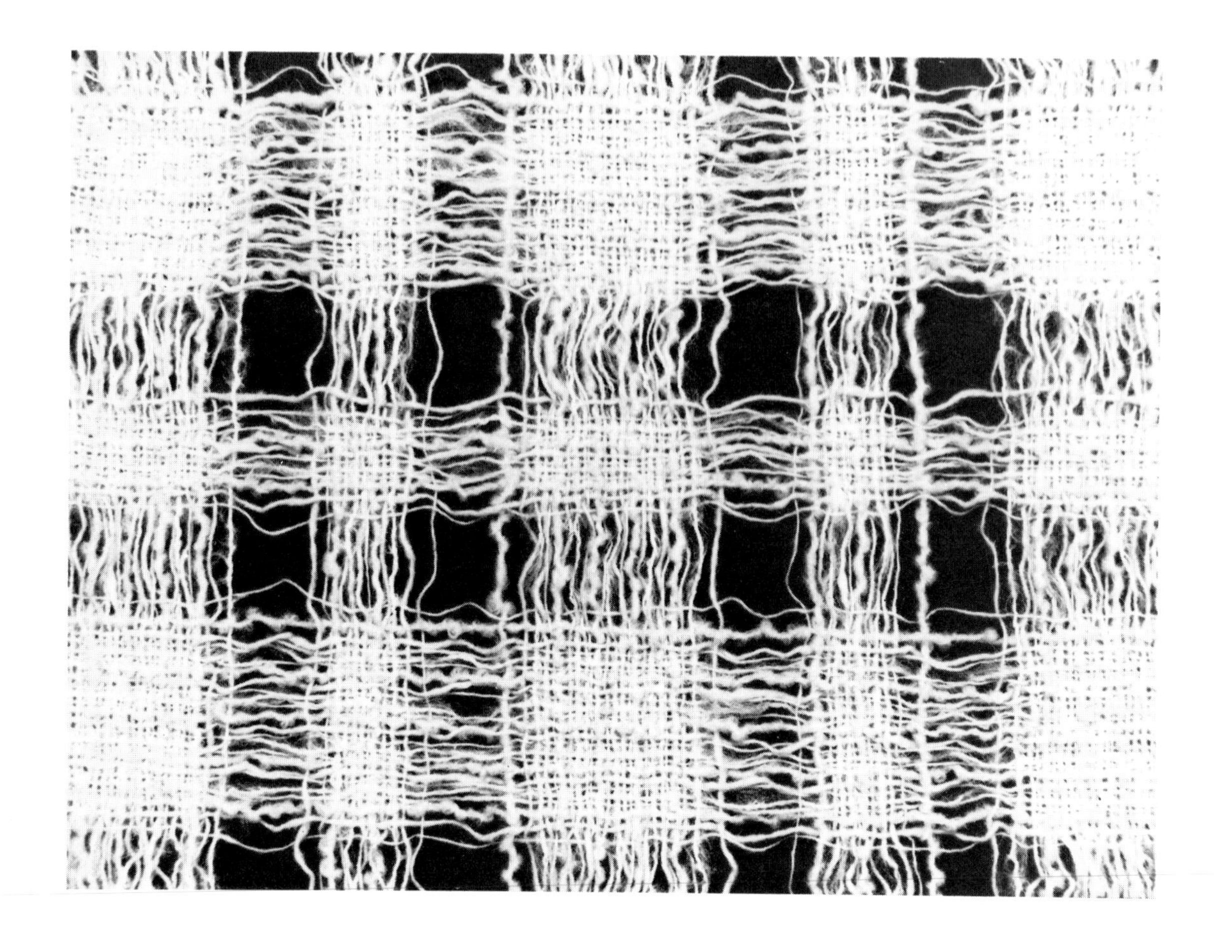

Fig 6 Plain weave with spaced warp and weft

according to the weaving width of your loom. The teeth of the comb are metal and called reed wires. The spaces between the reed wires are called slits or dents. The number of dents per cm or inch determine the reed count and this number is usually engraved on the ends of the reed. Old reeds are sold with reed counts per inch, while modern reeds are calculated as dents per 1 cm or per 10 cm. All sett calculations (see Chapter 5) should be worked out in the same system as your reed counts.

A different reed is required for every different sett that you might weave. As reeds are expensive, it is impractical to own very many. Three is probably the minimum necessary. If medium- to heavy-weight fabrics are to be woven, these could be a 2/cm (6/inch), 3/cm (8/inch) and 4/cm (10/inch). These reeds will cover a wide range of setts, if threaded (sleyed or dented) one end in every other dent, one per dent, two per dent, three per dent or four per dent. Table 1 shows the range of setts per cm or inch possible with these reeds.

Setts of 1, 1.5, 2, and 3 per cm, or 3, 4, 5, 6 and 8 per inch can cope with most weft faced rugs and very thick fabrics.

Setts of 3 to 6 per cm, or 8 to 18 per inch are suitable for medium weight cloths.

Setts of 6 to 9 per cm, or 18 to 24 per inch weave finer cloths.

Setts of 9 to 16 per cm, or 24 to 40 per inch are for very fine fabrics.

If necessary reeds can be sleyed with a different number of ends per dent, for example 2 ends in one dent 3 ends in next dent, repeat. In a 2/cm (6/inch) reed sleyed in this manner, a sett of 5/cm (15 ends per inch) would result.

It is better if possible to sley ends in a reed double rather than single per dent. This makes a more even spread of the ends over the fabric and reed marks, which are lines running up the fabric, are less likely to occur. On the other hand, once as many as 6 or 8 ends are sleyed together, reed marks might show again.

Deciding which reed to choose for which sett is also governed by the hairiness of the yarn and the number of knots there might be. If a hairy yarn is

Table 1

Ends sleyed	Ends PER CM	Ends PER INCH	Ends PER CM	Ends PER INCH	Ends PER CM	Ends PER INCH
One every other dent	1	3	1.5	4	2	5
REED COUNT One per dent	2	6	3	8	4	10
Two per dent	4	12	6	16	8	20
Three per dent	6	18	9	24	12	30
Four per dent	8	24	12	32	16	40

being used, a slightly coarser reed should be chosen as a fine reed will cause unnecessary friction.

Some weaves have several ends working in identical order next to each other. If possible, it is advisable to allow the reed wires to split these similar ends so that they do not roll over each other in the cloth and thus show up as faults.

DESIGNING WITH THE REED

The reed is one of the few pieces of equipment which can be used directly to design with.

1 *Spaced sleying*

Every dent in the reed need not hold an end. If quite small gaps (up to 6 cm, $2\frac{1}{2}''$) are left in the reed before normal sleying resumes, the woven cloth would have stripes of normal fabric alternating with long weft floats. If the picking and beat-up is broken in a similar manner, a lacy open work cloth results (Figure 6).

2 *Uneven density*

The reed can be sleyed to produce a variety of cloth densities or setts across its width. Certain sections are sleyed oversett and gradually the sleying passes through normal sett to undersett. If this is combined with a twill weave, an undulating line occurs (Figure 7). Plain weave also reacts well to this treatment.

Fig 7 3/2/1/2 twill with uneven sleying giving an undulating twill

2 FIBRES AND YARNS AND THEIR INFLUENCE ON DESIGN

Fibres and yarns are the raw material of the weaver. The choice of fibre is perhaps the most important consideration in the design of a fabric. The inherent characteristics of the fibre are the basis to the quality and properties of the fabric. Although spinning, weaving and cloth finishing processes can vary, the appearance and texture of the fibre, its intrinsic features, cannot be changed. There is a reasonably large variety to choose from. All have distinctive characteristics and degrees of versatility which enables a constructive decision about their suitability in any cloth to be made.

Experience in using a variety of materials is the best aid to choosing the correct fibres and yarns for a particular design, while a knowledge of fibre properties and spinning methods is also necessary. Experience enables one to understand the behaviour and appearance of fibres in different situations and thus allows one to assess their suitability for a particular project.

This experience, however, can only be built up slowly. Initially, I would advise beginners to restrict themselves to two or three basic yarns within one fibre range and experiment completely with these before moving on to something different. It is only after weaving several items with the same materials, and watching the reaction, that one can truly begin to design with them. Slowly, additional yarns and fibres can be introduced as new ideas emerge.

Awareness can also be built up by collecting examples of the many fibres and yarns that are available, and continually trying to get the feel of their different properties. Yarn and fibre examples can easily be obtained from suppliers, while actual fabric samples, from shops, show the traditional uses and handle of many fibres and yarns.

For handweavers it is wise to choose the best quality fibres and yarns that are available, assuming they are also the most suitable for the project. The amount of time and effort involved in handweaving something warrants this quality. It is very important, however, that the final choice made should excite and inspire you to use it in a cloth.

Fibres

Textile fibres are generally thin and hair-like and have sufficient length and flexibility to be able to be spun into yarns. The fibres available to the handweaver fall into two main groups; the natural fibres and the man-made fibres.

Natural fibres have been used to make textiles for thousands of years and are obtained from animal, vegetable and mineral sources. Man-made fibres have been developed since as early as the 1880's. They are manufactured by machines either from cellulose or protein materials which are not fibre-shaped (known as Regenerated Fibres), or from chemical compounds based on substances like coal or petroleum (called Synthetic Fibres).

All man-made fibres can be perfectly controlled during manufacture and their evenness and quality guaranteed. Natural fibres, on the other hand are produced in a range of qualities determined by the wide difference in growing conditions around the world, plant varieties and breeds of animals.

Table 2 lists the fibres most commonly available and used by hand weavers.

The individual fibres within the natural or man-made groups can be of two types; either filament or staple.

FILAMENT

Filament fibres are very long and continuous in length. Silk, the only natural filament fibre, varies from about 1000 m–3000 m in length. Man-made fibres are manufactured as filaments and can be several kilometres long.

STAPLE

Staple fibres are of limited length, in practice from about the 10 mm of a short cotton fibre up to about 900 mm of flax fibre. To make a continuous length, these short fibres have to be spun and twisted together. All the natural fibres other than silk are staple fibres, although waste silk obtained during silk production are short. Man-made fibres can be converted into staple by cutting them into short lengths.

Fig 8 Wool staples
From left to right: Border Leicester, Dorset Horn, Black Welsh Mountain. Bottom row: Southdown.

Animal Fibres

WOOL

Wool is obtained from the fleece of the domesticated sheep. It is widely available in both fibre and yarn form. It is an exceedingly versatile fibre and can be used for all kinds of end uses from fine delicate shawls to hardwearing carpets. Wool has a number of excellent natural properties including exceptional resilience and elasticity; these are due mainly to the spindle-shaped cells of the fibre's structure and the waviness called crimp inherent in the fibre. It has an ability to shed water and will absorb excess moisture without feeling cold and clammy. It is an excellent insulator, is crease-resistant and flame-resistant. It has an unusual natural tendency to felt or mat together when under

Table 2 *N.B.* *F* = Filament S = staple

NATURAL FIBRES				MAN-MADE FIBRES	
Animal		*Vegetable*		*Regenerated*	*Synthetic*
Silk	(F)	Cotton	(S)	Rayons	Polyamides (Nylon)
Wool	(S)	Flax	(S)	Acetates	Polyesters
Mohair	(S)	Jute	(S)	Triacetates	Acrylics
Cashmere	(S)	Hemp	(S)		Modacrylics
Camel	(S)	Ramie	(S)		Elastomeric
Alpaca	(S)				
Angora	(S)				
Goat	(S)				

the influence of heat, moisture and movement. This property, caused by the minute overlapping scales on the individual fibres, can be used to excellent design effect if done under controlled conditions, but it also creates wool's main disadvantage of requiring careful cleaning and laundering. It has a good affinity to dyes so that yarns are usually available in a wide range of colours. Its natural colours range from creamy whites through beautiful browns and greys.

It grows to a variety of staple lengths ranging from about 25 mm–400 mm (1″–16″) (Figure 8). The shortest fibres from 25 mm–100 mm (1″–4″) are the finest and warmest, they have the most crimp, but are not the strongest or the most durable. As the staple length gets longer, the fibres increase in strength, resilience and thickness, but diminish in softness and crimpiness. Some longer fibres have an attractive lustre to them. Some fleeces contain kempy fibres. These are white, brittle fibres which do not take colour during dyeing, giving subsequent yarns a very rough, tweedy appearance.

HAIR FIBRES (Figure 9)

Hair fibres are obtained from the coats of a variety of animals other than the sheep. In general they are used for speciality and luxury purposes as they are more expensive than wool. They are quite often blended with wool before spinning, but they can be spun alone. Interesting designs based on the interplay of textures can be created by weaving wool yarns and hair yarns together.

The properties and characteristics of hair fibres are described below.

Mohair

Mohair is obtained from the coat of the Angora goat. The properties which make mohair interesting and valuable are its long length—up to 250 mm (10″),—strength and soundness of fibre, springy and resilient nature, and in particular an excellent lustre. Once spun it produces a very attractive and manageable yarn which does not felt easily. The natural fibres are usually white and can, therefore, be dyed to many beautiful colours.

Cashmere

Cashmere fibres come from the undercoat of the Kashmir or Tibetan goat which lives in Northern India and Asia. These extremely soft downy fibres are between 40 mm–90 mm ($1\frac{1}{2}$″–$3\frac{1}{2}$″) long and vary in colour from brown to greyish white, and have a slight lustre. They produce an extremely warm and soft handling yarn and fabric. The outer coat hairs are longer and coarser.

Alpaca

Alpaca is obtained from the Peruvian llama. The fleece consists of two parts, a coarse outer hair and a soft, highly lustrous undercoat which has little crimp and does not felt easily. This hair is sometimes white, but more usually brown, grey or black, and since it is impossible to bleach, alpaca is used in its natural colours or in blends of these. Alpaca is softer and less resilient than mohair, but not as soft as camel or cashmere.

Camel

The best fibres are obtained from the Bactrian camel from Central Asia. The outer coat is very coarse and tough, but the undercoat is beautifully soft, short and fine. Like Alpaca it cannot be bleached and is, therefore, usually available only in the natural colours of beige through to brown.

Other hair fibres

There are a number of other more unusual animal hairs available which may be of interest to the handweaver. These include goat hair and reindeer hair, which are both coarse. They are usually blended with wool and produce a very tweedy appearance.

Angora rabbit hairs are long and suitable for conventional spinning if blended with wool. They are fine, soft and fluffy.

Wool and Hair Yarns

Wool and hair fibres are spun into yarn by two distinctive spinning methods which considerably affects the final appearance of the yarn and thus the fabric. The shorter fibres are usually spun on the woollen system, resulting in a fibrous and lofty yarn. The longer and more lustrous fibres are usually spun on the worsted system which maintains the lustrous appearance and creates a compact and fairly smooth yarn.

WOOLLEN SPUN YARNS (see photo, p. 20)

Wool or hair fibres spun on the woollen spinning system produce a hairy, springy yarn. During preparation for spinning, the fibres are carded by brushing them between metal wires which creates a thin web of fibres pointing out in all directions. This is called a sliver. The sliver is eventually drawn out into a roving and then twisted into a yarn. Also, prior to carding oil is added to the fibres to prevent fibre breakage during carding and to aid in the drawing out of the fibres (drafting) during spinning. It is the carding process that creates the fibrous and high loft texture of a woollen yarn.

Woollen spun yarns maintain any shrinkage and felting properties inherent in the fibres and therefore weaves, which base their effect on the differential shrinkage of floats work well if woollen spun yarns are used. These yarns also retain good resilience and elasticity, which makes working with them very easy and manageable.

A woollen spun yarn is extremely useful and suitable for many handweaving projects when a warm, soft, hardwearing, flame resistant result is required.

WORSTED SPUN YARNS (see photo, p. 20)
The longer and more lustrous wool and hair fibres are usually spun on the worsted system. This is a more complicated system than woollen spinning and involves a process called combing. After carding, the worsted sliver is deliberately combed straight and parallel, which removes any short or broken fibres and leaves the longer ones of more uniform length to be drawn out and spun. The parallel nature of the fibres enables a much smoother and more compact yarn to be produced of a different appearance to a woollen thread. It also enables much finer yarns to be spun as the fibres are more ideally arranged and the natural lustre present in some qualities of fibres can be preserved. Worsted spun yarns are nearly always supplied as a plied yarn which reinforces the smooth and even character, and also improves on the strength of the thread, as is particularly necessary with a very fine thread.

The colours of worsted spun yarns are usually much clearer and brighter than a woollen yarn, which has the distraction of a hairy surface. Any shrinkage and felting tendencies of the fibres are reduced by worsted spinning. The elasticity, resilience and insulation properties, however, are maintained. Worsted spun yarns are generally more expensive than woollen spun yarns, but are extremely hardwearing and very easy and manageable to work with. They should be chosen if a crisp, smart, hardwearing, crease-resistant fabric is desired.

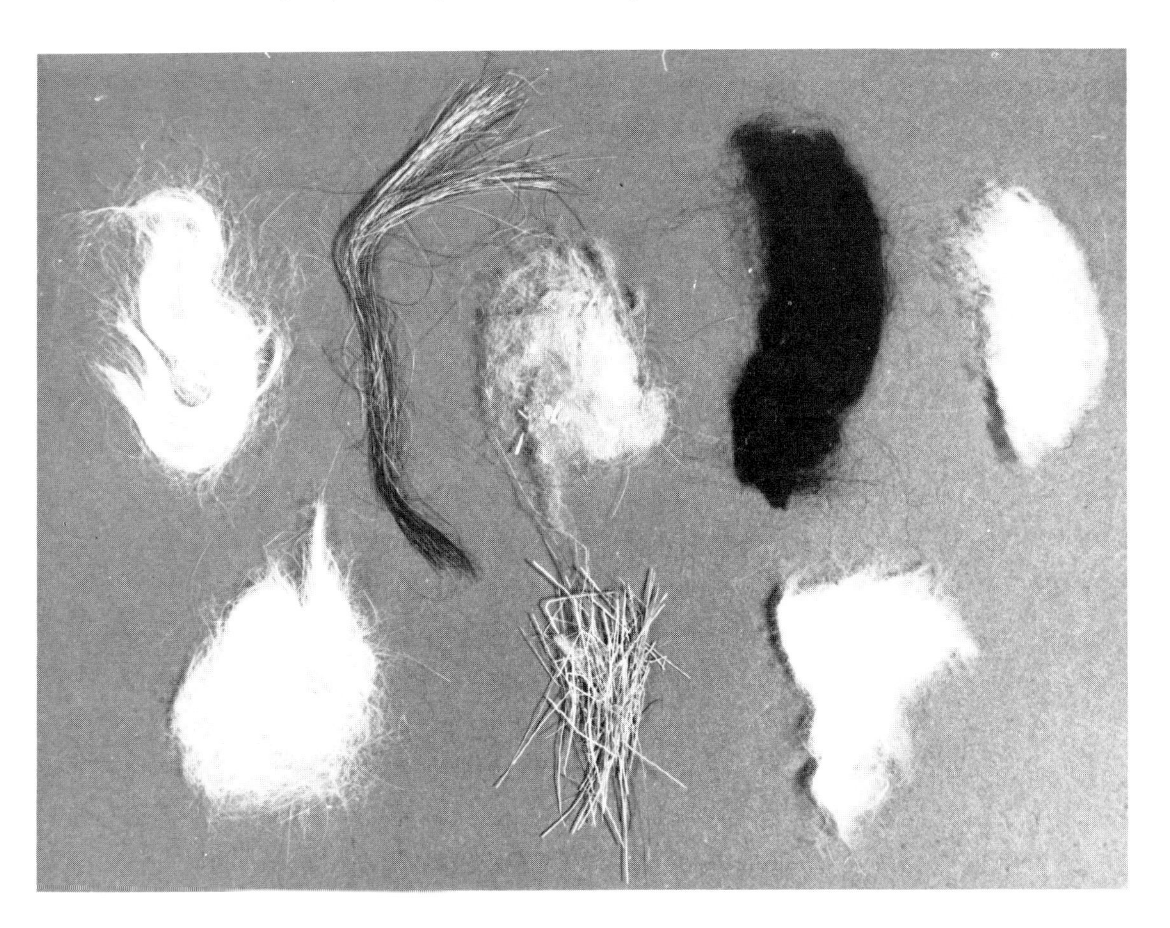

Fig 9 Hair fibres
From left to right top row: Mohair, Goat, Camel, Black Alpaca, Cashmere. Bottom row: Rabbit, Deer, Angora.

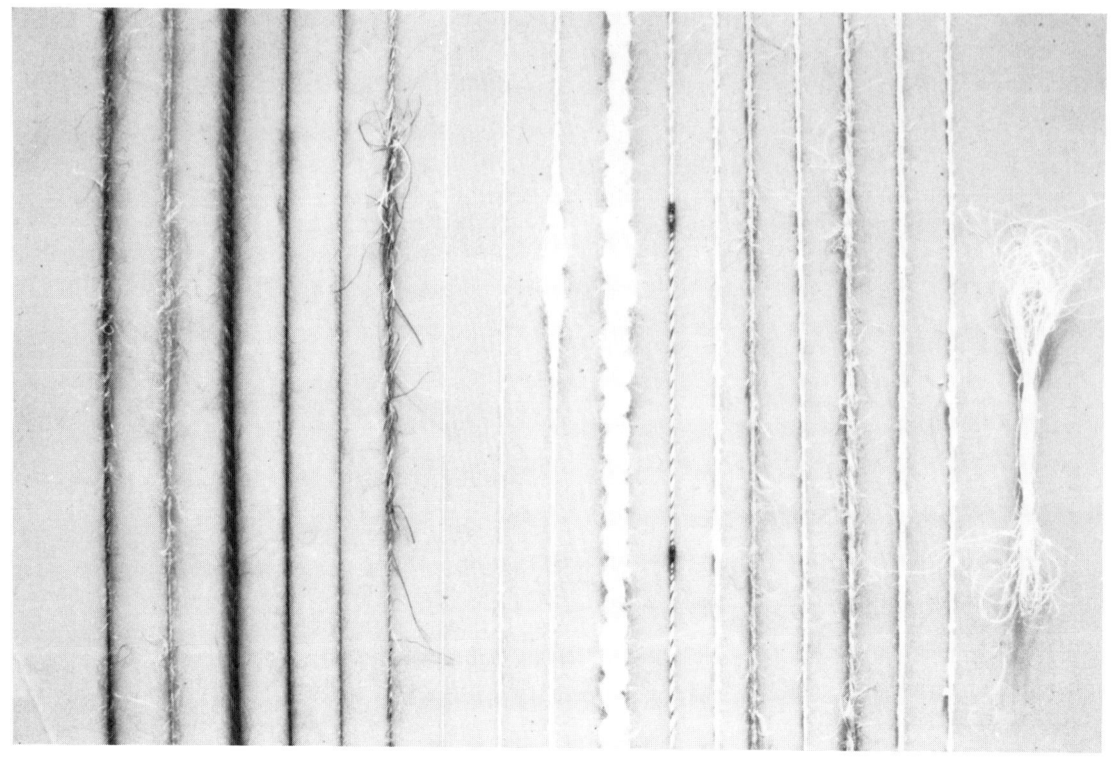

Yarns. From left to right: 9^{c} Woollen; 18^{c} Shetland; 2/2½ Worsted; 2/20 Worsted; 2/32 Worsted; Goat hair; 2/200 Denier Viscose Rayon; 2/20 Mercerised Cotton; 2 Cotton; ¾ Cotton gimp; Cotton knop grandelle; Line/Wool blend; Rough spun linen; 16/2 lea linen; Jute; Silk/Worsted mixture; Spun silk; Raw silk.

Silk

Silk is the only natural filament fibre. It combines the useful qualities of strength, fineness, lustre and elasticity. It is soft and delicate to handle and has superior draping qualities; it has natural crease resistance and warmth without weight. The natural fibre is usually creamy white in colour, but silk yarns can be dyed to beautifully rich colours. The bulk of the world's supply is obtained from the cocoon of the caterpillar of the silk moth, *Bombyx mori*. The fully grown caterpillar makes a cocoon as part of its life cycle in order to change into a chrysalis and then a moth. It extrudes twin silk filaments (fibroin) and a gummy substance (sericin) from two glands on its head. Its head moves from side to side in a figure of eight motion, while the cocoon builds up around it, and the sericin hardens. The final cocoon is about 3 cm in length (Figure 10).

In order that complete cocoons are available for silk yarn production, the chrysalis must be killed by a process called stifling. After stifling, the cocoon can be unreeled. Several cocoons are put into hot water which softens the sericin, and with the aid of brushes the outer layers are removed and a single end of silk found. Five, six or seven ends are then reeled off simultaneously, with the sericin binding them together. The resulting thread is known as 'raw silk'.

Raw silk is turned into silk yarn (nett silk) by the process called throwing, which doubles and twists the thread into many different weights and textures.

Most silk fabrics woven commercially are woven from continuous filament silk, which, unless it has been dyed prior to weaving, still has the natural gum present in the yarn. Handweavers, however, usually use spun silk as it is more easily available and is thicker in count.

Spun silk is produced from waste silk, such as the rough outer parts of the reeled cocoons, damaged cocoons, or any other precious bits of silk from any of the previously-mentioned processes.

The waste silk is collected, the natural gum and other impurities removed, and then the resultant fibres are combed into bundles of lustrous silk which is cut into staple lengths. The longer fibres are then spun in a similar manner to worsted yarns and retain much of the natural lustre of silk. The shorter fibres, however, lose a lot of their lustre and other natural characteristics through spinning.

Tussah silk is reeled from the cocoon of the wild and uncultivated silk moth caterpillar. It produces a

Fig 10 Silk and cotton fibres
From left to right: Tussah silk, Cultivated silk, Silk cocoon, Cotton.

coarse and less lustrous filament yarn which is creamy brown in colour.

In its finest counts, silk requires great care and patience to deal with the enormous number of ends and picks involved. If care is taken, however, there are few problems in warping and weaving as silk is kind and manageable to work with.

The natural lustre of the fibre should be used to the full when designing. Weaves where there are longish floats on the surface are ideal for showing off this fibre, e.g. satin and sateen. Shot silk is a traditional fabric using silk yarns of contrasting colours in warp and weft and plain weave. Silk's lustre brings an unusual shimmering effect to the colour mix.

Spun silk combines well with worsted and hair fibres in fabrics. The natural shrinkage of raw silk is nil, while spun silk will shrink around 8%–12%.

Vegetable Fibres and Yarns

COTTON

The raw material is the soft downy hairs found in the seed pods of the cotton plant (Figure 10). It is grown in many parts of the world, chiefly in sub-tropical lands. The very finest is long-stapled cotton—up to 55 mm ($2\frac{1}{2}''$) long—known as Sea Island cotton and grows in the West Indies. Fine cottons are also grown in Egypt and Sudan, while the USA grows the bulk of the strong medium-stapled cottons and India the short-stapled and coarser fibres. The average staple length is about 25 mm (1″).

The longer fibres are usually combed before being spun in a similar way to worsteds, producing a very compact and smooth yarn. The shorter fibres are carded before spinning.

Cotton's qualities are that it is soft, strong and durable. It is extremely easy to launder and takes readily to bleaching and dyeing as well as being highly absorbent and cool to the touch. It is widely available and the cheapest of the natural fibres. Cotton's main disadvantage is that it has little resilience and tends to crease easily.

Cotton yarns are usually sold plied, giving them greater strength and smoothness. They can be spun very fine, very thick, or with interesting textures (photo, p. 20).

They are also available mercerised, which indicates that the yarns have been passed through a cold solution of caustic soda, causing it to contract considerably. It is then stretched to about its original length, during which time the threads take on a permanently silky lustre. The yarn is then neutralised and washed.

Cotton is a very adaptable fibre and should be chosen if strength and durability are important, if the item will need frequent washing, and if a clean fresh and comfortable fabric is desired. The rich variety of colours available allows colour to be a chief factor in designing. It is a very easy yarn to work with.

Bast Fibres—Fibres obtained from the Stems of Plants

FLAX

Linen is spun from flax, a fibre found in the stems of a plant, *Linum Usitatissimum*. The fibres are very long—up to 900 mm (35″)—and have to undergo elaborate operations before being spun into yarn. These processes involve removing the bundles of fibres from the woody stems of the plant and then splitting the bundles into individual long fibres and removing the uneven or broken ones. Yarns and fabrics produced from the long fine fibres are called line and are very fine and smooth. Those produced from the shorter irregular and broken fibres are called tow and are thicker and rougher in appearance.

Linen yarns are very strong but are non-elastic. They have a beautiful natural sheen and are very smooth, with virtually no projecting fibres. This smoothness is one of its most distinguishing features (photo, p. 20).

All fabrics woven with a fine linen thread have a clear surface, with the weave creating the design and texture. The sheen exaggerates the influence that the weave has over the design. The smoothness also means that the fabric soils less quickly and creates the cool, clean, crisp feeling of a typical linen cloth. Linen fabrics are fairly hardwearing and have a natural readiness to absorb water, making them useful for towels. They launder easily and if done with care this can even improve the fabric.

Its main disadvantages are that it creases easily and its non-elastic properties create difficulties with tension during warping and weaving, when great care is necessary.

It can be dyed to many attractive colours and is also bleached to varying shades of brilliant white, beige and silver grey.

HEMP, JUTE AND RAMIE

These are other bast fibres which produce linen-type yarns, but which have limited use in fabric weaving.

Hemp fibres cannot be bleached without loss in strength so they are only available in darkish colours. It is not a very flexible yarn and is not usually suitable for fine textiles, but can sometimes be used as a substitute for coarser flax.

Jute like hemp can be dyed, but does not bleach well. It is a coarse fibre and is therefore only suitable for coarse textiles. It is not very strong and deteriorates under the influence of moisture. It tends to be fluffy also and can clog up heddle eyes if they are not big enough.

Ramie can be treated to produce a white and extremely lustrous fibre from about 25 mm–300 mm (1″–12″) in length and reasonably fine. It can be spun alone or mixed with flax and wool. It is strong, durable and easily dyed and therefore has many good characteristics, although it is not easily available. Its principal disadvantage is its lack of elasticity.

Man-made Fibres

Man-made fibres cover an enormous range of different textures and characteristics. Because they are chemically manufactured, practically any effect or property can be incorporated. They were initially developed in the early 1900's to find a material which could imitate silk. The chemists were fairly successful, but the artificial silk was always inferior to the real thing. Nowadays imitation is not an important criterion and both regenerated and synthetic yarns have unique characteristics which in certain projects may give advantageous reasons for their use. They are very easily available. The prices of the different man-made fibres vary, but in general they are less expensive than the natural fibres.

Visually some man-made yarns are similar to the natural ones. Some rayons look like silk, acrylics can be like wool and the polyesters are similar to cotton. Other man-made yarns like nylon, lurex or polypropylene threads have no natural counterpart and if they give the desired effect, they are the correct choice of material to use (photo, p. 25).

Blends and Mixtures of Fibres and Yarns

Usually one fibre is spun into a yarn, but sometimes a combination of fibres in one yarn or a combination of yarns in one fabric is beneficial and attractive to the design. This involves the blending and mixing of fibres.

Blending is the mixing of fibres before spinning so that the individual yarn contains two or more different colours or fibre types. Mixing is the term used when two or more different fibres are used in a fabric, but each fibre has been spun into a separate yarn.

Fibre blending is done for many reasons. Firstly, it can make an expensive fibre into a more economic yarn if a less expensive fibre is blended with it in a small quantity. The proportion of fibres in a blend is crucial, though, to ensure that the important visual and handling properties of the expensive fibre is not superseded by the other. In general a quantity of less than 10% will have little noticeable effect, but above 20% the handle and appearance of the main fibre is affected.

Secondly, fibre-blending combines different properties within one yarn. An ideal yarn can be produced in this way: one perhaps which has the natural beauty of wool and the strength of nylon, or in a blend of wool and linen, the wool giving a little elasticity to the linen without losing too much of the sheen or cleanliness of the linen.

Thirdly, blending and mixing produces decorative effects. Some fibres have a distinctive appearance, lustre or texture, or they vary in their affinity to dyes. A blend of wool and linen can make an attractive yarn because the two fibres dye to different shades and therefore an unusual two-tone yarn can be produced.

Colour blending is very common with wool fibres. Several shades or tones of one colour, or of totally different colours, are carefully combined during carding, before spinning. Very rich and attractive yarns result, either apparently of one colour or with a multicoloured tweedy look.

Mixtures, such as combining yarns spun from wool with hair fibres or spun silk in a striped cloth will help to exaggerate the lustre of the more expensive fibres, while the wool will economise on the total cost of the fabric.

Mixing yarns in one cloth, whether of different fibres or yarn thicknesses, must be done with care, ensuring that the shrinkage and sett of the yarns will combine without causing fabric distortion.

Twist in Yarns

Twist is the means of giving fibres strength and cohesion, enabling them to be formed into yarns which must be continuous in length and be able to withstand tension. Filament fibres are simply grouped together to produce the thickness required and then lightly twisted to ensure that they stay together. Strength is normally naturally present in the fibres, but the twist will increase the strength of the yarn.

Staple fibres on the other hand must be twisted

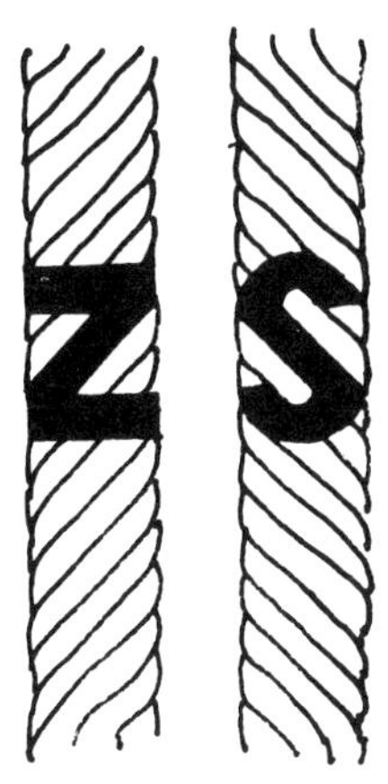

Diag 1 Z and S twist

together to make them cohere and to give them strength. The twist is inserted while the fibres are being spun or drawn out into a continuous length. They are usually spun into a singles yarn which can range from a very thin thread to a thick thread depending on the fineness of the original fibre, but this singles yarn will only be strong if a reasonable amount of twist has been inserted.

There is an optimum amount of twist at which the maximum strength is obtained for any size of yarn. If twist is continued beyond this point, the yarn will become harder and brittle but not stronger.

Twist can be inserted in two directions (Diagram 1). If the fibres are turned to the right, the angle of inclination of the twist up the yarn is the same as the slope of the crossing bar of the letter Z, and if turned to the left, the inclination is the same as the slope of the crossing bar of the letter S. Another term for Z or S twist is Openband or Crossband respectively. The majority of singles yarns are spun as Z twist. In most situations the direction of twist does not affect the appearance of the fibre, yarn or fabric. In other cases, when weaving twills or crepe fabrics in particular, the direction of twist can be used for specific design effects and then both Z and S twist yarns must be available. These effects are discussed under the specific weave headings. The amount of twist that is inserted during spinning affects the fibre's and yarn's characteristics. A soft, full-handling, lightly-twisted yarn has only the minimum amount of twist inserted to give it cohesion, and the fibres textures will be clearly seen. A firm, strong yarn would require more twist. This extra twist, however, would suppress some of the fibre's visual and handling properties.

Plied and Folded Yarns

The spinning process makes fibres into singles yarn. For reasons of strength, texture or colour mixing, it is often desirable to combine yarns together by plying or folding.

It is almost impossible to spin a perfectly even singles yarn from staple fibres. By plying two singles together, the thicker parts of one have a good chance of coinciding with the thin places of the other, so a 2-ply yarn will produce a stronger and more even thread than a singles yarn of equivalent thickness. If roundness and evenness are particularly important, three or more yarns can be plied together.

Generally a 2-ply yarn is created by twisting two Z twist singles in an S direction or two S twist singles in a Z direction. This produces an evenly balanced strong thread. A harder and less flexible yarn is produced if the doubling twist is in the same direction as the component singles yarn.

When yarns of different colours are plied together, the attractive result is called a grandelle yarn. When two or more yarns are plied together but are fed into each other at different speeds or tensions, unusual textured yarns are made.

Folding yarns can be simply achieved by a weaver at home. It involves winding together two or more singles yarns and imparting a few turns of twist to ensure that they form one thread. This is a useful technique for producing grandelle type yarns quickly, or for doubling up a thin yarn to use in combination with a thicker yarn in a cloth. It also enables one to increase the choice of colours available to use in a cloth, as several shades and tones of colours can be produced by folding coloured yarns together in varying proportions with each other. For example, a 3-fold yarn of 2 blue threads and 1 green would give quite a different colour from the same yarns folded in a proportion of 2 green and 1 blue. Folded yarns are really only suitable for weft.

The obvious method to fold yarns is to wind onto a shuttle bobbin two, three or more yarns, whose cones are standing on a creel, each passing through its own guide hole. A problem arises, however, when the combined yarns run off at different tensions, resulting in loops occurring in the folded yarns. This problem can be overcome slightly if the original cones hold a similar circumference of yarn.

A better method is to place a cone of yarn on a temporary shelf, made from two pieces of wood laying side by side between two uprights (e.g. chairs or boxes). A second cone is placed directly below the first with its end of yarn passing between the two pieces of wood and through the central hole of the upper cone. The two threads then pass through the same guide hole in an adjacent creel and are then wound onto a bobbin. This method imparts a few turns of twist into the folded yarn and lessens the looping problem (Diagram 2).

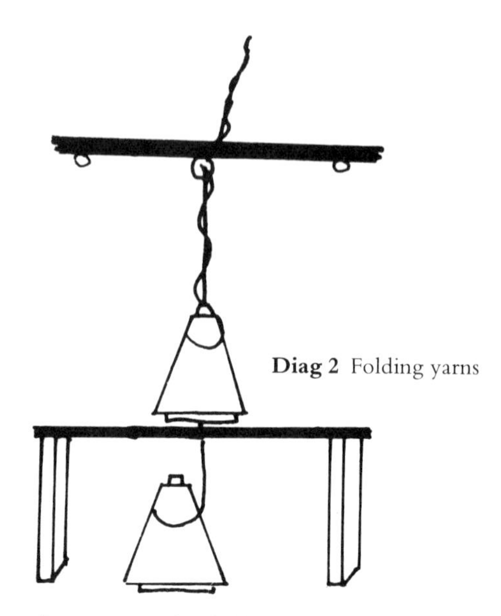

Diag 2 Folding yarns

Textured Yarns

Yarns can be spun to create unusual textured or coloured effects which are interesting and fun to use. They are known as fancy yarns. They range from being very fine to very thick and bulky, but the fibre's characteristics have their normal influence on the yarns. Some of the principle types are illustrated on pages 20 and 25.

DESIGNING WITH FANCY YARNS

Fancy yarns should be used initially with moderation. Usually the point of using them is to provide additional interest in a fabric. Their use in any cloth can dominate the appearance and handle, therefore care should be taken when designing with them if a subtle texture is intended.

Weaves which allow the textured yarn to lie on the surface are best for showing off their particular qualities. The 1 Face 3 Back self-stitched double cloth (Chapter 14) is ideal for this purpose. Other weaves like distorted thread effect (Chapter 11), weft figuring (Chapter 13) or summer and winter (Chapter 13) when the extra threads are a fancy yarn and the ground is smooth, also give the textured yarn prominence (Plate 9). Some of the simplest and most attractive designs are created when thick fancy yarns form widely spaced stripes or overchecks on a fine ground fabric.

Lightweight fancy yarns can be used quite freely and in reasonably large quantities in simple weaves like plain weave and 2/2 twill. Once thicker boucles are introduced in large quantities, however, very spongy handling, unattractive fabrics can result.

Yarns. From left to right: 100% Polypropylene; Single spun wool fancy; Brushed mohair; Mohair loop; Wool grandelle; Wool gimp; Chenille; Worsted slub; Worsted spaced dyed; Snarl; Fancy knop; Fine boucle; Coarse boucle; Loop/snarl; Wool marl; Lurex; 100% Viscose.

Careful setting and choice of weave can give the same visual effect without yarn wastage or excessive weight.

Traditionally mohair loop yarns are brushed or raised after weaving to produce a hairy surface. Brushed yarns can be used to give a similar effect but should be inserted in the weft only, otherwise a clean shed is almost impossible to achieve due to ends sticking together. Most looms work better if the textured yarns are used in the weft, because they can cause poor sheds. If used in the warp the eyes of the heddles must be large enough to allow the thick slubs, knops or curls to pass through.

Warp Yarns

Warp yarns need to be firm, compact and strong and preferably have some elasticity in order to withstand the continual movement of the shafts and the beat-up of the reed. Elasticity is a natural property in some fibres, in particular wool, cotton and silk. There is none in flax and the other bast fibres and variable degrees in man-made fibres. Strength is achieved by the amount of twist that is inserted into the yarn, and not necessarily the thickness. A fine thread with a high number of twists per inch will certainly be stronger than a thick thread that is little more than a roving.

To test a yarn for warp strength, simply hold quite a long piece taut between two hands and gently apply tension by moving the hands apart. If the fibres start to drift apart, the yarn is not suitable for a warp. If a reasonable amount of tension can be exerted before the thread finally snaps, it will be a suitable warp yarn. The warp yarn should not be too hairy, otherwise the reed and heddles may clog up with fibres, and the heddle eyes need to be large enough for the ends to pass through easily.

WEFT YARNS

Weft yarns can be almost anything that is available. They are not under tension during weaving and therefore need not be exceptionally strong. They can be much softer twisted and more bulky in texture. Materials not usually associated with weaving like ribbons, leather, rags, grasses, string or polypropylene are all possible.

3 COLOUR AND TEXTURE IN WEAVING

Colour

Colour is usually the most dominant feature of any cloth. It is the first aspect which attracts attention and decisions about liking or disliking a fabric can be determined by this factor alone, and only afterwards are features like pattern, handle, texture, suitability for purpose or expense considered.

One's reaction to colour is personal and is influenced to a certain extent by fashion. It is impossible, therefore, to lay down rules to assist in the actual choice of colour. During weaving, colours change depending on the fibre, texture and weave. Certain phenomena tend to occur, however, when colours are combined on the loom and a few are discussed below. Experience will help to build up confidence in the choice of colour combinations.

COLOUR THEORY

Colour has been described and measured accurately by scientists for many years and their theories are interesting and in certain cases can be directly used by the weaver to achieve attractive colour schemes.

There are basically two colour theories, one based on 'Lights' and the other on 'Pigments'. When combining differently coloured lights the mixture of all the rays produces a white light. This is known as a process of addition and the actual colour of something is determined by the character of the light it reflects. When mixing coloured pigments, as in dyeing or painting, the process is called subtraction since one colour completely absorbs the other. Colour is applied to fibres with the use of dyes and therefore the subtractive pigment theory is relevant and involves the mixing of three primary colours or hues, red, yellow and blue. These primary hues cannot be created by the mixing together of other pigment colours, but by mixing them together in different proportions and with the addition of black and white pigments almost all other colours can be produced. This can be visually appreciated by painting or examining a colour wheel.

THE COLOUR WHEEL

Hue

Hue is the term to describe the actual colour by name—e.g. red. The three primary hues of red, yellow and blue are positioned equidistantly around a large circle. Each hue spreads out in either direction, gradually changing colour with the increasing influence of its neighbour, as one primary is absorbed by another. The adjacent colours eventually meet to form the secondary hues. Red and yellow become orange, yellow and blue become green, and blue and red mix to form purple. The colour wheel will now show a scarlet red merging through vermilion, orange and amber before losing all its warmth as it reaches a pure bright yellow. The yellow begins to absorb blue and takes on a greenish tinge as it turns from lime through grass green and turquoise to reach the primary blue. Blue moves back around to red passing through violet, purple and magenta.

Tone

Any one of these hues can become paler or darker in tone by the addition of white or black respectively. On the colour wheel the paler colours or tints move towards the centre, eventually reaching white, while as the colours move outwards they become darker in tone until becoming black. These deeper colours are known as shades.

From a completed colour wheel it is possible to examine the tonal path of many hues, either based on one particular colour by following it through from its very palest tint to a deep shade, or by remaining at one level of tone and moving to the right or left through a quarter or half turn of the wheel.

These colour combinations are extremely harmonious and can be very successfully used in weaving.

It can also be seen from a colour wheel that some colours are brighter than others even though they are on the same tonal level around the circle. Yellow is the brightest colour, while purple is the least bright. The brighter colours tend to predominate when used in colour combinations.

The colours obtainable from a tonal colour wheel are numerous and exciting, but in no way cover all the possible dyes in yarns that the weaver is likely to find or want. We have not begun to mix opposites of the colour wheel in various degrees. When the three primaries are mixed together in equal proportions, the dominance of one is absorbed by the others and a neutral or grey colour results. If one primary is mixed in slightly greater proportion than the others, the grey moves towards this colour, so cool greys results as blue is added, browny greys emerge when red is stronger and khaki when there is more yellow.

Moods

Different moods are generated by one's impression of a colour, feelings of brightness, warmth or nearness. Red is a cheerful colour and gives the impression of warmth. It is a powerful colour and tends to advance towards the observer. Yellow is luminous and bright. It is not as warm as red, but appears to stand out more. Blue is a cold colour and recedes from the eye. Green is a receding and slightly cold colour, but fresh. Orange is strong and warm, but not as intense as yellow. Purple is a beautiful rich and deep colour.

Natural colours

All animal and vegetable fibres have their own natural colour. When these fibres are spun into yarns without being dyed, these natural colours are available for the handweaver to use.

They usually fall into a group of colours ranging through white, creams, browns, greys and blacks and always produce less crude colours than any similar colour produced by dyeing.

Fibre blending before spinning can expand these natural colours into an even greater choice of subtle variations of the creamy, brown and grey tones.

Natural colours always give a successful, subtle colour combination in fabrics and also enhance any other strong colour that may be used in combination with them.

Colour in Weaving

As handweavers we are dealing with building up a cloth from several different threads and colours rather than applying areas of solid colour to the cloth. Colour mixing occurs during weaving, particularly when using simple weaves with neat interlacing in a square sett and a fine thread. A primary yellow warp crossed by a blue weft will give the effect of a green cloth, especially if viewed from a fair distance. However, true colour-blending has not taken place as in the colour wheel, because on closer inspection the individual yellow and blue can quite clearly be seen, the green tinge becoming less prominent. The thicker the yarn or the longer the weave float, the less obvious the mixing becomes.

This colour change makes it possible to weave a cloth which appears to have three colours, but in fact is made up of only two. A simple example is a regular checkerboard check in yellow and blue (Diagram 3). When the yellow weft stripe crosses a yellow warp stripe a pure yellow results, when the blue weft stripe crosses the blue warp stripe a pure blue results, but where yellow and blue cross each other, the greenish tinge will appear. This colour mixing in a cloth is a unique feature of weaving and should, therefore, be used for design effect. The double plain fabric shown in Plate 2 relies entirely on this phenomena for its design.

Diag 3 Colour interaction in check designs

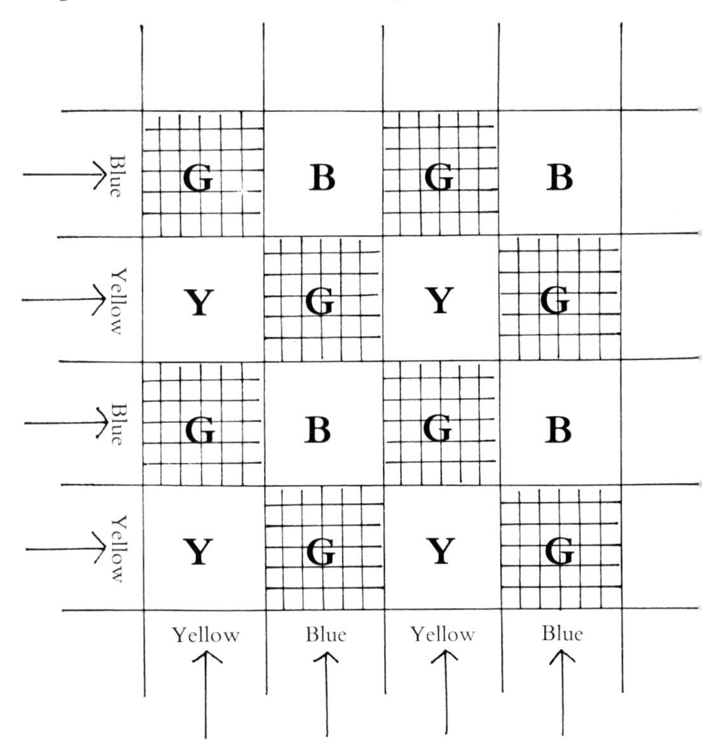

Plain weave cloths with a warp of one colour crossing a weft of another can have a powerfully vibrant effect, particularly when the colours are strong, close in intensity and near each other on the colour wheel. Fine silk is often woven this way and the lustre increases the liveliness. A slightly less dazzling effect will be achieved by combining colours from opposite sides of the colour wheel, while a more subtle scheme can be composed by balancing tones from opposite sides.

When yarn of the same colour is used in both warp and weft, the shadows created by the texture of the structure's interlacings appear to make the colour less intense. A richer and stronger effect results if the warp is crossed by the same yarn, but one in which the colour is a fraction deeper in tone. The same thing occurs to a much lesser extent with weaves which bring one set of threads more prominently to the surface like satin and sateen and 3/1 twill.

On all cloths where the warp and weft show equally on the surface and are of different colours, it is generally better if the warp is the lighter of the two. A lighter coloured weft shows any uneven beating during weaving. Also long weft floats, e.g. on a point join of 2/2 twill, always show up more obviously than a similar light-coloured warp float.

Creams and off-white warps are usually more successful in a cloth than a bleached white, unless the cleanliness of the bleached white is important in the design, A bright white warp tends to cheapen or give the crossing colour a chalky appearance. Black warps on the other hand appear to brighten and enrich the colours that are crossing it, especially if they are strong colours initially.

The stage at which the dye is introduced to the fibres affects the final appearance and colour. Dyed fibres can be blended together before spinning. The resultant multicoloured yarns, whether a blend of one hue or of various colours, have a depth and richness that is not present when dyeing takes place at the yarn stage.

Piece dyeing, which takes place after the cloth is woven, produces a very flat and even colour. If the cloth has been woven with several colours or with various fibres which take up dye differently, piece dyeing creates a subtle tonal change within the colour of the dye used. All the colours of the original cloth become a tint or shade of that dye colour. This is a fairly safe way of ensuring that all the colours will mix together, although it is a very subtle blend. It is especially effective if natural yarn colours like the white, grey and brown of natural wool are combined in a cloth and then piece dyed.

VISUALISING COLOURS BEFORE WEAVING

A simple way of visualising how colours will mix in a cloth is to twist a few strands of yarn together in your hand. A general feeling of liveliness or dulness will immediately occur and by twisting in alternative or unusual colours a gloomy combination can be made to sparkle. Different proportions of colour can be indicated by twisting two or more strands of one colour compared to another. It is easier to perceive intricate colour combinations this way rather than by laying large cones of yarn next to each other.

Yarn card winds are the easiest way of trying out coloured stripe patterns or for comparing the reaction of large areas of colour to one another (Chapter 10).

BACKGROUNDS

In some weaves such as weft figuring, a ground cloth is woven and shapes or patterns are interwoven on top. A background colour which is attractive and exciting by itself will not remain unaffected when these extra picks are inserted, but will alter as the new colour relates with it. No one colour is better than another, although some are easier to work with. Neutral backgrounds, or colours chosen from the grey colour wheel, can provide an interesting and subtle choice. They have a natural affinity with the colours from which they derive as well as being a subdued contrast to others.

Lighter-toned backgrounds are slightly easier to work with than darker tones. There is a greater choice of colours which look attractive and stimulating with them. The background is allowed to enliven the fabric, but not to take over. On a white ground colours appear deeper and darker. Darker backgrounds like navy, brown or maroon, on the other hand, can dominate the design so that the motif colours need careful selection to withstand the competition and still look interesting. On a black ground, colours look brighter and lighter than usual. Pure colours can make dramatic backgrounds for tonal schemes of black, grey and white, but again great care and confidence is required to overcome the contrasts of a more complicated combination, and experiments should always be woven before weaving a major piece.

It is important when designing with colour to be sure you like the choice before you start. It is difficult to improve on one during weaving. This need not mean that you cannot design for other people who insist on a colour that is not your favourite. Within any range of a colour some will attract and inspire you as a weaver, and with these you can create good design.

As in all aspects of design, one should try not to be too complicated with colour, and be aware at all times of the other main factors in a cloth of texture, weave, fibre and suitability for purpose. If colour is to be an important feature, use it strongly. If other aspects are more important, give colour a decisive but not competing role. Texture is an ideal occasion to allow colour to play an equal role. When weaving a self-coloured cloth with different yarns and textures, the mood generated by the colour chosen will be able to speak and the texture will enhance the colour.

Texture

Texture can be perceived in a cloth by two senses—by touch and by sight. Touching is one of the easiest and most pleasing ways of recognising and reacting to fabrics.

Texture is inherent in all woven textiles, simply by the interlacing of the threads. This natural tendency can be emphasised or subdued and thus texture can be used in designing. Fibres, yarns, colour and weave structure are all possible tools in the creation of texture. Finishing techniques are also a considerable influence on the final appearance and thus on the texture of a cloth.

We have seen that some fibres and yarns are naturally more textured than others. If a rough texture is important, then woollen spun yarns or an unevenly spun yarn should be chosen. Worsted spun yarns are smoother, but not as even or lustrous as some mercerised cottons, silk or good quality linens. Fancy yarns are spun to produce texture and can change these naturally smooth fibres into very textured materials (see photos on pages 20 and 25).

Combining two fibres of different character is a simple way of emphasising texture—a shiny one with a matt one (Plate 3). Combining different yarns of the same fibre will give a similar but less contrasting effect. Two yarns with differing shrinkage used in the warp or weft in a narrow stripe will cockle when washed, producing a slight seersucker effect. If intended this creates an interesting fabric and texture, but if not done carefully can look scruffy.

Textured weaves include crepe weaves (Figure 78), Huckaback (Figure 83), mock leno (Figure 85), honeycombs (Figure 82), distorted thread effects (Plates 5+9) and bedford cords (Figure 69). These weaves are constructed to have an irregular surface by combining floats of different lengths, or by joining together sections of tight interlacings and loose interlacings which distort on relaxation and shrinkage. Except for honeycomb they are usually quite subtle and fairly shallow in texture. Textured yarns will emphasise the roughness.

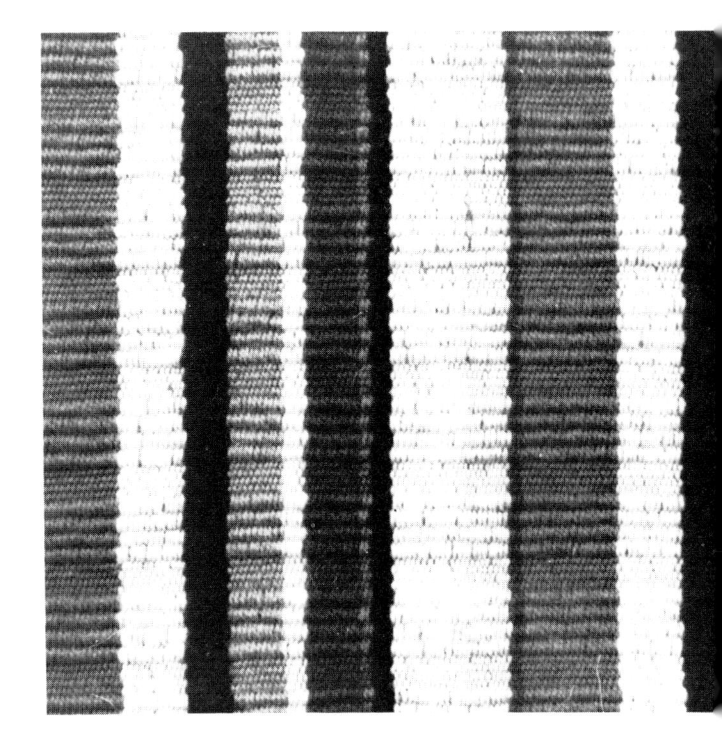

Fig 11 Warp rib weave using wefts of varying thickness

Warp and weft rib weaves usually use smooth yarns to create a strong directional texture of ribs. These ribs can be of various sizes by combining different thicknesses of yarns (Figure 11). The addition of wadding threads into bedford cord weaves or horizontal interchanging double plain can change a comparatively flat surface into quite a bumpy one, although again with a strong directional pattern. These bumps will be smooth unless fancy yarns are used for additional texture (Figure 70).

Simple weaves like plain weave, twill or satin and sateens can be made textured by the use of fancy yarns (Figure 6). They can also be given the visual appearance of texture which is not tactile, when random-dyed or marl-coloured yarns are used in warp or weft. The light and shade of the colours and their haphazard distribution can give a feeling of texture.

As with other aspects of design, limitation is the key to success. If texture is to be an important criterion, let it speak for itself and create it in a simple way. Do not get too sophisticated and combine textured fibres, textured yarns, textured colours and textured weave together in a complicated stripe or checked pattern.

DESIGNING ON PAPER

To be able to design on paper is the key to being able to control the fabric that is to be woven on the loom and thus create new and individual results. It also encourages records to be kept of past work and so enables experiences and references to be stored, but more importantly it allows weavers to pre-think their ideas and 'try them out' before spending time and money dressing the loom.

The ability to visualise a fabric from a weave diagram written on paper can only be learnt by seeing the threads interlace on the loom, so the initial steps in designing on paper should also involve sample weaving and experiment.

After constructing a fabric on paper, there is a systematic and logical procedure to find out drafting plans and lifting plans required to actually produce the fabric on the loom. A knowledge of the mechanisms of your particular loom are necessary to put the drafting and lifting plans into use.

In no way does designing on paper restrict the freedom of a weaver to change ideas and design on the loom. On the contrary, a thorough understanding of a weave construction, and the method you have adopted to convert it to a cloth on the loom, opens up opportunities to experiment with the interlacings of the warp and weft and create new effects.

Weave or thread interlacings, drafting plans and lifting plans are recorded on point paper. Point paper is graph paper divided in $\frac{1}{8}''$, $\frac{1}{2}''$ and $1''$ squares. This paper in pads is becoming increasingly difficult to obtain due to metrication, but it is well worth hunting for. The majority of weaves repeat on multiples of four and so fit into point paper with ease and logic. Normal graph paper divided into 1/10th is not only smaller in scale, but illogical for writing weave diagrams and therefore mistakes are more likely to be made.

The Weave Diagram

The notations used in writing weave interlacings on point paper are reasonably universal.

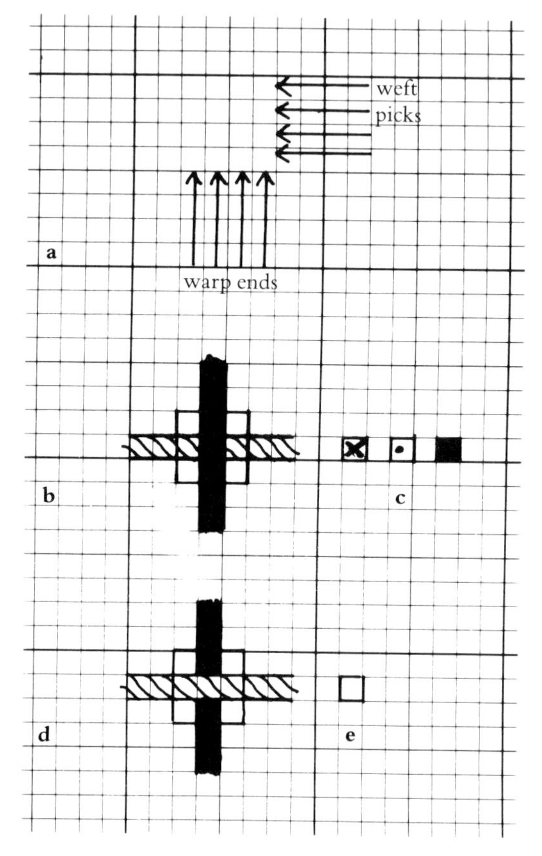

Diag 4 Weave notation

The weave is the interlacing of two sets of threads at right angles to each other. The length-wise threads are known as the warp and are made up of individual threads called ends. The crossing weft is made up of individual threads called picks.

On point paper each vertical row of squares represents one warp end and each horizontal row of squares represents one weft pick (Diagram 4a). Where the two rows meet a square is formed which represents the point of interlacing of one end and one pick. Only two things can occur at this point.

1 Either the end can pass over the pick—allowing

the end to show on the surface (Diagram 4b).

2 Or the end can pass behind the pick—allowing the pick to show on the surface (Diagram 4d).

On point paper, when a designer wishes the warp end to show on the surface of the cloth, he places a mark at the point of intersection, e.g. an x, a dot or by filling it in as a solid (Diagram 4c). When a designer wishes the weft to show on the surface, the point of intersection remains blank (Diagram 4e).

By this method, the surface pattern of a cloth, which has an equal number of ends per cm/inch as picks per cm/inch, can be visually represented on paper. (As soon as the sett of a cloth, i.e. the number of ends and picks per cm/inch, is unbalanced, this visual patterning is distorted or lost, even though the actual interlacings of the ends and picks remain accurate. Double weaves and other more complicated constructions need experience to recognise immediately a fabric's appearance from the weave diagram).

Throughout the past history of weaving numerous standard weaves have been constructed and these are now the building bricks for the modern designer. All these weaves are discussed in detail in the following chapters, but Diagram 5 illustrates some of the simplest and most common weave diagrams.

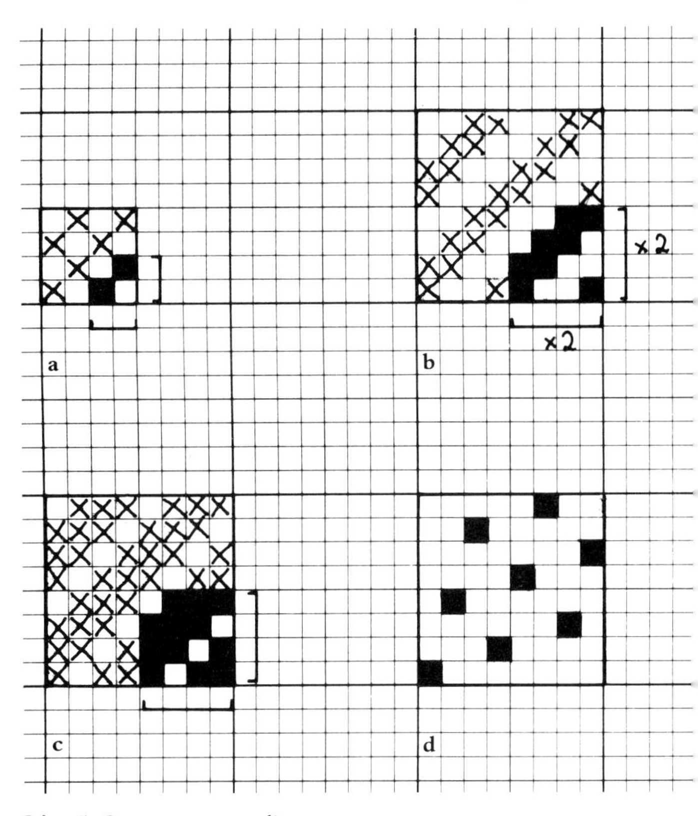

Diag 5 Common weave diagrams

Diagram 5

a. Plain Weave or Tabby Weave

Every alternate end is raised for every alternate pick. There is an equal proportion of marks to blanks on the diagram. At a glance it can be seen that if the warp is black and the weft is white, equal amounts of each colour will show on the surface in a minute chequerboard pattern.

b. Common Twill or 2/2 Twill

Again there is an equal proportion of marks to blanks, therefore equal amounts of warp and weft are showing on the face of the cloth, but this time a fine diagonal line from bottom left to top right forms the surface pattern. Each end is floating over and under 2 picks.

c. 3/1 Twill

There are more marks than blanks in the weave diagram, therefore the fabric will be dominated by the colour and texture of the warp yarn. The surface pattern will be diagonal lines from bottom left to top right. Each end is floating over 3 picks and under 1 pick.

d. 8 end Sateen

There are more blanks than marks in the weave diagram. The fabric will be dominated by the colour and yarn of the weft, with an indistinct all over surface pattern. Each end is floating under 7 picks and over 1 pick.

It must be realised that the scale of point paper relates to a cloth sett of 8 ends and picks per inch. If the actual cloth to be woven has a sett of 16 ends and picks per inch, the weave diagram is twice the actual size of the cloth pattern. The visual impact of the weave diagram is, therefore, closely related to the sett of the cloth.

REPEATS

When designing weaves on point paper it is vital to recognise the weave repeat. This is the point along the width and height of the weave diagram where an exact replica of the previous section begins. This original section can be multiplied infinitely across the fabric without altering the surface pattern.

On the examples given in Diagram 5a, b and c two complete repeats in both height and width are illustrated. Diagram 5d shows only one complete repeat of the 8 end sateen. Generally only one repeat needs to be written down, if the same weave is covering the total cloth. On occasions when several different weaves are combined, perhaps in a stripe or check, it is necessary to indicate each separate repeat within the total design by inserting brackets below and to the side of the weave diagram, and noting how many times each section is repeated (e.g. ×2 in Diagram 5b means that section is to be repeated twice).

It should be noted that a weave can repeat on either an equal or unequal number of ends and picks, but a complete repeat must form a square or a rectangle in format to accommodate every interlacing of all the ends and picks at right angles to each other.

Joining Weaves

Designing on paper does not only amount to writing standard weaves out on point paper. It starts to become creative when experimenting by combining weaves together is tried.

When manipulating weaves, combining them or reversing them it is important that care is taken at the joining points so as to avoid ugly long floats occurring. The designer must beware of long weft floats (a horizontal line of blanks) when joining weaves side by side and of long warp floats (a vertical line of marks) when joining weaves one on top of the other.

If possible, at the join no float should be longer than any float in the body of the main weave.

Diagram 6 explains the point. There are four possible ways of joining 2/2 twill to the right with 2/2 twill to the left to form a warp stripe. It should be noted that there is no float longer than 2 in both weaves.

In diagram 6

a. Produces a weft float of 3
b. All floats at the join are either 2 or under
c. Produces a weft float of 3
d. Produces a weft float of 4

Diagram 6b would create the neatest join, while d. would be quite unattractive especially if the weft was of a light colour.

Diagram 7 illustrates 3/1 twill combined with 2/2 twill to form a weft stripe. a. and d. would produce perfect cloths, but b. and c. produce a long warp float of 5 which would show up surprisingly prominently and unattractively on a cloth.

A very long float at a join also creates a weak spot in the cloth construction which can be caught and snagged.

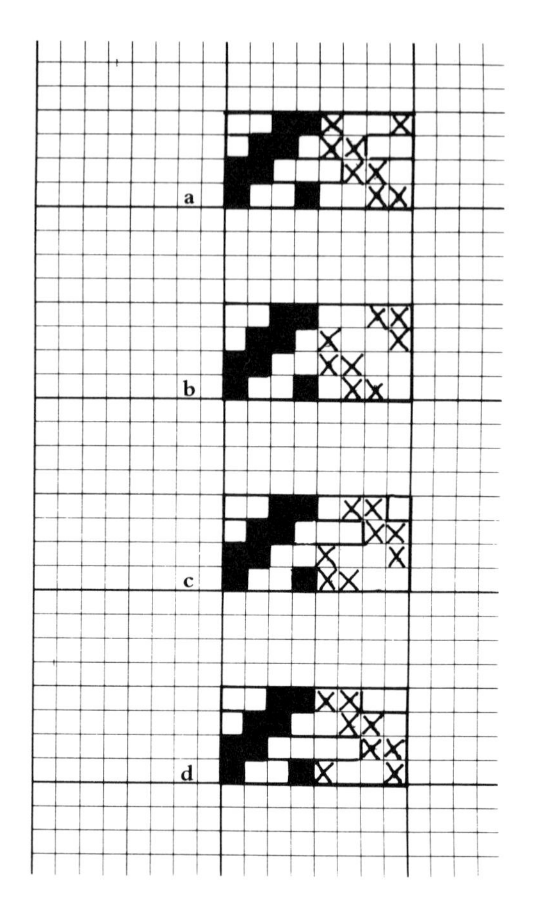

Diag 6 Joining weaves to form a warp stripe

Diag 7 Joining weaves to form a weft stripe

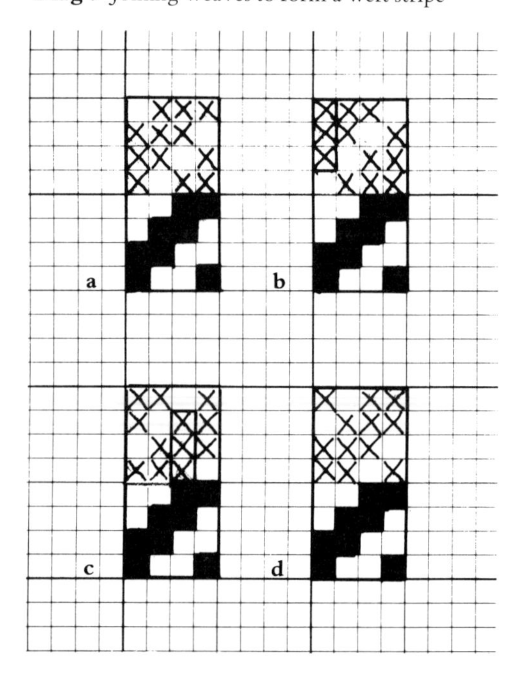

Designing Within the Capabilities of your Loom

Constructing and manipulating weaves on point paper can be absorbing and exciting. However, it is of little use designing a beautiful weave only to discover that it cannot be woven on the specifications of your loom. A thorough understanding of the basic weave constructions can usually overcome this problem, but it is important to determine at an early stage the number of shafts required to weave a particular design and for owners of counterbalance and countermarche looms, the number of pedals required. This can be quickly established from the weave diagram by a process called DRAFTING. Drafting is also the first stage of working out the appropriate drafting plan and lifting plan of a particular design which enables the loom's mechanisms to actually weave the design.

DRAFTING

During weaving when a shaft rises, all the ends that are drawn through the heddles on that shaft are raised also. Each shaft works independently from the others, but all ends drawn onto any one shaft are working in unison, and therefore must be interlacing in an identical order with the weft. The weave diagram represents the order that the ends interlace with the picks. All the ends that interlace in an identical order can be allocated to one shaft on the loom. The number of different end interlacing sequences found in the weave diagram, therefore, equals the number of shafts required to weave it.

A similar relationship exists between picks and pedals. Each pedal on the loom can lift up a different selection of shafts to produce the shed for the pick to pass through. The number of different pick interlacings found in the weave diagram, therefore, indicates the number of different pedals required. It should be remembered, however, that in certain cases and on some looms, two or more pedals can be depressed simultaneously for enlarging the scope of lifts that a loom can perform.

The procedure for drafting is described below and illustrated in Diagrams 8a, b and c.

a. Look at the first end on the right-hand side of the weave diagram. Mark underneath this end with the No. 1. Note the order that this end is interlacing with the picks. Mark No. 1 under any other end that is interlacing in an identical order (i.e. over 1, under 2, and over 1).

b. Mark the second end from the right No. 2. Look for other ends interlacing in an identical order and mark them No. 2 also.

c. Continue in this manner until each end has a

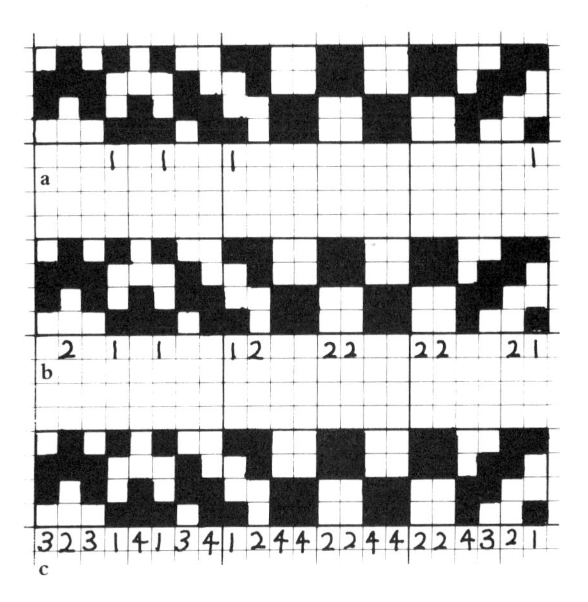

Diag 8 Weave drafting

number beneath it. The maximum number reached indicates the minimum number of shafts required to weave it. If 4 different interlacings are found, then four shafts are required. If 6 interlacings are found and your loom can only accommodate four shafts, then that particular design cannot be woven. The weave will need to be redesigned.

All the weave diagrams in this book have been drafted according to this method and the numbers underneath each diagram indicate the number of shafts required to weave that pattern.

A similar drafting method should be adopted with the picks if it is necessary to determine the number of pedals required. This may be easier to do if the weave diagram is turned a quarter turn around. Countermarche looms with four shafts and eight pedals can cope with 14 different lifting sequences, as can counterbalance looms with six pedals by depressing two or more pedals at a time.

Drafting Plans and Lifting Plans

These are the vital plans which refer to a particular weave, and which indicate how the ends and picks are arranged in relation to the shafts, to enable the loom to produce the desired cloth.

Unlike weave notating, which is fairly universal, there are numerous methods for working out and notating the drafting and lifting plans. All methods arrive at the same end, but it is difficult to read them unless you know the method. If you have a method which you understand and like, please continue to use it. If not, my method is as good as any other. It is based on the Scottish System of Pattern Drafting.

In all sections the weave, drafting plan and lifting plan are read from right to left. Threading the loom (*heddling*) is done from right to left also.

THE DRAFTING PLAN

This indicates the order in which the ends are drawn through the eyes of the heddles on the shafts. The drafting plan, is therefore, only concerned with ends and shafts. On point paper, the vertical rows of squares represent ends, and the horizontal rows represent the shafts. One should try to imagine these horizontal rows as the actual shafts suspended in the loom. The drafting plan is written directly below the weave; the ends in the weave continuing straight down to use the same vertical row of squares in the drafting plan. Diagram 9 illustrates how a drafting plan is constructed from a weave diagram.

a. The weave is notated on point paper in the normal manner with any bracketing necessary. The picks are marked A, B, C, etc., up the right-hand side of the diagram starting from the bottom. A, refers to the first pick of the weave. The drafting procedure is completed so that the number of shafts required is known as is the order in which they are arranged.

b. Number each shaft i, ii, iii, iv, etc., on the right-hand side of the plan. Use Roman numerals to distinguish these numbers from the numbers underneath the weave diagram, which do not necessarily relate to the same shaft. The Scottish system of pattern drafting calls the shaft furthest away from the weaver while facing the front of the loom No. i, and the shaft nearest the weaver is the highest number so the numerals are listed from the top (Diagram 9b).

(The reason for this is that while heddling a simple straight draft from the right to left, it is physically easier, if you are right-handed, to draw from the back shaft to the front shaft, so it seems logical to be counting in a forward direction. If however, you find it more sensible, or natural, to call the shaft nearest the weaver i, and count backwards, then this is quite acceptable. It is in fact immaterial what you actually call a shaft as long as you are entirely clear in your own mind which number refers to which shaft.)

Look at the ends marked No. 1 on the weave plan above. Place all the ends marked No. 1 onto the same shaft on the drafting plan. It does not particularly matter which shaft they go on, as long as they are all drawn onto the same one. Mark the

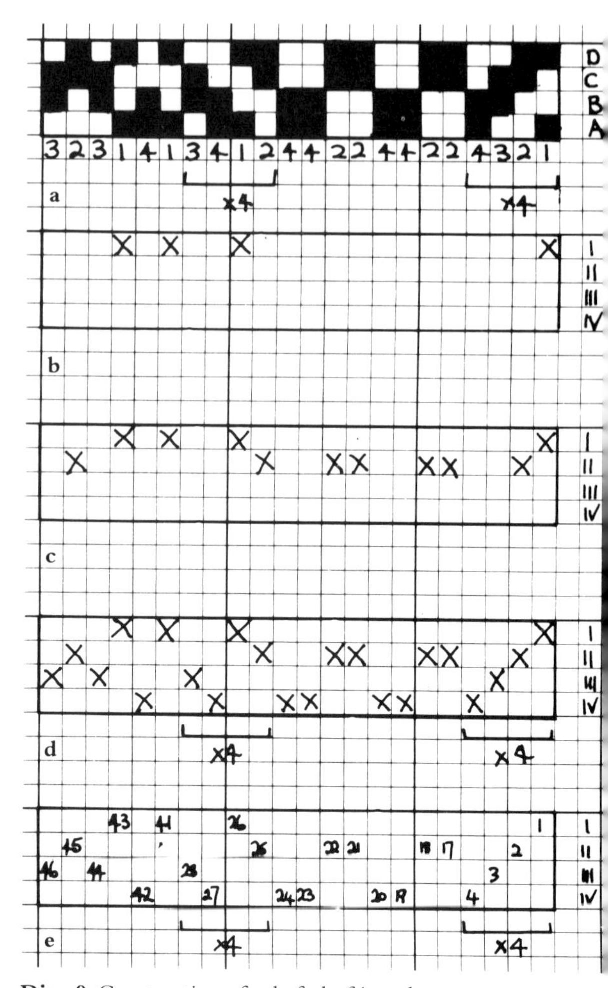

Diag 9 Construction of a shaft drafting plan

squares with an x (Diagram 9b).

c. Place all the ends marked No. 2 onto another shaft (Diagram 9c). Place all the ends marked No. 3 onto a different shaft. Continue in this manner until all the ends in the weave diagram have been allocated a shaft (Diagram 9d). No end can be drawn onto more than one shaft. The draft repeats on the same number of ends as the weave does, so any bracketing up of the weave must be transferred onto the drafting plan also.

d. On long drafts such as the one shown in Diagram 9d, it is easier for heddling if the draft is rewritten by numbering each consecutive end along the repeat. It enables one to follow and check a draft quickly (Diagram 9e).

N.B. Numbers have been allocated to all ends, even those which are repeated within the bracketed sections. The maximum number reached in the draft equals the number of ends in one repeat of the weave, including any repeated sections.

Drafting plans should be constructed primarily for ease of heddling, but also they should allow the mechanism of the loom to work smoothly. It is easier to heddle if the draft follows some logical pattern if this can be arranged. Also, if you are left-handed it may be easier to heddle from left to right.

The straight draft follows the most straightforward arrangement for heddling (Diagram 10a). The first end on the right is drawn onto the back shaft, the second end is drawn on the shaft in front of it, etc. Most simple basic weaves can be drafted to suit this arrangement. Block weaves (Chapter 13) usually fall into block drafts which are made up of short straight drafts on separate groups of shafts (Diagram 10c). The Point draft results from weaves which are reversed or mirrored in some way (Diagram 10b). Sometimes it is impossible to construct a neat and logical draft as in Diagram 9d, and great concentration is required during heddling to ensure that mistakes are not made.

The loom will generally work better if the following considerations can be incorporated in the draft (Nos 1 and 2 are particularly important on looms which create a rising shed):

1. If more ends are drafted onto one particular shaft, make this shaft the front shaft.

2. If some ends in the warp are weaker than others, put these onto the front shaft.

3. If there are more than 12 heddles per shaft per inch, it is wise to halve the density of the heddles per shaft by allocating two shafts to one particular lift on the plan. This reduces the overcrowding on the shafts which may cause warp breakages. Plain weave can initially be drafted onto two shafts, but is normally drafted onto four shafts for this reason.

4. Many weaves can be woven using identical drafts and therefore one should be aware while designing of the other possibilities and weave combinations open to you on the same warp.

THE LIFTING PLAN

The lifting plan indicates the order in which the shafts rise and fall to allow the pick to be inserted. The lifting plan is, therefore, only concerned with shafts and picks. On point paper, the vertical rows of squares represent the picks and the horizontal rows the shafts. The lifting plan is written immediately to the right of the drafting plan, thus allowing the same horizontal rows representing the shafts in the drafting plan to continue across to be used as shafts in the lifting plan. Diagram 11c

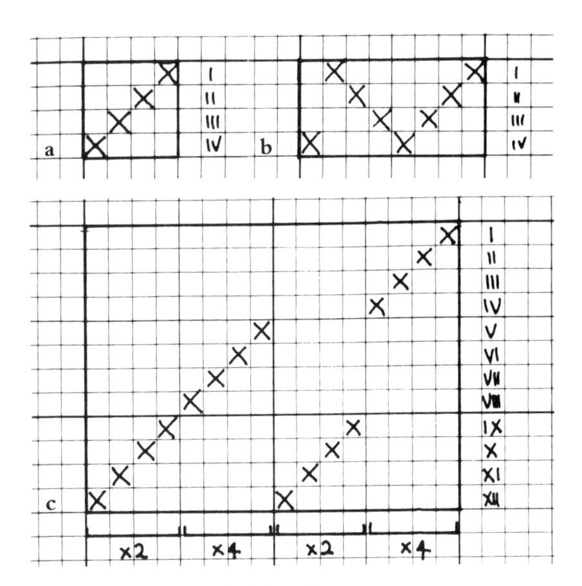

Diag 10 Common drafting plans

illustrates the construction of a lifting plan from a weave and drafting plan.

1. Number the shafts i, ii, iii, etc., as before.

2. Indicate the picks A, B, C, etc. underneath the lifting plan repeat. (A must be marked at the furthest point to the right of the repeat, for the lifting plan to be consistent with the other parts of the pattern drafting method, and to be read from right to left.)

3. Look across to the drafting plan (Diagram 11b). Take any end that is drawn onto shaft i. Follow this end up to the weave above (Diagram 11a), and note how it is intersecting with the picks. In the example in Diagram 11a, all the ends on shaft i are interlacing over picks A, under picks C and B and over pick D. Transpose the same marks from the weave diagram onto the same picks on shaft i of the lifting plan (Diagram 11c—shaft i shows marks on picks A and D).

4. Do a similar thing with any end drawn onto shaft ii (crosses in Diagram 11c) and then with shaft iii (dots in Diagram 11c). Continue in this manner until each shaft on the lifting plan has been filled with the appropriate intersections found from the weave diagram.

5. The lifting plan is now complete. It is read from right to left, with each vertical row representing the shaft lifting sequence for each pick. The bottom row of squares is the front shaft on the loom and the top row of squares the back shaft. In the example in Diagram 11c, Pick A requires shafts i and iv to rise and ii and iii to remain down or fall. Pick B requires

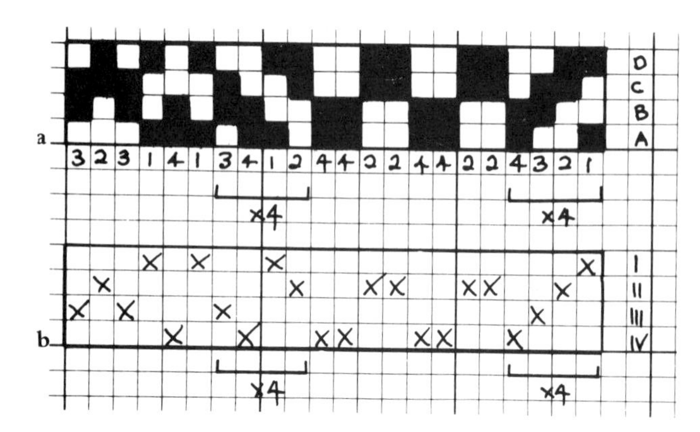

Diag 11 Construction of a lifting plan

shafts iii and iv to rise and i and iv to remain down or fall etc.

It depends on the type of loom you own as to the way you actually achieve the action of the shafts rising and falling for each pick.

For owners of counterbalance looms, countermarche looms and jack looms a similar drafting procedure with the lifting plan, to that followed on the weave diagram, is necessary to establish the number of different pedals the design requires, and the order that the different shedding actions are performed. For example:

1. Mark Pick A of the lifting plan No. 1. Look for any other pick which has an identical shedding action and mark No. 1 also.

2. Mark Pick B No. 2. Look for any other pick which has an identical shedding action and mark No. 2 also.

3. Continue in this manner until each pick has a number beneath it. The final number reached indicates the variety of different lifts a design is composed of.

Sleying Plan

The sleying plan indicates the order that the ends are sleyed through the dents of the reed. In most cloths the reed is sleyed evenly across the width, with 1, 2, or 4 ends per dent. This information can be simply noted by writing the reed number and the ends per dent alongside, e.g. if there are 12 ends per inch in the cloth, then a 6's reed would be sleyed 2 per dent. The sleying plan would read 6/2.

If, however, a more complicated and uneven sleying order is required, for example in a huckaback weave, a longer sleying plan needs to be written. Underneath the weave diagram the groups of ends to be sleyed in the same dent should be marked by looped brackets (Diagrams 89b and c) and the order noted.

A graduating sett across a cloth as is necessary for an undulating twill might have a sleying plan like this. 6's reed 1/1/2/2/3/3/4/4/4/3/3/2/2/1/1/0/1/0 (Figure 7).

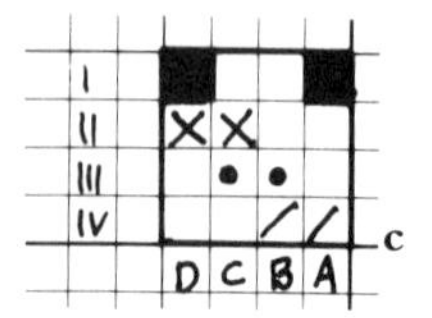

Warping and Wefting Plans

It is necessary to note down the warping and wefting plans, which denote the yarns and colour orders of the ends and picks, at the time of designing the weave. Except for self-coloured warp and wefts, it is vital to synchronise end 1 on the warp and end 1 of the draft, and similarly pick A of the lifting plan with pick A of the colouring plan.

WARPING PLAN

List all the colours and yarns that are being used in the warp. The number of ends in each colour is written against the appropriate name as they occur in vertical columns. Any groups that are being repeated are bracketed up as shown. The sum of the ends in each colour and the sum of the ends in the total repeat, is recorded at the end of each line and under the final column as shown.

Diagram 12 shows the warping plan for a colour and weave effect with a simple overcheck. It is read in the following manner, taking each vertical row in succession. 2 red, 2 white repeated 8 times, followed by 2 red and 4 blue. 2 red, 2 white is then repeated 8 times followed by 2 red and 4 navy. There are 76 ends in the total repeat of this plan.

WEFTING PLAN

The wefting plan is written in a similar manner.

Diag 12 Warping plan

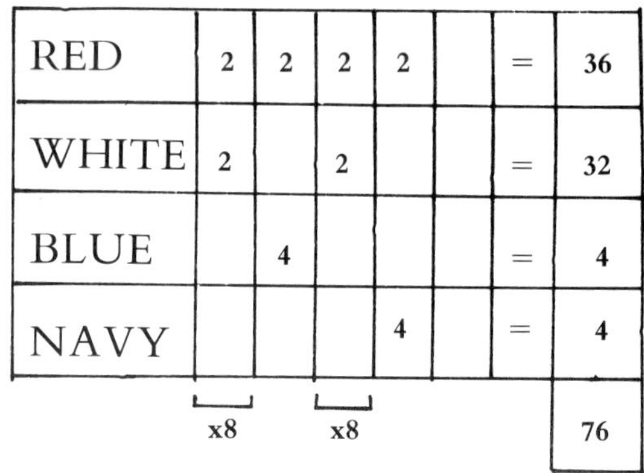

RED	2	2	2	2		=	36
WHITE	2		2			=	32
BLUE		4				=	4
NAVY				4		=	4
	x8		x8				76

END IN REPEAT WARPIN PLAN

5 CALCULATIONS

Yarn Count

Yarns vary in thickness. The yarn count number indicates the thickness of a yarn and is based on a relationship between length and weight. A good mill or yarn supplier will sell yarn with a count number so that the exact thickness of the yarn will be known and thus comparisons between yarns can be accurately made. The count number is also useful for calculating the sett of a cloth, and the weight of yarn required to weave a length of cloth.

Different yarn counting systems have been developed in many of the industrial textile centres of the world, based on fibres and spinning methods, and this has resulted in a variety of systems which can be confusing to the handweaver. The Tex system is an internationally recognised counting method based on metric figures, and it can be applied to all types of yarns regardless of spinning method or fibre content. This should simplify the situation except for the fact that many of the old systems are still widely used.

There are two main approaches to yarn-counting systems. The fixed weight method whereby the count depends on the number of unit lengths which balance to a fixed weight, usually of 1 lb. The fixed length method calculates the count number depending on the number of unit weights which balance a fixed length of yarn.

THE FIXED LENGTH SYSTEM

The fixed length method calculates the count number depending on the number of weight units that are required to balance a fixed length of yarn (Diagram 13). The two systems that fall into this group are both based on metric weights and lengths. The Tex system is applicable to all fibres and spinning methods. The Denier system is used with all continuous filament yarns including reeled silk and man-made extruded yarns.

In both systems the lower the count number the finer the yarn. As the count number increases the yarn becomes thicker.

The Tex system

The Tex system uses a fixed length of 1000 metres and weight units of 1 gramme each. A 12 Tex yarn means that 1000 metres of yarn weighs 12 grammes. A 50 Tex yarn means that 1000 metres of yarn weighs 50 grammes. The 50 Tex yarn is therefore much thicker than the 12 Tex yarn.

When a yarn is plied, the resultant count of the ply is given, followed by the number of component threads and the direction of twist. For example, R 22 Tex/2 S means that 2 threads of 11 Tex count have been twisted together in an S direction to form a yarn with a resultant count of 22 Tex.

The Denier system

The Denier system uses a fixed length of 9000 metres and weight units of 1 gramme each. Thus a 12 Denier yarn means that 9000 metres of it weighs 12 grammes.

THE FIXED WEIGHT SYSTEM

The fixed weight method calculates the count number depending on the number of unit lengths which balance to a fixed weight (Diagram 14). Table 3 shows some of the most common systems

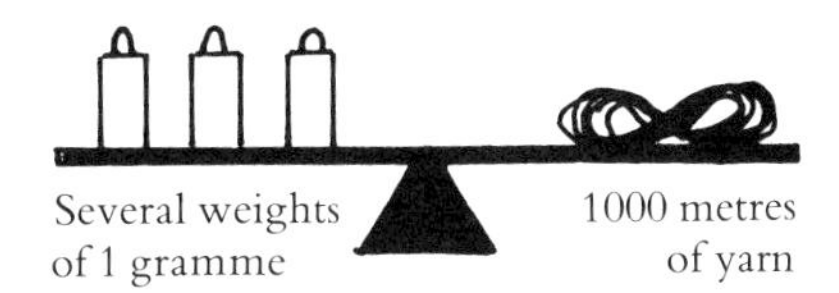

Diag 13 Fixed length counting system

Diag 14 Fixed weight counting system

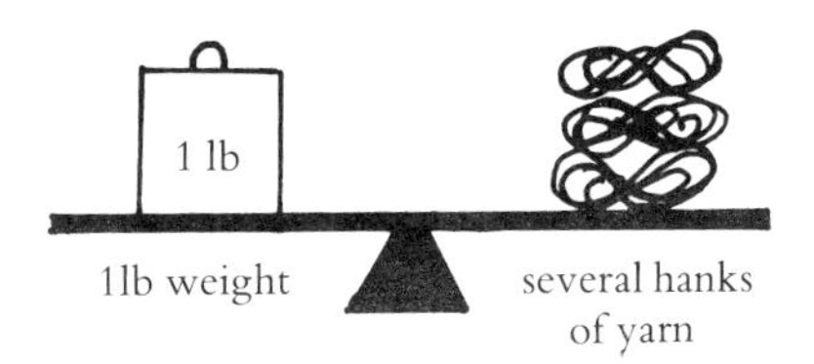

that fall into this group. The table is based on an imperial weight of 1 lb and lists the various unit lengths in yards per lb of the different systems depending on fibre content or spinning method. In all cases, the low count numbers indicate the thicker yarns. As the count number increases, the yarn becomes finer.

Table 3

	Unit length per lb
Woollen spun yarns—Galashiels cut (G^c)	200 yards
Woollen spun yarn—Yorkshire woollen skein (YSW)	256 yards
Woollen spun yarn—West of England hank	320 yards
Worsted yarns (Wrst)	560 yards
Linen yarns (lea)	300 yards
Cotton yarns (C)	840 yards
Spun silk yarns	840 yards

An 8's cotton yarn means that 8 hanks of 840 yards weigh 1 lb or there are 8 × 840 = 6720 yards per 1 lb of yarn.

An 8's Yorkshire woollen skein (YSW) yarn means that 8 hanks of 256 yards weigh 1 lb or 8 × 256 = 2048 yards in 1 lb of yarn.

A fixed weight system using metric figures is in use, principally in Europe. The count number is calculated on the number of hanks measuring 1 Kilometre which balance against a fixed weight of 1 Kilogram.

When a yarn is plied, the resultant yarn will be twice as thick as before. The count number is notated by writing the ply number first followed by the singles count of the yarns plied. The actual resultant count will, therefore, be half the count number of the component yarns. For example 2/32's Worsted means that 2 threads of 32's Worsted have been plied together making a yarn equivalent to single 16's Worsted. A 3-ply yarn would have a resultant count of 1/3rd of the component count, e.g. 3/48's Worsted means that 3 yarns of 48's Worsted form a yarn equivalent to single 16's Worsted. The 2/32's Wrst. and the 3/48's Wrst. are therefore of identical thickness, with 16 × 560 = 8960 yds/lb.

The above notation for plied yarns is the case with all fixed weight systems except spun silk. On this occasion the resultant count of the two component yarns are written preceding the ply number. For example, 20/2 Spun silk means that 2 single threads of 40's count have been spun together to produce a yarn of 20's Spun silk count. The yards per lb of this yarn would be 20 × 840 = 16800 yards.

Sett

The sett of a cloth is the correct number of ends and picks per cm or per inch required to weave a fabric in a specific yarn to produce the desired result in weight and handle. It is directly related to the following factors: the count and texture of the yarn, the weave, the firmness and handle of the cloth that is required and the amount of shrinkage that may occur during wet finishing.

The sett is a very important aspect of designing a cloth. It can drastically alter the appearance and handle of a fabric, making it either attractive and useful or ugly and impractical.

There is an upper limit to the number of ends and picks per cm/inch that can be put into a cloth, depending on the count of the yarn and the weave to be used. This upper limit is called maximum sett. Maximum sett can be assessed by a simple calculation, but experience and experiment also play a large part in choosing the most appropriate sett for a cloth.

A cloth woven at maximum sett is very firm. The further below maximum a cloth is sett the softer and fuller in handle it becomes, wearing and draping qualities gradually deteriorate, but with less ends and picks being inserted, a less expensive cloth is produced. All cloths are woven slightly below maximum sett. A furnishing fabric or a cloth needing similar hardwearing qualities should be sett between 5% and 12% below maximum. A clothing fabric might be sett as far as 10% or 15% below maximum. By 20% a very much softer and lofty handling cloth results. Blankets may suit this weight. Scarves and shawls can be sett as low as 30% or 40% below.

A further percentage reduction needs to be taken off maximum sett to allow for any shrinkage that may occur during the wet finishing processes. Woollen fabrics in particular, which undergo a milling process, may shrink from 15% to 30%, while normal shrinkage on other fabrics will reduce maximum sett by only 2% to 5%. This shrinkage figure can only be correctly determined by weaving a sample of the cloth and comparing the width in loom with the finished width and the woven length by the finished length. If a sample was woven 20″ × 20″ and after finishing it measured 19″ × 19″, a shrinkage of 1″ out of 20″ had occurred, which equals 1/20th × 100 = 5%.

The basic theories for the calculation of maximum sett deal with simple weaves using the same counts of yarn in warp and weft, and having equal numbers of ends per cm/inch to picks per cm/inch. This situation is known as a square sett cloth. The appropriate setts for more complicated weaves and those which combine different counts in warp and weft are deduced by comparison with these simple designs.

Maximum sett is calculated in two stages:

1. Find the number of yarn diameters that fit into a unit space of 1 centimetre or 1 inch.

2. Multiply this number by a fraction, which is dependent on the relative firmness of the weave to be used.

TO FIND THE NUMBER OF YARN DIAMETERS WITHIN A UNIT SPACE

The number of threads which can lay side by side within a unit space of 1 centimetre or 1 inch is dependent on the count of the yarn. Fine yarns have a smaller diameter than thick yarns, therefore more threads of finer count yarns fit into the same space as thicker count yarns (Diagram 15).

When the count of the yarn is not known, the number of yarn diameters can be determined by winding a thread around a ruler and counting the number of threads that fit into the unit space of either 1 centimetre or 1 inch as required. The threads must be wound very evenly around the ruler and as close together as possible, but without allowing them to roll over each other (Diagram 16). A more accurate assessment of the number of diameters will be obtained if an area of 10 centimetres or 2 inches is covered with threads, the total threads counted, and an average figure taken for 1 centimetre or 1 inch.

When the count of the yarn is known, the number of yarn diameters within a unit space can be determined by a calculation. Arthur Ashenhurst, who pioneered cloth setting theories, found that the diameters per inch equals the square root of the yards per lb, with certain deductions depending on whether it is a woollen, worsted, cotton, linen or silk yarn. His formulae for fixed weight counts and imperial measures are:*

Woollen Diameters per in. $= 0.85\sqrt{\text{yards per lb}}$

Worsted ,, ,, $= 0.9\sqrt{\text{yards per lb}}$

Cotton, silk and linen ,, ,, $= 0.92\sqrt{\text{yards per lb}}$

Example: Find the diameters per inch of a 9 cut Galashiels Woollen yarn.

Yards per lb $= 9 \times 200 = 1800$

Diameters per inch $= 0.85\sqrt{1800}$

,, ,, $= 0.85 \times 42.4$

,, ,, $= 36$

(*N.B.* Diameters per centimetre $= \dfrac{\text{Diameters per inch}}{2.5}$)

Ashenhurst formulae converted to accommodate Tex counts and metric measures are:

Woollen Diameters per cm $= \dfrac{240}{\sqrt{\text{Tex count}}}$

Worsted ,, ,, $= \dfrac{254}{\sqrt{\text{Tex count}}}$

Cotton ,, ,, $= \dfrac{259}{\sqrt{\text{Tex count}}}$

Example: Find the diameters per centimetre of a 225 Tex woollen yarn

Diameters per cm $= \dfrac{240}{\sqrt{225}}$

$= \dfrac{240}{15}$

$= 16$

(*N.B.* Diameters per inch = diameters per cm $\times 2.5$)

*1 The square root sign is $\sqrt{\ }$. The square root is the figure which results when a number is multiplied by itself. For example the square root of 16 ($\sqrt{16}$) = 4, because $4 \times 4 = 16$. Square root tables or a good calculator must be used to find the square root of numbers which cannot be done mentally.

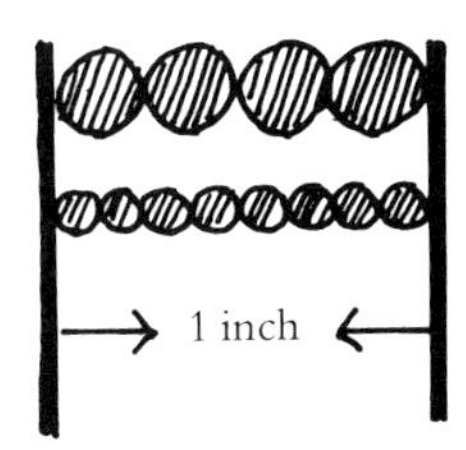

Diag 15 More threads of a fine yarn, than of a thick yarn fit into the same unit space

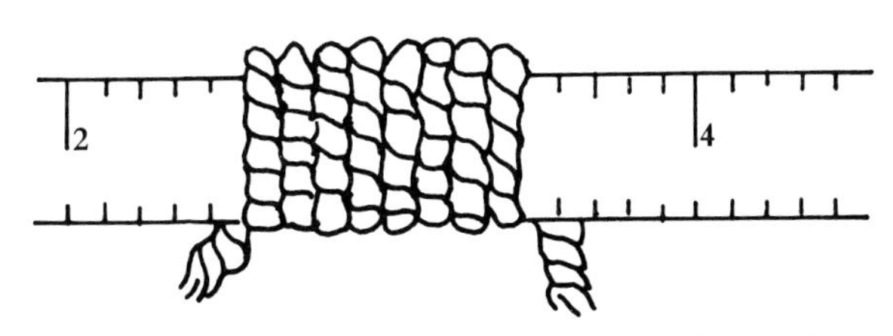

Diag 16 Finding the diameters per cm/inch of a yarn by winding it around a ruler

WEAVES FIRMNESS FORMULA

When a weave diagram changes from marks to blanks and vice versa, the warp threads are changing from one side of the cloth to the other, or they intersect each other. Each thread must make at least two intersections in a complete repeat of the weave. One passes from the face to the back and the other returns the thread from the back to the face of the cloth to start the next repeat. The intersections of the threads give the cloth firmness, the more frequent the intersections are, then the firmer the cloth.

In a square sett cloth with the warp and weft of similar counts, each intersection of the weft causes the ends to separate by about the diameter of one thread. Therefore, the more frequently the weave intersects, the further apart the ends should be sett.

Diagram 17 illustrates the ends and intersections of different weaves. The top lines represent the diameters per cm/inch and the lower lines show the necessary spacing of the warp to allow for the intersections of a pick.

a. In one repeat of plain weave, the two ends plus the two intersections which occur use up the equivalent of four yarn diameters. There are, however, only two actual ends in the repeat, therefore the maximum sett of the cloth = $\frac{2}{4}$ or $\frac{1}{2}$ of the actual diameters per cm/inch.

b. In one repeat of 2/2 twill the four actual ends and the two intersections that occur, use up the equivalent of six yarn diameters. Maximum sett of the cloth is, therefore, $\frac{4}{6}$ or $\frac{2}{3}$rds of the actual diameters per cm/inch.

c. In one repeat of 4/4 twill, the eight actual ends plus two intersections use up 10 yarn diameters. Maximum sett = $\frac{8}{10}$ or $\frac{4}{5}$ths of diameters per cm/inch.

d. In one repeat of 3/2/1/2 twill, the eight ends plus four intersections use up 12 yarn diameters. Maximim sett $\frac{8}{12}$ or $\frac{2}{3}$rds of diameters per cm/inch.

Ashenhurst formed an equation for determining the above fraction by which diameters per cm/inch must be reduced to allow for the relative firmness of weaves.

Weave firmness formula

$$= \frac{\text{Nos of threads in repeat of weave}}{\text{Nos of threads in repeat of weave} + \text{Nos of intersections per repeat}}$$

Therefore Plain weave $= \frac{2}{2+2} = \frac{2}{4} = \frac{1}{2}$

Maximum sett $= \text{diameter} \times \frac{1}{2}$

2/2 twill $= \frac{4}{4+2} = \frac{4}{6} = \frac{2}{3}$

Maximum sett $= \text{diameter} \times \frac{2}{3}$

8 end satin $= \frac{8}{8+2} = \frac{8}{10} = \frac{4}{5}$

Maximum sett $= \text{diameter} \times \frac{4}{5}$

The Actual Sett

Once maximum sett has been calculated, the actual sett of your cloth must be assessed. Reductions in maximum sett need to be made to allow for handle, drape, take-up and shrinkage as mentioned earlier. The amount by which to reduce maximum sett is the most difficult decision for a beginner to hand-weaving to make, and only with experience or after several samples have been woven can a sensible judgement be made.

Initially, I think that most handweavers over-sett their cloths. Do not be afraid to reduce maximum sett by a reasonable amount. One or two ends and picks per cm/inch less may be all that is needed to turn a stiff boardy cloth into an attractively draping skirt length.

Once weaving is in progress, it is vital to ensure that your beat-up is producing the correct picks per cm/inch, as determined by the sett calculations. All too often this figure is not maintained, resulting in a distortion of the pattern and a deterioration in handling qualities.

When different square sett weaves are being combined in a single cloth, the sett should be based on the tightest interlacing. For example, a combination of 2/2 twill and plain weave should be sett as for plain weave.

Setting of Non-uniform Cloths

When yarns of different counts are being used together in a cloth, and a square sett is still desired, the number of diameters per unit space can be determined in the following manner: Either wind around a ruler the different threads in the same proportions as they are being used in the cloth and count the number that fit into 1 centimetre or 1 inch, or calculate the diameters per cm/inch for each yarn separately using Ashenhurst's formulae and then multiply each figure by the proportion that each yarn is being used in the cloth; the sum of all these numbers is the diameters per cm/inch. These

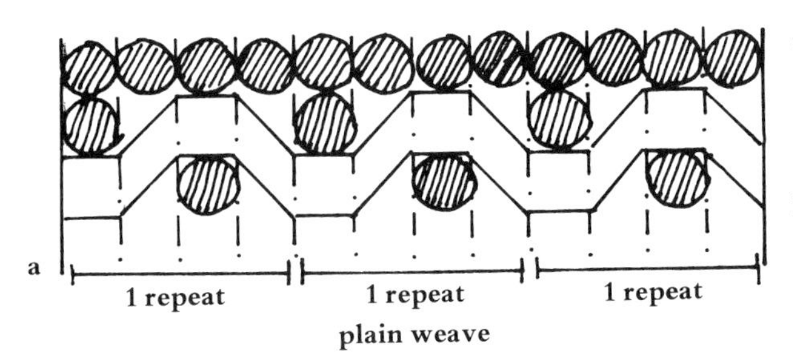

end diameters per cm/inch

pick intersecting the ends

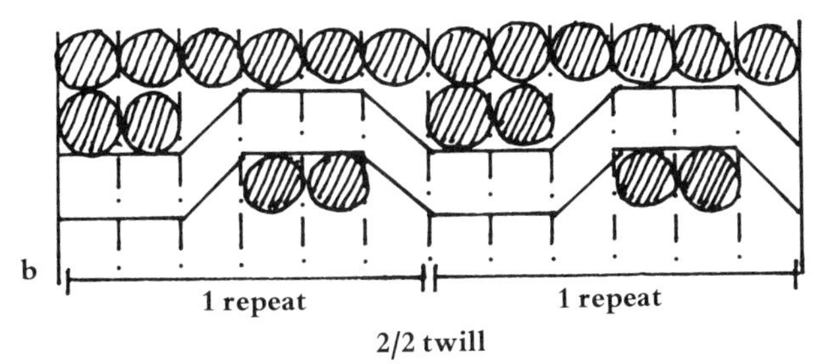

end diameters per cm/inch

pick intersecting the ends

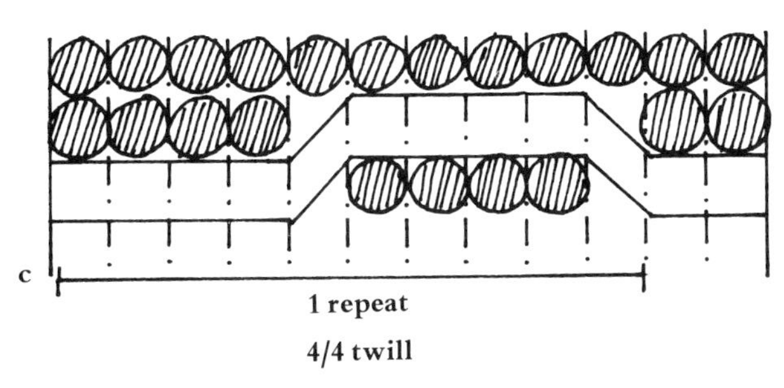

end diameters per cm/inch

pick intersecting the ends

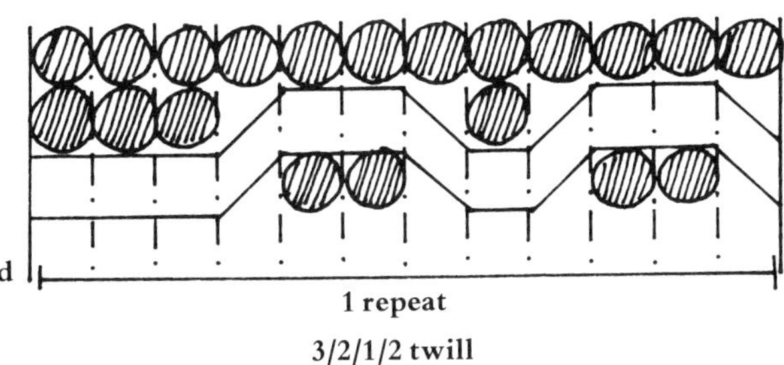

end diameters per cm/inch

pick intersecting the ends

Diag 17 Weaves firmness formula

diameters are then reduced by the weave firmness fraction to obtain maximum sett.

For example:

Warping plan

9^c Wool	2
2/20 Worsted	1
	3

Diameters per inch of 9^c wool $= .85\sqrt{9 \times 200}$
$= .85\sqrt{1800}$
$= .85 \times 42.4$
$= 36$

Proportion of diameters per inch $= 36 \times \frac{2}{3}$
$= 24$

Diameters per inch of 2/20 worsted $= .9\sqrt{10 \times 560}$
$= .9\sqrt{5600}$
$= .9 \times 75$
$= 67.5$

Proportion of diameters per inch $= 67 \times \frac{1}{3}$
$= 22.3$

Total diameters of the two yarns	$= 24+22$
	$= 46$
Maximum sett of plain weave	$= 46 \times \frac{1}{2}$
	$= 23$ per inch
or	$23 \div 2.5$
	$= 9$ per cm

N.B. The proportions that each yarn is being used in a cloth can be found by studying the warping and wefting plans.

The setting of non-square cloths is usually assessed by comparison with square sett cloths. It is always advisable to try out different setts by sample weaving before starting a major piece.

Warp and weft rib structures are woven with an unbalanced sett. Warp rib structures allow the weft to lie straight and only the warp threads bend, while in weft rib structures the warp lies straight and only the weft bends. A basic guide for setting these cloths is that the number of threads in the bending series can equal the actual diameters per cm/inch of the yarn, while the threads lying straight are calculated in the ordinary way using the weave firmness formula. This is the basis, whether the same yarns are used in both warp and weft or if the straight threads are thicker or thinner than the bending ones. This maximum sett can be reduced slightly to make a more pliable and softer fabric as desired.

The closer together the warp and weft setts become, the higher sett yarn shows less prominently on the surface and the low sett yarn becomes more apparent. In all weaves where one set of threads is wanted to predominate on the surface of a cloth, then these threads should be sett higher than the less prominent threads.

Specific setting details for all weaves are given under the individual weave chapters.

Warp Calculations

Before weaving can begin it is necessary to make certain simple calculations in order to establish the width of your warp and the number of ends which will create that width, and the length of warp that needs to be made.

The width and length of a cloth in loom must always be greater than the desired finished width and length of a cloth. The width and length of the warp is affected by the take-up of the weave during weaving and the shrinkage that may occur after any finishing processes. With balanced weaves and square setts, the take-up and shrinkage is identical in both directions. On warp-faced weaves, the take-up and shrinkage is greater in the length direction, while on weft-faced weaves, take-up and shrinkage is greater in the width. Only by weaving a sample of a cloth and measuring the width in reed compared to the finished width and the woven warp length with the finished warp length, can an exact percentage allowance for shrinkage and take-up be known. On average a figure of 10% needs to be added onto the desired finished width and length of a warp.

The warp length needs an additional 1.50 m added to it to allow for tying up the ends to the front stick, and wastage at the end of the warp due to the back stick not being able to pass the shafts. This wastage is called thrums. In fact it is always worthwhile being generous with the warp length, in order to overcome wasted length at the beginning of the warp due to mistakes needing correction, and any excess warp remaining after the piece is completed is useful for trying out ideas that may have occurred to you while weaving the main piece.

The number of ends in the warp can be determined by multiplying the width in loom of your cloth by the sett. For example, a cloth to be 150 cm in loom, with a sett of 8 ends per cm will have $150 \times 8 = 1200$ ends in the warp. Selvage ends must be added as extra.

The above calculation is adequate except that the ends in the warp should coincide with an exact repeat of a weave. It is, therefore, necessary to know in addition the number of ends in each repeat of the draft and the number of repeats of the draft in the width of the cloth, before the exact ends in the warp can be calculated.

For example, if a draft repeats on 54 ends and the width in loom is 150 cm and the sett is 8 ends per cm, there are 1200 ends in the warp. The number of repeats of the draft in that width will be $1200 \div 54$ which equals 22 repeats with 12 ends over. In order to get a complete repeat of the draft in the design, the warp can either have 22 repeats or 23 repeats.

22 repeats $= 22 \times 54 = 1188$ ends in the warp with a warp width of $1188 \div 8 = 148.5$ cm

23 repeats $= 23 \times 54 = 1342$ ends in the warp which equals $1342 \div 8 = 167.75$ cm width in loom

Heddle Calculations

It is simple to calculate the number of heddles required on each shaft of the loom from the drafting plan.

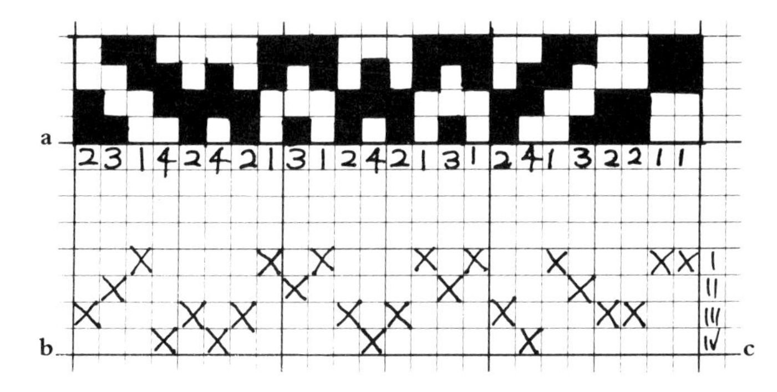

$8 \times 10 = 80$
$4 \times 10 = 40$
$8 \times 10 = 80$
$4 \times 10 = 40$

Diag 18 Heddle calculations

The drafting plan shows one repeat of the weave. For each shaft, add up all the ends that are drawn on that shaft, including any repeat bracketing that is indicated, and write the total number down (Diagram 18). Multiply each number by the number of repeats across the width of the cloth, including any half repeats that are indicated. Any selvage threads must also be allocated a shaft and thus a heddle each.

Diagram 18 illustrates a typical calculation.
The weave (Diagram 18a) and the drafting plan (Diagram 18b) repeats on 24 ends.

Cloth is 48 cm (20″) wide with 5 ends per cm (12 ends per inch).

Total ends in warp $= 5 \times 48 = 240$ ($12 \times 20 = 240$) plus 2 selvage ends on each side of each shaft $= 16$ ends

No. of repeats of drafting plan across piece $= 240 \div 24 = 10$

Shaft i needs 80 heddles + 4 selvage heddles

Shaft ii needs 40 heddles + 4 selvage heddles

Shaft iii needs 80 heddles + 4 selvage heddles

Shaft iv needs 40 heddles + 4 selvage heddles

TOTAL = 240 heddles + 16 selvage heddles

Most looms work better if the heddles are evenly distributed across a shaft. If there are more heddles per shaft than are actually required, half of the unused heddles should be left empty on either side of each shaft. This also ensures that the warp is centralised in the shafts.

Calculations to Establish the Weight of Yarn Required to Weave a Fabric

Before warping or weaving begins, it is essential that you have enough yarn in all the necessary colours and textures to complete the project. Repeat dye batches can be fractionally different from each other and will spoil a cloth if combined. The formulae for calculating the weight of yarn required are given below. They are slightly different, depending on whether you are using metric measurements and Tex counts, or imperial measurements and fixed weight counts.

1. Weight of warp in grammes

$$= \frac{\text{Ends per cm} \times \text{width in cm} \times \text{length in m} \times \text{Tex count}}{1000 \text{ metres}}$$

2. Weight of weft in grammes

$$= \frac{\text{Picks/cm} \times \text{width in cm} \times \text{lengths in m} \times \text{Tex count}}{1000 \text{ metres}}$$

Example: What weight of warp is required to weave a fabric using 130 Tex yarn with 10 ends per cm, a warp width of 100 cm and a warp length of 6 metres?

Weight of warp

$$= \frac{10 \times 100 \times 6 \times 130}{1000} = 780 \text{ grammes}$$

3. Weight of warp in lbs

$$= \frac{\text{ends/inch} \times \text{width in inches} \times \text{length in yds}}{\text{yards per lb of yarn}}$$

4. Weight of weft in lbs

$$= \frac{\text{Picks/inch} \times \text{width in inches} \times \text{length in yds}}{\text{yards per lb of yarn}}$$

Example: What weight of warp yarn is required to weave 8 yards of material 42″ wide using 6's cotton yarn with 30 ends per inch?

Yards per lb of 6's cotton $= 6 \times 840 = 5040$ yards per lb.

$$\text{Weight of warp} = \frac{30 \times 42 \times 8}{5040} = 2 \text{ lbs}$$

When two, three or more yarns or colours are used in the warp and weft, it is necessary to establish the weight of each individual component. Each yarn must have its total weight calculated separately, and then this figure is multiplied by the proportion of each yarn or colour in the warping and wefting repeat.

For example, if a warp is made with the same specifications as the cloth above but with the warping plan as follows:

6' cotton				
	Red	2	2	= 4
	Yellow	1		= 1
	Blue		1	= 1
				6

The warp is made up of 4/6th red yarns and 1/6th of the yellow and blue yarns each. Therefore:

the weight of red yarn in warp

$$= \frac{30 \times 42 \times 8}{5040} \times \frac{4}{6} = 1.33 \text{ lbs}$$

the weight of yellow yarn

$$= \frac{30 \times 42 \times 8}{5040} \times \frac{1}{6} = .33 \text{ lbs}$$

the weight of blue yarn

$$= \frac{30 \times 42 \times 8}{5040} \times \frac{1}{6} = .33 \text{ lbs}$$

total = 1.99 lbs

If the count of your yarn is not known, it is extremely difficult to determine the weight of yarn required to weave your cloth. The table 4 below is designed to give an approximate worsted or Tex count figure which can be used in a warp and weft weight calculation. It is based on the diameters per cm or per inch of the yarn to be used which will have been determined by winding the yarn evenly and closely around a ruler as described earlier in the chapter. The table should be used in the following way:

1. Choose a diameter per cm or inch in the table that is as close to the actual diameters of your yarn to be used. If in doubt about which one to choose, pick a slightly lower figure as this will result in a more generous yarn quantity.

2. Note either the worsted or Tex count number of the yarn which produces this diameter and use it in your weight calculations.

Selvages

Selvages are the two firmly-woven outer edges of a cloth. They are usually about ½" wide, and may not be in the same weave or yarn as the main cloth.

Selvages are necessary for several reasons. They should produce a neat and strong edge to the cloth as well as providing a base to hold a temple in place during weaving, and tenterhooks in place during finishing. They are best woven with a strong smooth yarn, and sleyed at twice the density of the main cloth.

On a plain or simple twill weave, it is usually sufficient to continue the same weave right through the selvages and simply sley the reed twice as dense for the first and last half inches. Warp and weft faced weaves, however, need a selvage of 2/2 hopsack weave, otherwise the edges tend to curl when taken off the loom. Additional shafts will be needed to accommodate the selvage ends which are lifting in a different order to the main weave.

2/2 hopsack should also be used as the selvage with any weave which does not produce a neat selvage naturally. A neat selvage is automatically produced if each pick turns around the outer ends before returning through the next shed. If extra shafts are not available in these situations, floating ends can be implemented.

A selvage is double sleyed in the normal manner using the weave of the main cloth, but the first and last ends of the warp are not heddled onto any shaft although they are sleyed through the reed. These ends will remain stationary no matter what the lifting sequence of the weave. The handweaver must pass the shuttle either over or under these ends manually to produce a neat edge with each weft turning around the outer ends. These floating ends can be doubled for additional strength.

Table 4

Worsted count	*Diameters per inch*	*Diameters per centimetre*	*Tex count*
1	20	8	875
1.50	25	10	580
2.25	30	12	400
3	35	14	290
4	40	16	225
5	45	18	175
6	50	20	145
7	55	22	125
8.75	60	24	100
10.25	65	26	86
12.25	70	28	72
14	75	30	64
16	80	32	56
17.75	85	34	50

Table 4: Approximate worsted and Tex count numbers in relation to the number of diameters per centimetre or inch of a yarn.

6 PLAIN WEAVE

Plain or tabby weave is the simplest of all weave structures. The ends and picks interlace in alternate order with each other, floating over one and under the next, creating the tightest of all interlacings and thus the most stable of all fabrics. When a square sett is employed and the warp and weft are of similar counts, a balanced cloth with equal amounts of ends and picks will show on both sides of the cloth and the take-up of the ends and picks during weaving will be identical. If the cloth is sett fairly close to maximum, then a firm, crisp handling fabric results. The further below maximum the cloth is sett, the softer, less stable and open textured is the cloth which is formed. All types of fibres and yarns can be used with this very adaptable weave, to produce a huge variety of weights, textures and patterns. The surface appearance of the weave is even, without any directional force, and this enables the character of the fibres and yarns chosen to determine completely the appearance and handle of the cloth. It should be realised, however, that because of the short float length and tight interlacing of the weave, there is little room for the more textured yarns to display their beauty.

The weave diagram for plain weave is given in Diagram 19, along with a pictorial representation of the weave. It should be noted that the weave repeats on two ends and picks and that there are only two different lifting sequences of the ends, which enables it to be woven on two shafts, or any multiple of two, should the closeness of the sett, the fineness of the warp, or the loom itself warrant the employment of four or more.

Balanced plain weave usually produces a perfect selvage. Should, however, the wefting plan compose of two shuttles crossing in alternate order, on one side of the warp the last end will not catch. This can be overcome by using a floating selvage (Chapter 5).

Diag 19 Plain weave

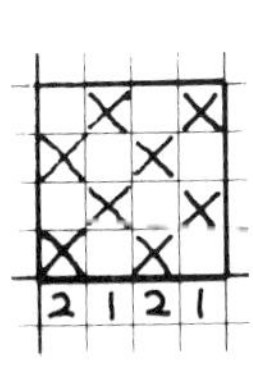

Designing with Square Sett Plain Weave

1. The warp and/or the weft can be varied in colour, fibre or count to produce stripes and checks (Figure 12).

2. The ends per dent in the reed, and/or the picks in a given space, can be varied, producing tight sections and loose sections, or lacy fabrics if large spaces are left (Figure 6).

Fig 12 Plain weave stripe

Fig 13 Regular warp rib

3. Crepe fabrics can be produced by warping alternate ends of Z and S twist yarns and using a similar wefting plan of alternate Z and S twist yarns.

4. Small repeating designs are available with colour and weave effect. These can also be combined in stripe and check patterns (see Chapter 8).

5. A combination of two or more of the above.

Sett
Maximum sett = $\frac{1}{2}$ of diameters per cm/inch.

Derivatives from Plain Weave

The next simple form of interlacing based on plain weave consists of extending each end and pick either vertically or horizontally in one direction or in both directions simultaneously, producing warp rib, weft rib and hopsack weaves respectively.

WARP RIB—HORIZONTAL RIBS WHICH ARE WARP-FACED

Regular warp ribs are constructed by extending each plain weave lift vertically by a regular amount, and simultaneously altering the sett of the cloth from a balanced sett to one with a high number of ends per cm/inch and a low number of picks per cm/inch.

The resultant cloth is similar in appearance on both sides. Horizontal ribs are formed made up of the colours and textures of the warp yarns (Figure 13). The weft does not show on the surface or the back at all. Shrinkage and take-up is greater in the length than the width.

The counts of the warp and weft can be similar or the weft can be thicker. The thicker the weft and the closer the beat-up of the reed, then the deeper the ribs will appear. A smooth, even warp yarn such as cotton, linen or tightly spun worsted is easier to work with than a hairy, rough yarn. The warp sett is relatively high so a clean shed can be difficult to achieve with a fibrous warp.

As can be seen from the weave diagram and pictorial representation (Diagram 20), two or more picks are inserted into the identical shed, creating one thick rib. This will cause selvage problems and a floating selvage should be incorporated. If desired, one very thick pick, either of a low count or several finer ones running together off the same shuttle, can be substituted for the multiple picks. This in effect reverts the weave diagram back to plain weave. Generally a softer handling cloth, but with less rounded ribs, results from using multiple picks, or

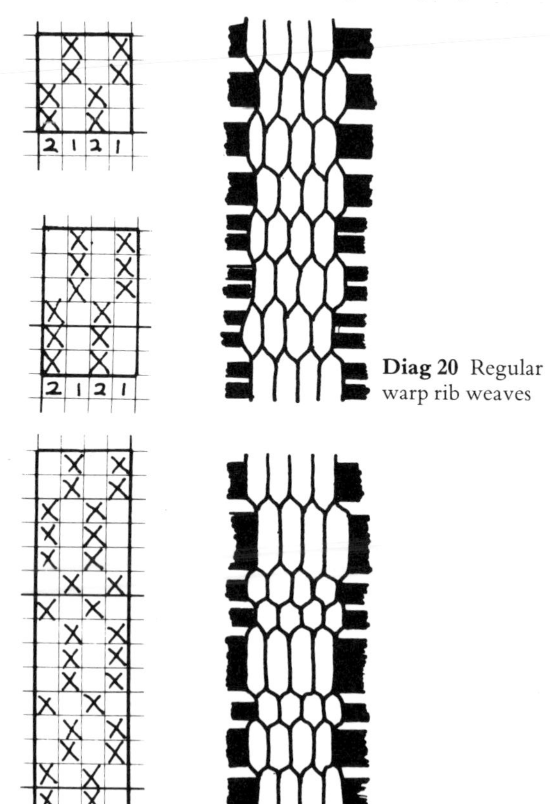

Diag 20 Regular warp rib weaves

Diag 21 Irregular warp rib weaves

one thick pick made up of multiple threads, than from using one solid thick thread.

Irregular warp rib is constructed, either by varying the length that each alternate end is extended on the weave diagram (Diagram 21), or by inserting picks of different thicknesses into a plain weave structure (Figure 11).

Sett

The setting of warp ribs is less straightforward than a balanced plain weave cloth, especially if an irregular warp rib is to be woven, and it is therefore worthwhile to weave a sample before weaving a major piece from which to make a decision. As a guideline, if the same yarn is to be used in warp and weft, then the warp sett equals diameters of yarn less 10–15%, and the weft sett equals diameters $\times \frac{W}{W+I}$ less 10–15%. (*N.B.* If weave is plain $\frac{W}{W+I} = \frac{1}{2}$). As the sett returns towards a more balanced sett, more weft yarn will appear on the surface of the cloth.

DESIGNING WITH WARP RIB

Designing with warp rib is based principally on the colours and order of colouring of the warp yarn. Pre-planning the design before warping or weaving is essential.

1. A self-coloured warp produces a plain coloured fabric, with the interest produced by the light and shade that the ribbed texture creates. A shiny or lustrous warp yarn will exaggerate this effect, as will making a warp of alternate ends of S and Z twist yarns. Varying the thickness of the picks by weaving an irregular warp rib provides additional textural interest to a plain coloured cloth.

2. A coloured striped warp, where at least two adjacent ends are of the same colour, will produce a richly coloured stripe along the length of the cloth. The stripes will be extremely clear as they do not have to mix or compete with the colour of the weft (Figure 13).

3. If two colours are warped alternately, one and then the other, every alternate rib in the fabric will be of one or other of the colours giving the effect of a fine horizontal stripe (Figure 14).

4. A similar warp, colouring plan to that in example 3, but woven with a weft of alternating, one fine pick, one thick or multiple picks, produces a cloth which is predominantly one of the colours on the face with the other colour on the back. By throwing two fine picks across in succession, the

Fig 14 Regular warp rib coloured 1 light, 1 dark in the warp

Fig 15 Horizontal stripes with irregular warp rib weave

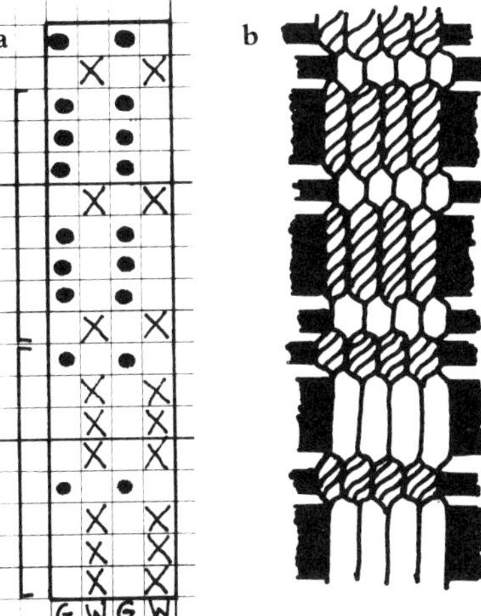

Diag 22 Horizontal stripes with irregular warp rib weave

colour which is on the face transfers to the back of the cloth and the colour on the back shows up on the face. Horizontal stripes of two colours in varying widths can now be woven (Figure 15). Diagram 22a shows the weave diagram with a warp coloured one white (W), one grey (G) and Diagram 22b a weave representation drawing to show the pattern. Note the two fine picks sent across in succession causing the change over of the colours. The width of the stripes can be increased by repeating the section of the weave (and the lifting plan) that is bracketed up.

5. Vertical stripes in two colours can be woven by reversing the lifting sequences of the irregular rib weave for alternate stripes. This means that the two ends at the joins of the stripes lift in an identical order. Diagram 23a illustrates the weave diagram. A warping plan of one light colour, one dark colour, as before, is used and as can be seen from the weave representation in Diagram 23b, one colour dominates in one stripe and the other colour predominates in the other stripe. The width of each stripe can be increased by repeating the section of the weave, that is bracketed up. This in fact means that the width of the stripes is determined while heddling the warp is taking place. Once the warp has been set up on the loom, the widths of the stripes cannot be altered. It should be noted from the numbers underneath the weave diagram that the drafting plan is no longer a straight draft on two shafts, but has become a block draft on two shafts.

A similar effect can be achieved by using an irregular warp rib weave throughout, but changing the warping plan from one dark, one light, to one light, one dark when a stripe is desired (Diagram 23c).

By throwing two fine picks across the warp in succession (Diagram 24a), the two colours in the

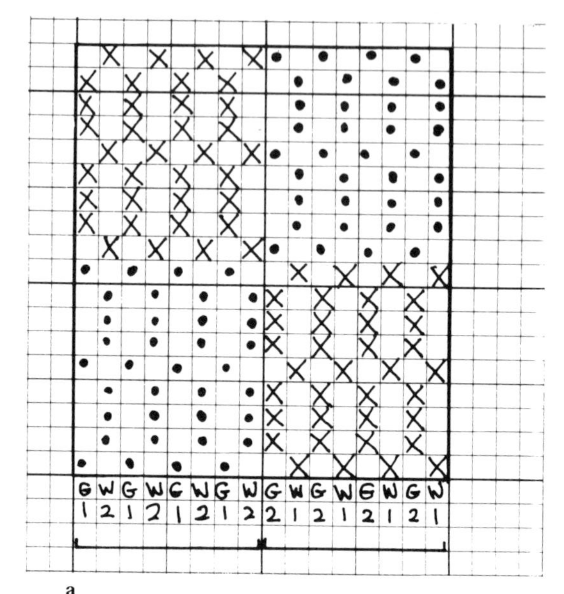

a

b

Diag 24 Rectangular shapes with irregular warp rib weave

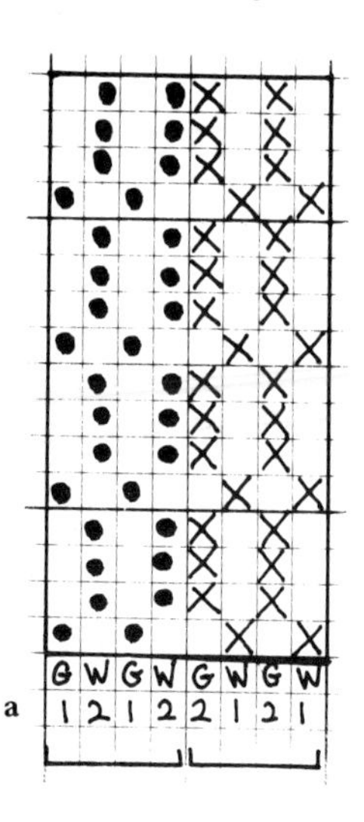

a

b

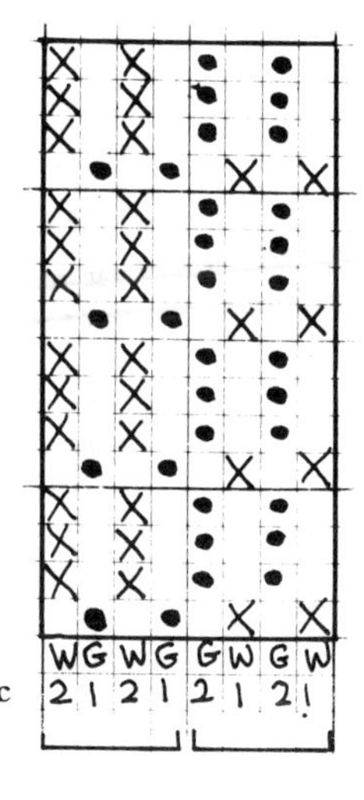

c

Diag 23 Vertical stripes with irregular warp rib weave

vertical stripes change positions, making it possible to weave square and rectangular shapes (Diagram 24b), (Figure 16).

6. A combination of the two ideas in sections 4 and 5 gives enormous scope for interesting patterning.

Diagram 25a illustrates the weave diagram of a typical combination, with a one white, one grey warp colouring plan, alternating with a one grey, one white warping plan and a one fine, one thick wefting plan. The upper section shows an ordinary rib producing the horizontal stripes and checks and the bottom section shows the rib weave lifts changing position in alternate blocks. It should be noted that the drafting plan of this combined pattern (Diagram 25b) will be a block draft on four shafts. Figure 17 shows a cloth woven in this manner.

7. As can be seen from above, with a 1/1 warp colouring plan of two colours, either colour can be made to show on the surface of the cloth by alternating the lifting sequence of the rib weave.

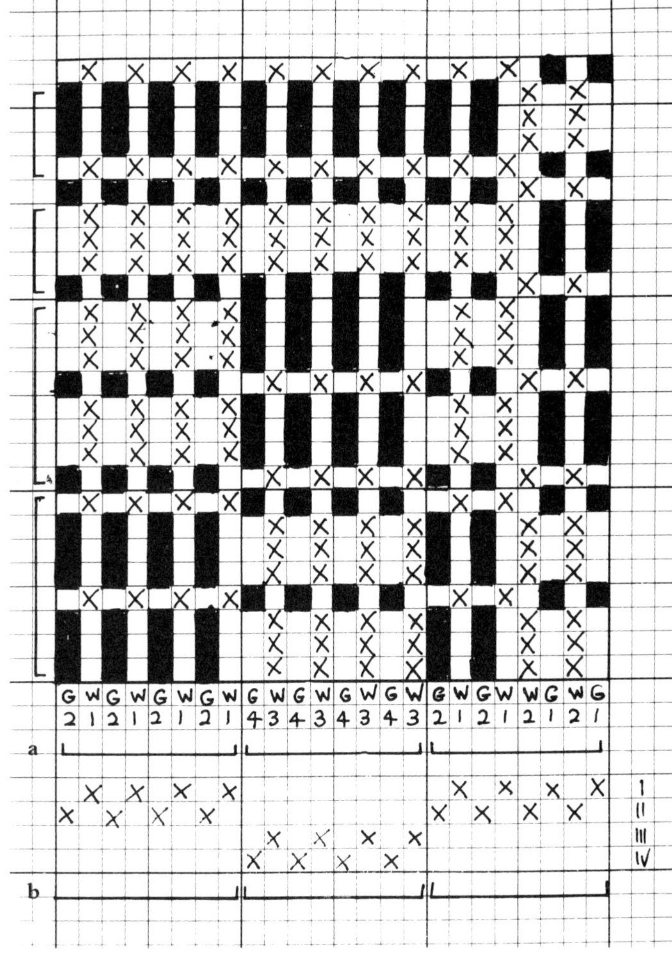

Diag 25 Irregular shapes with warp rib weave and drafting plan

Fig 16 Rectangular shapes with irregular warp rib weave below

Fig 17 Irregular shapes with warp rib weave

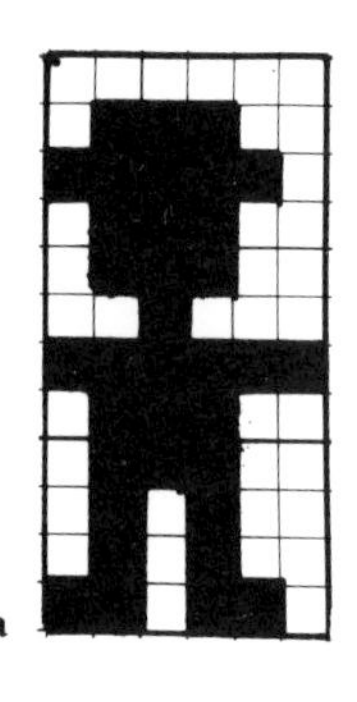

a

Diag 26 Man motif pattern in warp rib weave

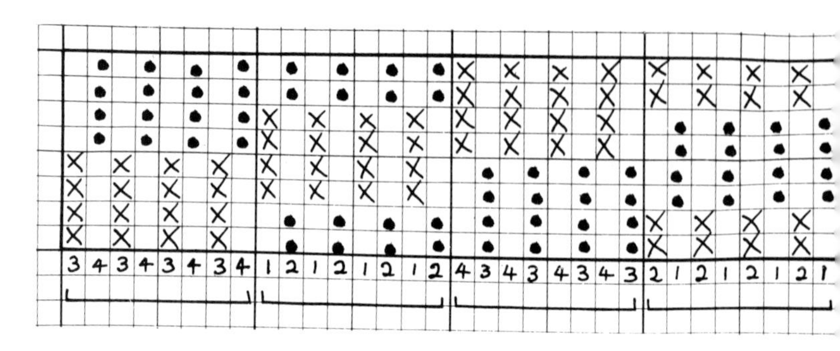

G W G W G W G W G W G W G W G W G W G W G W G W
4 3 4 3 6 5 6 5 8 7 8 7 6 5 6 5 4 3 4 3 2 1 2 1

b

Diag 27 Diagonal lines with warp rib weave

This construction, therefore, lends itself to the building up of large patterns from a motif shape as described in Chapter 12. Rib weave is inserted into each shape of a motif. In each repeat of the shaded areas, the first end on the left will lift under 1 pick and over 3 picks, while the first end on the left in the contrasting shape is lifting over 1 pick and under 3 picks per repeat.

Usually each individual block of a motif will require two shafts, although diamond shaped motifs may only require one shaft per block. Each block of the weave diagram can be increased in height or width by bracketing each repeat (Diagram 26b).

Diagram 26b illustrates the weave diagram of a man motif (Diagram 26a) on 8 shafts, and Plate 8 a fabric woven using this design.

8. Narrow diagonal lines are produced if the irregular warp rib weave is commenced in a different position in succeeding blocks and a continuous warping plan is followed of one and one colouring as indicated by the different marks in Diagram 27.

9. If very large ribs are constructed with long warp floats, it is wise to give the cloth some extra stability by interlacing the ends which produce the back cord in a plain weave order (Diagram 28). This will flatten the ribs slightly, but the surface colouring is unaltered although four shafts will be required to weave it. Soleil weave is the name for this construction, and is traditionally combined with a one and one order of warping with S and Z twist yarns in order to fully develop the rib lines.

WEFT RIB — VERTICAL RIBS WHICH ARE WEFT-FACED

Weft ribs are constructed by extending the basic plain weave picks horizontally and simultaneously reducing the ends per cm/inch and increasing the picks per cm/inch. The resultant cloth is similar in appearance on both sides and is made up of vertical ribs of only the weft yarn. The warp yarn does not

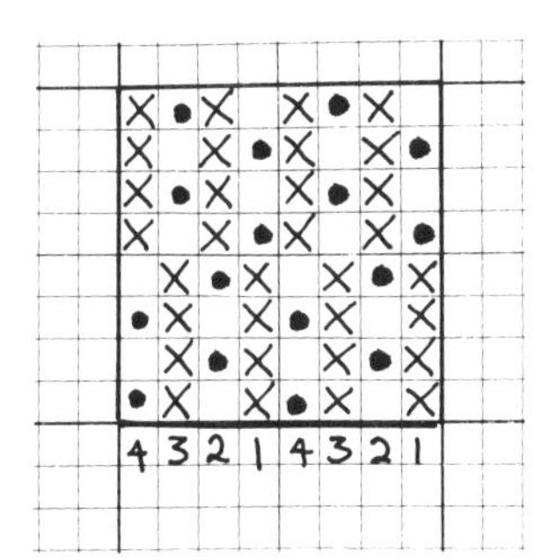

Diag 28 Soleil weave with warp rib

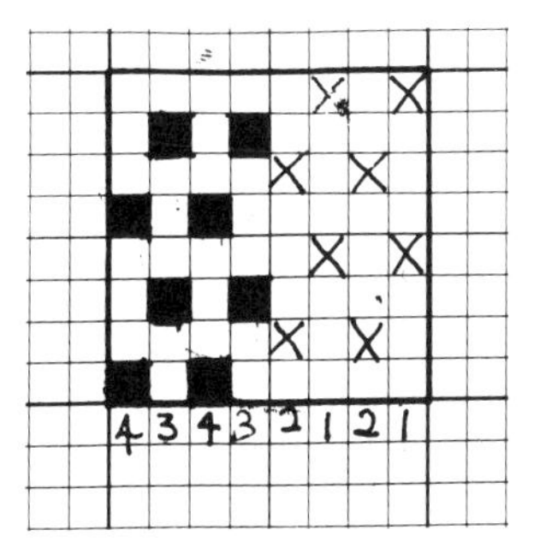

Diag 30 Soleil weave with weft rib

show on the surface. The take-up in the warp is very small, but a reasonable amount of extra weft will be required for each pick to allow it to bend around the ends. By beating up the weft while it is lying at an angle in the shed, or even undulating the weft in the shed for very coarse fabrics, should overcome the problem of the cloth becoming increasingly narrower as weaving progresses. Both regular (Diagrams 29a and b) and irregular (Diagrams 29c and d) weft ribs can be designed.

Colour and patterning depends entirely on the weft. Similar effects to warp rib weaves can be woven. Bold horizontal stripes will occur when several picks of one colour are followed by several picks of another, while a one-and-one coloured wefting plan produces narrow vertical lines. Because the warp is entirely hidden, and the visual effects are achieved by the weft, a certain amount of designing on the loom can take place.

The weft does have a tendency to slip over the warp unless the fabric is very firmly woven. Interlacing the back rib as plain weave overcomes this problem (Diagram 30).

Maximum sett

Yarn counts similar in warp and weft.
Warp = $\frac{1}{2}$ diameters per cm/inch
Weft = diameters per cm/inch

Diag 29 Regular and irregular weft rib weaves

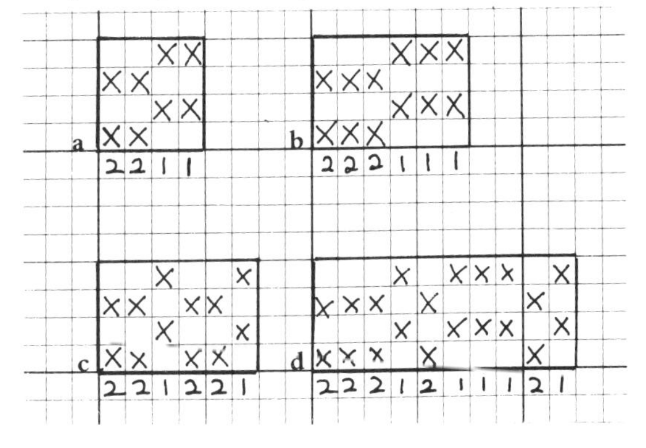

Combining warp rib and weft rib

It is obviously impossible to combine a true warp rib and weft rib in the same cloth as the setts are so incompatible. If, however, they are combined in a checkerboard arrangement and a square sett employed, a rib type of effect is achieved. If the warp and weft is coloured one light and one dark, a basket effect of vertical and horizontal lines results. If the two warp colours are different from the two weft colours, a four-colour basket weave is formed as illustrated in Figure 18. Diagram 31 illustrates the weave diagram of a 3/3 warp and weft rib checkerboard arrangement. Each section commences, however, with a float of 2 in order that no float longer than 3 occurs at the joins. It requires 8 shafts to weave it.

PLAIN AND ORNAMENTAL REPP

Repp weaves in their simplest form are usually warp-faced. They produce a fabric with a similar effect to warp rib weaves except that only the face of the cloth is deeply ribbed with horizontal ribs, and the weft is visible on the back of the cloth. The warp is very closely sett.

The weave has a warp and weft of alternating, one fine thread with one, two or more thick threads. Ideally the finer warp should be run from a separate beam and tensioned tighter than the thick warp. Diagram 32 illustrates two simple repp weave diagrams. The fine pick is made to float under the

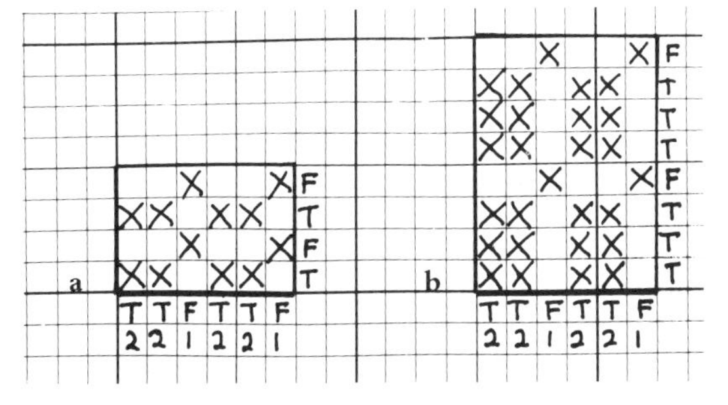

Diag 32 Simple repp weaves

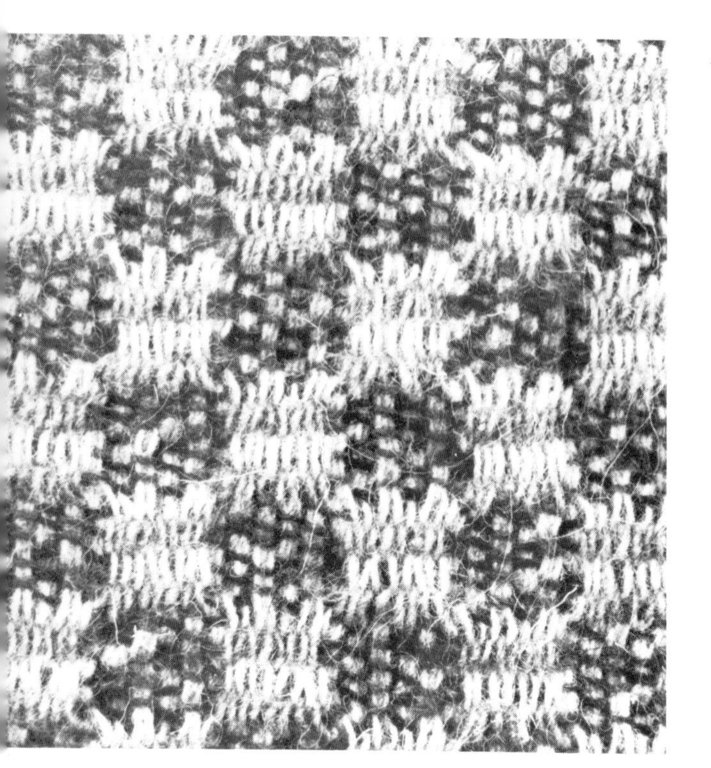

Fig 18 Warp and weft rib combined

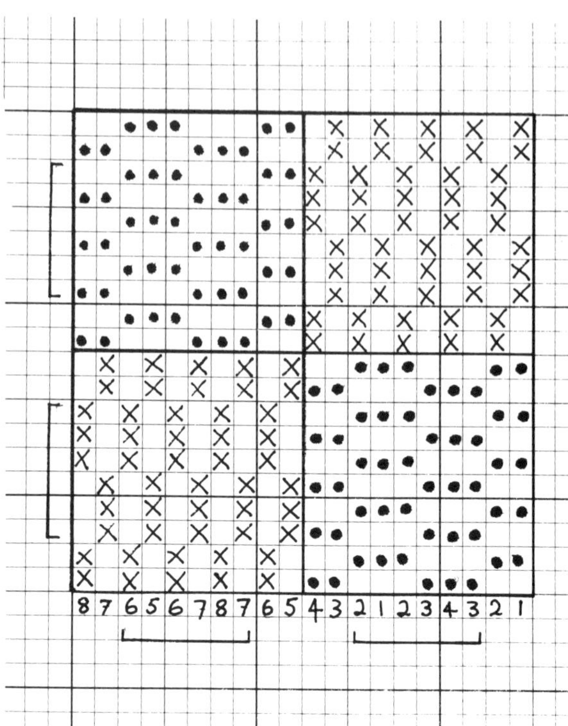

Diag 31 Warp and weft rib combined

Diag 33 Checkerboard patterns in ornamental repp weave

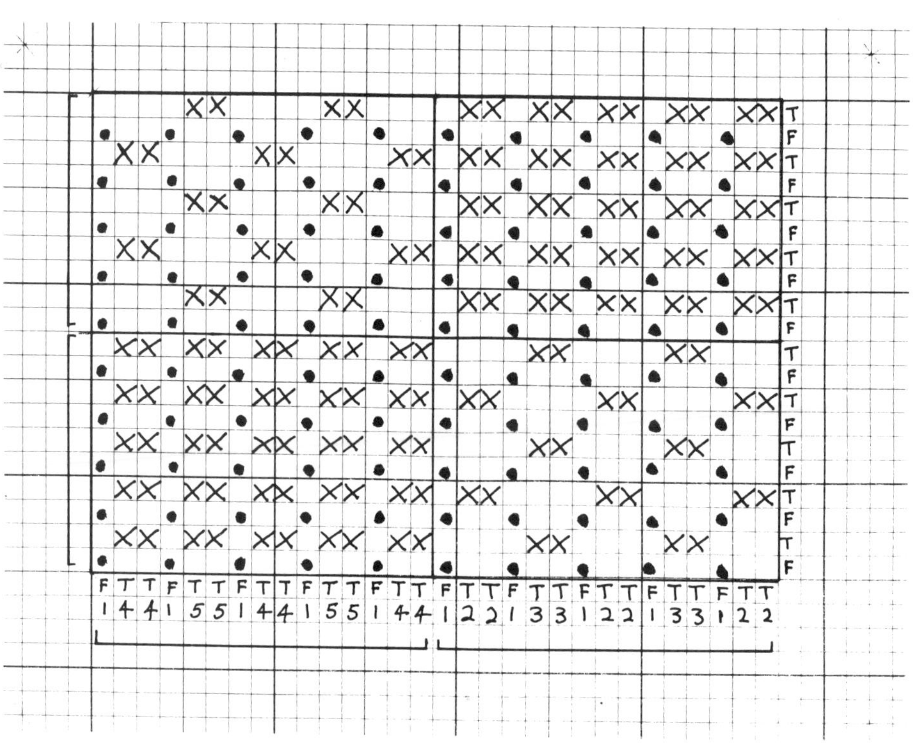

fine ends and the thick or multiple picks are made to float under the thick ends. The fine thread should be strong and tightly twisted. The thick threads can be three or four times the weight of the fine thread. Plate 13 illustrates a jacket woven in simple repp, additional interest achieved by making a warp stripe.

Normally the thick weft threads do not show on the surface of the cloth. They can, however, be brought to the surface if desired to create a pattern or motif. A warp-faced repp which brings thick picks normally hidden on the back to the face, is a very versatile construction with which to design.

Diagram 32a illustrates a small repeat of a simple warp faced repp. The warping plan is one fine (F) end to two thick (T) ends and the wefting plan is one fine one very thick as indicated. If this weave is drawn out in a large repeat and any of the warp-up marks on the thick ends are removed from the weave diagram to show as blanks, the thick crossing pick will peep out onto the surface at that point.

No more than two adjacent groups of warp-up marks on one pick should be removed at a time, otherwise very long weft floats will occur. Any number of warp-up marks in a vertical direction, however, can be removed. A row of these removed results in a pattern of narrow vertical lines. An all-over dotted effect is achieved by removing alternate groups of warp-up marks on every other thick pick. Diagram 33 illustrates a checkerboard with opposing squares in either normal repp or dotted effect. Removing warp-up marks in a diagonal direction enables large zig-zag and diamond shapes to be formed on a comparatively low number of shafts compared to other weave constructions. Diagrams 34a and b illustrates diamond patterns using these techniques and Figures 19 and 20 two cloths woven with these designs.

The fine end is lifting in an identical plain weave lift across the cloth, and can therefore be drafted onto the same shaft. Each unique lifting sequence of the thick ends will need one shaft each.

The fine ends and picks do not effect the pattern of the cloth and should therefore be similar in tone and colour to the thick warp ends. They need to be a strong, fairly tightly-spun yarn.

The thick warp ends will need to be smooth and straight to enable the high warp sett to weave cleanly. It is also best if it is contrasting in colour or fibre to the thick weft to allow any design to show up.

The thick weft can be of any quality or colour and can be of as many different colours as the design warrants. A thick lustrous weft yarn when allowed to show up on the surface can make a fabric appear

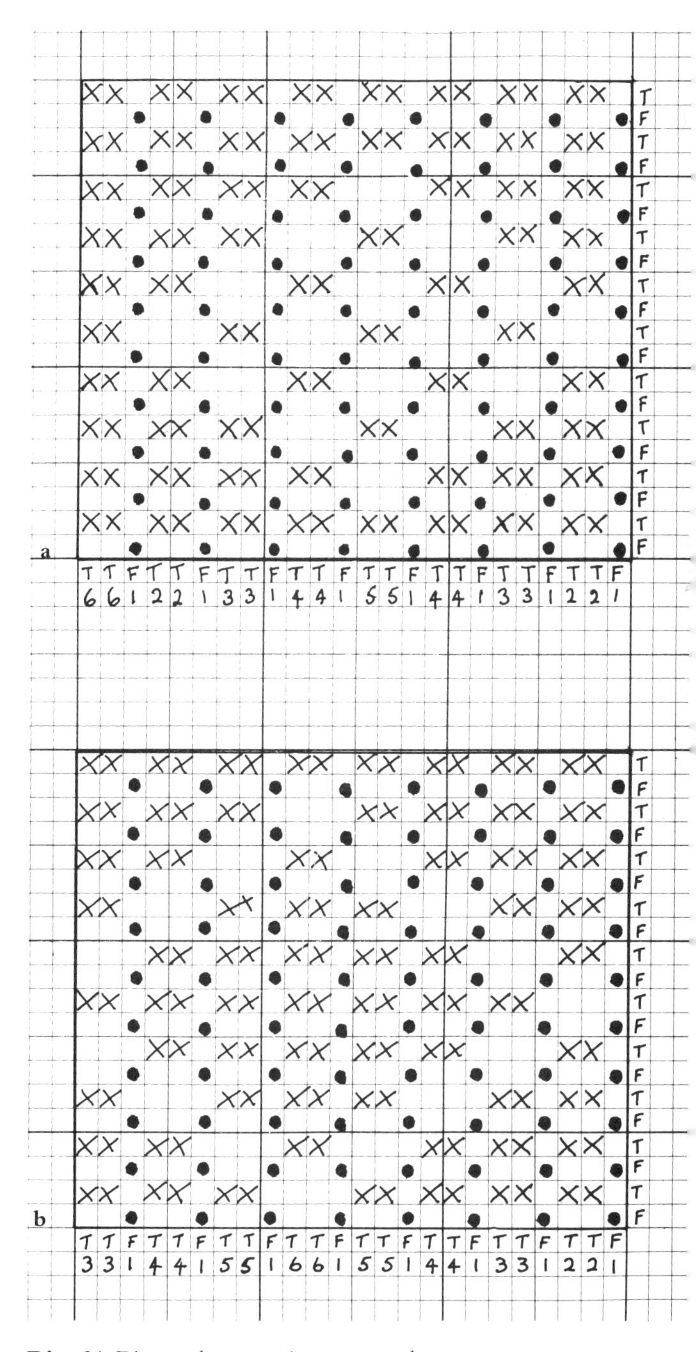

Diag 34 Diamond patterns in ornamental repp weave

to be covered in many 'blobs' of bright jewels. Plate 1 shows a fabric giving this effect.

Sett

Maximum sett is based on the normal sett of a warp faced rib fabric. i.e. Warp = diameter per cm/inch of yarn. Weft = $\frac{1}{2}$ of diameter per cm/inch.

Fig 19 Diamond pattern in ornamental repp weave

Fig 20 Diamond pattern in ornamental repp weave

Hopsack or Matt Weaves

In their simplest form, these weaves are merely an enlarged plain working. The ends and picks of plain weave are extended both vertically and horizontally. To be true hopsack the adjacent threads at each new lift must always be exact opposites from each other. 'Clean cuts' is the term given to this phenomenon. Similar counts are used in warp and weft and are usually employed with a square sett. Hopsacks fall into two groups: regular hopsacks and irregular hopsacks.

In regular hopsack the warp and weft show equally on the surface on both sides of the cloth in the form of small equal sized squares. Diagram 35a illustrates a weave representation of 2/2 hopsack and Diagram 35b its weave diagram and Figure 21 the woven cloth. Irregular hopsacks form unequal sized squares and rectangles (Diagram 36 and Figure 22).

The handle of hopsack is softer and more flexible than plain weave fabric, because the weave interchanges less frequently and the floats are longer. Especially with large hopsacks, for example one that interlaces over six ends and picks and then under six ends and picks, or 6 and 6 hopsack (Diagram 35d), very loose and unstable fabrics can result and these large designs are only suitable for very fine yarns.

Hopsacks lend themselves well to coloured stripe and check designs, while regular 2 and 2 hopsack produces many interesting effects from the colour and weave interlacings (Chapter 8).

Yarns of similar colour but different lustres or textures combine well with hopsack weaves if one type is in the warp and the other in the weft. The long floats in the weave show off lustrous yarns which contrast distinctly against a matt yarn, giving designs which rely on light and shade reactions.

The ends which work similarly together tend to roll around each other as the cloth is being woven and can appear as faults in the cloth. This can be remedied by ensuring that while sleying, the reed wires separate the ends which are working similarly whenever possible. The sley marks (dashes) indicated below the 2 and 2 hopsack weave diagram (Diagram 35b) show where the reed wires should occur. A neat selvage can only be achieved if a separate shuttle is used for each similarly lifting pick, or a floating selvage is implemented.

Maximum sett

2 and 2 hopsack square sett = $\frac{2}{3}$ of diameters per cm/inch. Other hopsacks square sett = diameter $\times \frac{W}{W+I}$.

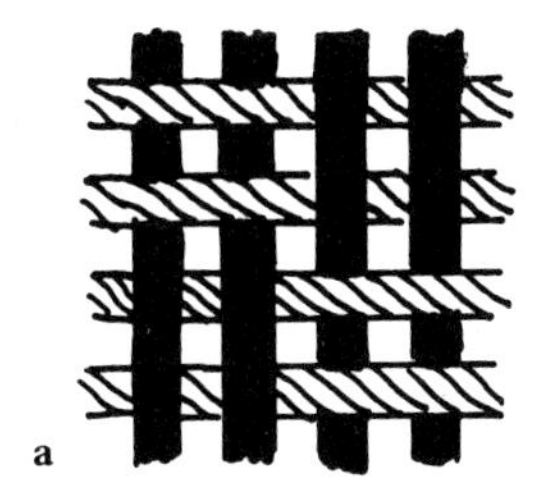

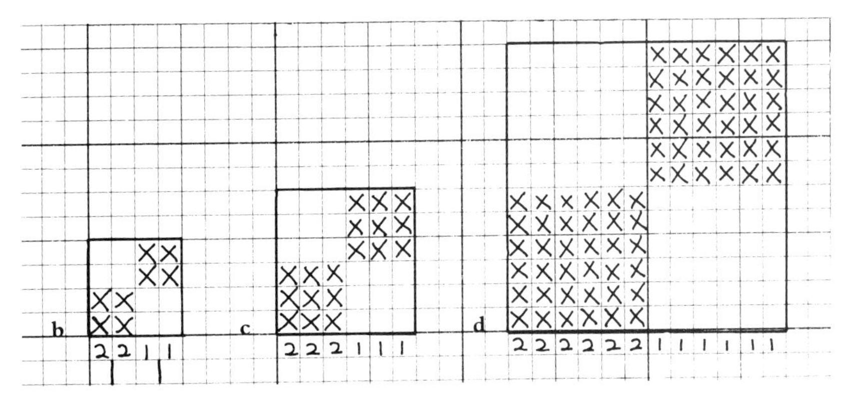

Diag 35 Regular hopsack weaves

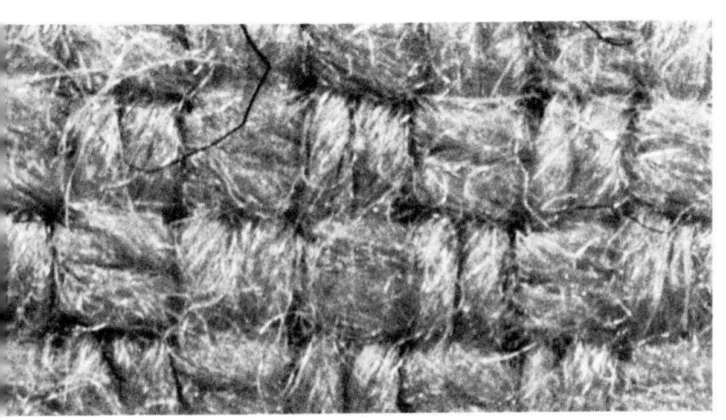

Fig 21 2/2 hopsack weave

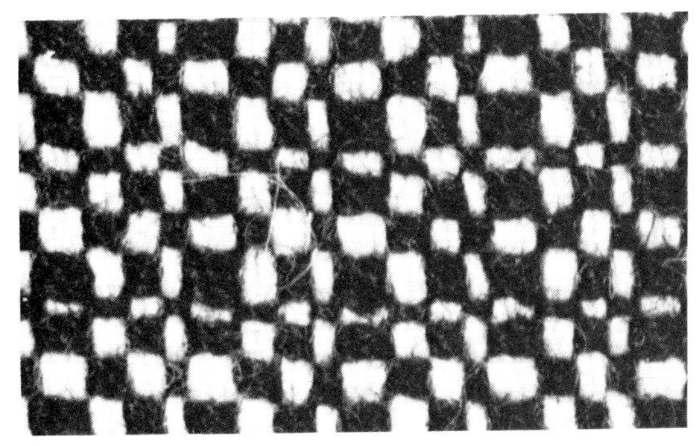

Fig 22 Irregular hopsack weave

COMBINING PLAIN WEAVE WITH HOPSACK AND WARP OR WEFT RIB

Plain weave is the tightest of all interlacings and therefore it shrinks less than any other weave. If combined with a looser structure which has longer floats such as hopsack, the difference in shrinkage can produce interesting distorted effects which are rich in texture. Combining regular hopsack and plain weave in a checkerboard arrangement is the simplest and perhaps the most effective pattern.

Construction of simple weave diagram (Diagram 37)

1. Measure complete repeat size on point paper and divide this up into appropriate sized quarters. It is important that each quarter in the design repeats on an even number of ends and picks.

2. Fill in plain weave in two diagonally opposing corners.

3. A regular or irregular hopsack is inserted in the remaining quarters. Both quarters can show the identical weave or be different weaves, and either show one large hopsack design or be filled with several repeats of a smaller weave.

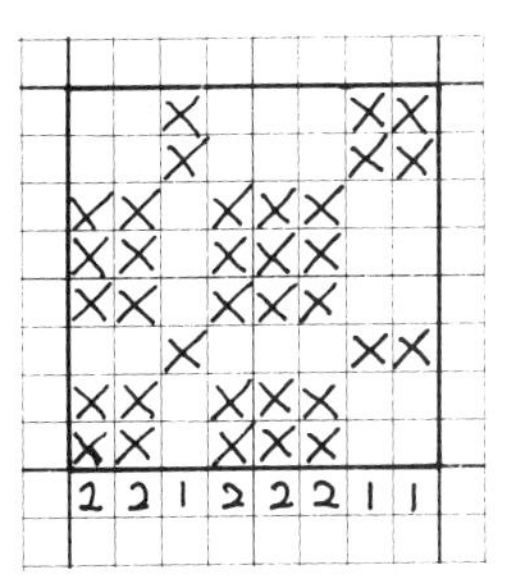

Diag 36 Irregular hopsack weaves

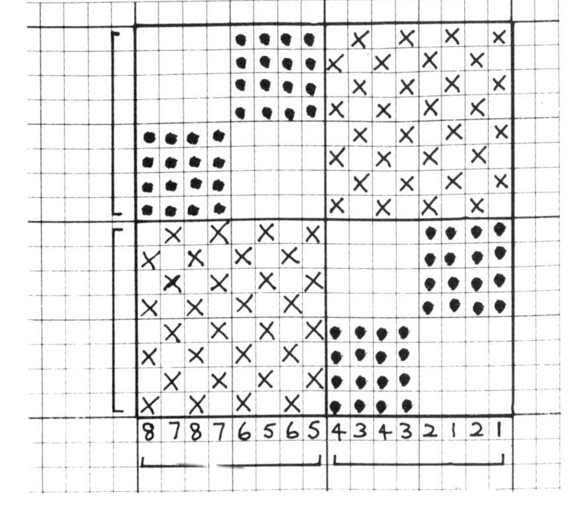

Diag 37 Plain weave and 4/4 hopsack combined

Diagram 38 illustrates another weave combining hopsack and plain weave (R = red, W = white). The illustration on the front jacket shows a fabric woven with this design.

On relaxation of the fabric and full shrinkage after finishing, the plain weave areas appear to bulge out into a circular shape while the hopsack areas converge in on themselves. The distortion can be emphasised by making the first end and pick in each quarter of the design a different colour to the main fabric, and if the reed is sleyed so that the reed wires coincide with the change in the weaves.

The warp and weft yarns should be of similar count, but can of course be of different fibre, and coloured stripes and checks can be easily incorporated. As the weave itself is creating so much texture, it is unnecessary to use very fancy yarns.

Similar distorted effects occur if the two opposite quarters to plain weave are filled with warp rib, weft rib or both. Diagram 39 illustrates this idea and Figure 23 shows a cloth woven to this design.

In all cases the size of each quarter can be increased by bracketing up each individual repeat of the weave diagram as necessary.

Sett

The maximum sett of a design which combines plain weave with another construction is always based on a normal plain weave sett (i.e. $\frac{1}{2}$ of diameters).

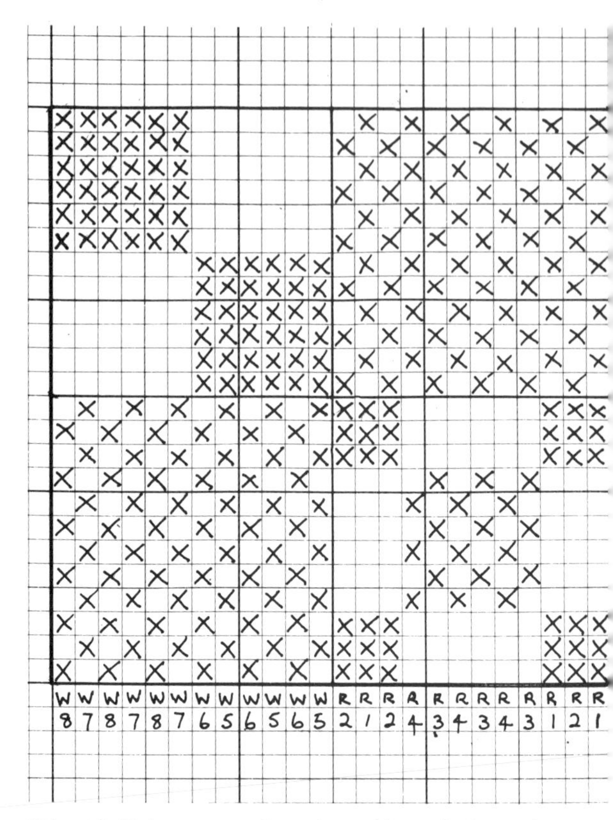

Diag 38 Plain weave and regular and irregular hopsack combined

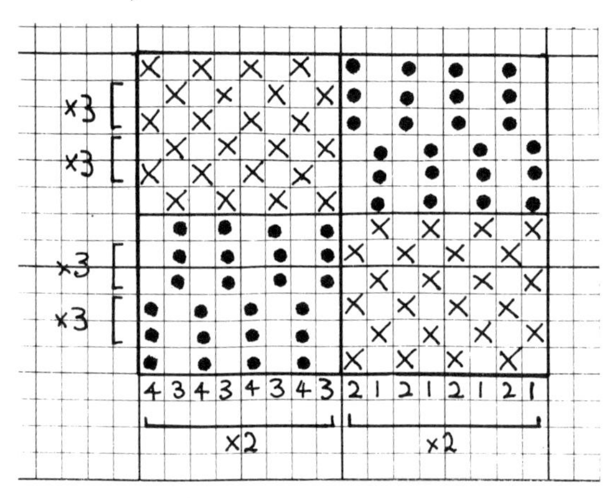

Diag 39 Plain weave and warp rib combined

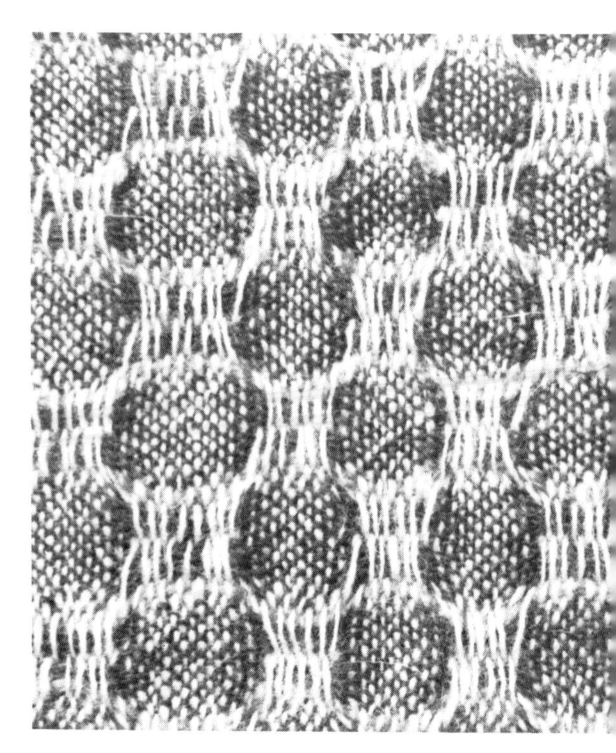

Fig 23 Plain weave and warp rib combined

7 TWILLS

All twill weaves are characterised by diagonal lines of warp and/or weft. In the basic weaves, these lines are continuous and run at an angle of 45° to the horizontal. They usually run from bottom left to top right, but they can run in the other direction. The direction of twill on the underside of the fabric is opposite to that on the face. A simple twilled fabric is softer, heavier, and more flexible than a plain weave fabric woven with the same yarn and sett reductions.

Basic twill weaves repeat on the same number of ends as picks, the smallest possible repeat being three ends and three picks. The largest repeat size that can be woven is limited only to the specifications of your loom, because for each end in the weave repeat an additional shaft on the loom is required. A four-shaft loom can therefore only weave twills which repeat on 4 ends or less. Basic twills are woven with a square sett, which in the simple weaves repeating on four ends and four picks equals $\frac{2}{3}$ of diameters of the yarn, less reductions for shrinkage and handle.

The diagonal line is achieved by moving identical end intersections progressively one pick up and to the right across the weave. On point paper the weave is constructed by marking out the repeat size and inserting on the left-hand edge the first end intersection. This same intersection is repeated on the next end to the right, but starting one pick up. This continues until the total repeat is completed (Diagram 40).

Basic twills are described numerically by listing the standard end interlacing of a particular weave, starting with a warp float first. For example, 2/2 twill is a twill weave in which each end is floating over two picks and under two picks, per repeat. A 3/1 twill is one in which each end is intersecting over three picks and under one pick, and a 3/2/1/2 twill is one where each end is intersecting over three picks, under two, over one and under two per repeat. The total sum of the numbers recorded equals the size of the repeat and the number of shafts required to weave it.

Basic twills fall into four main groups:

1. Simple twills are twill weaves which have only one size of float used in both warp and weft. In a square sett cloth they produce patterns with equal amounts of warp and weft showing on the surface. Simple twills can only be constructed on an even repeat size. Examples of simple twills are 2/2, 3/3, 4/4 etc. (Diagrams 40a, c and d). The larger the repeat of the twill, the less stable and practical the fabric progressively becomes because of the long floats involved. They are also very extravant on shaft requirements. Diagram 40b illustrates a weave representation of 2/2 twill and Figure 24 a 2/2 twill fabric.

2. Simple warp-faced twills are twill weaves which have one size of warp float and one size of weft float, but the warp float is longer than the weft float. The

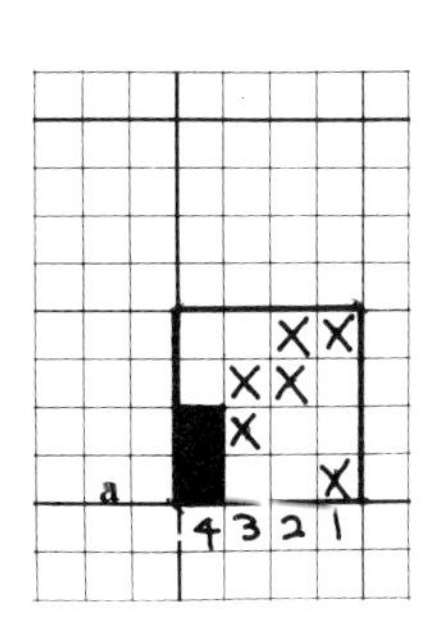

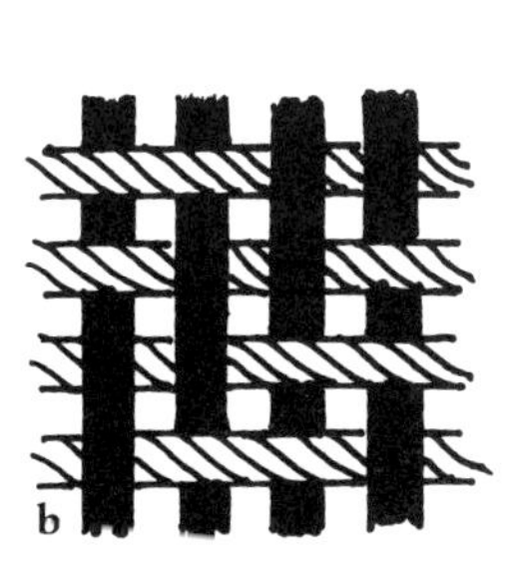

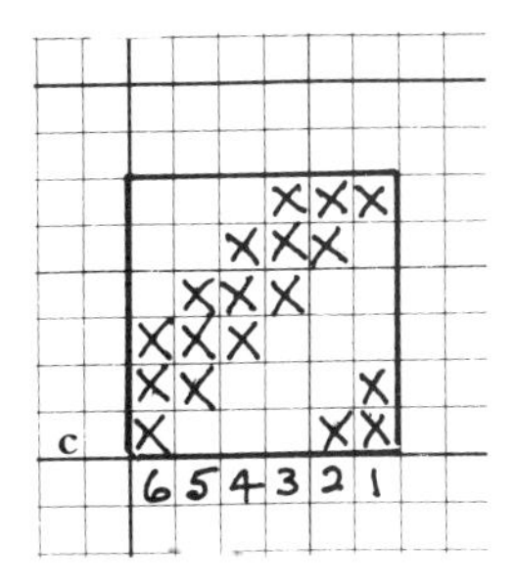

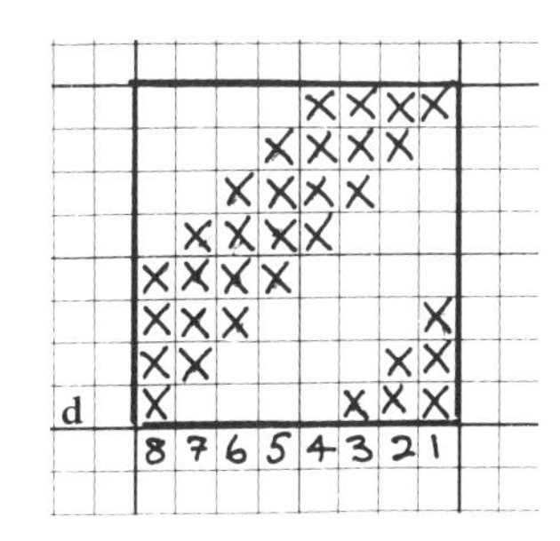

Diag 40 Simple twill weaves a 2/2, b 3/3, c 4/4

Fig 24 2/2 twill weave

Fig 25 3/1 twill weave

surface appearance of the cloth is dominated by the colours and textures of the warp yarn. The underside of the cloth is dominated by the weft yarns. Examples of simple warp-faced twills are 2/1, 3/1, 3/2, 4/2, etc. (Diagrams 41a, b, c, d). Figure 25 illustrates a striped fabric in 3/1 twill.

3. Simple weft-faced twills are twill weaves which have only one size of warp float and one size of weft float, but the weft float is longer than the warp float. The surface appearance of the cloth is dominated by the colours and textures of the weft yarn. Examples of simple weft faced twills are 1/2, 1/3, 2/4, 2/6, 1/7 (Diagrams 42a, b, c, d, e).

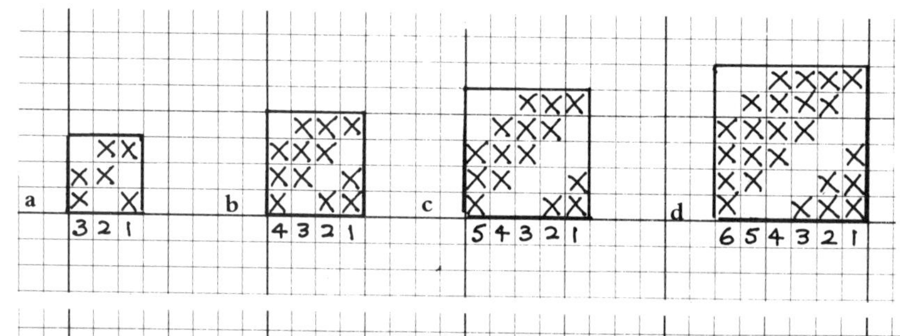

Diag 41 Simple warp-faced twills a 2/1, b 3/1, c 3/2, d 4/2

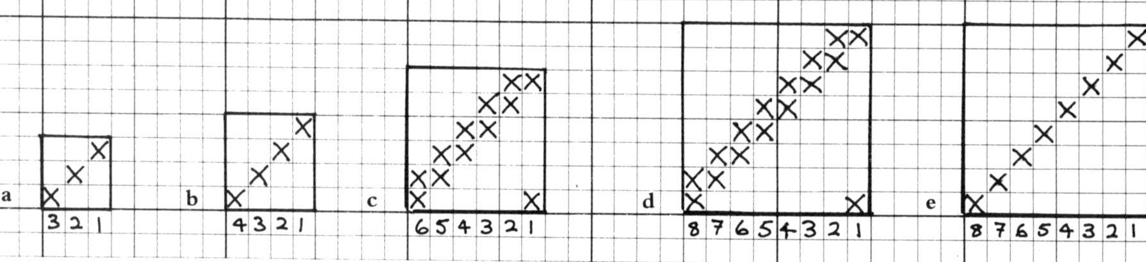

Diag 42 Simple weft-faced twills a 1/2, b 1/3, c 2/4, d 2/6, e 1/7

Fig 26 3/2/1/2 twill weave

Fig 27 Stripe with 2/2 twill

4. Multiple twills are twill weaves which have two or more sizes of warp float and weft float, thereby making fabrics with twill lines of many different sizes. Examples of multiple twills are 3/2/1/2, 4/1/1/2/1/3 (Diagrams 43a and b). Figure 26 illustrates a cloth woven with 3/2/1/2 twill.

Designing with Twills

Twill weaves offer enormous scope for hand-weavers to design with. They can be woven in their original straightforward form, or they can be manipulated to create interesting effects. As previously stated, each end of a twill weave repeat requires one shaft, therefore a four-shaft loom can only weave twills which repeat on four ends and picks. This rule continues when manipulating and designing with the majority of twill weaves. If you only have a four-shaft loom, you can only modify 2/1, 1/2, 2/2, 1/3 or 3/1 twill weaves.

DESIGNING WITH BASIC TWILLS

1. Two distinct diagonal lines result from a self-coloured warp which is crossed by a self-coloured weft of a darker or lighter colour (Figure 24).

2. Coloured yarns in warp and/or weft produce stripes and checked patterns (Figure 27).

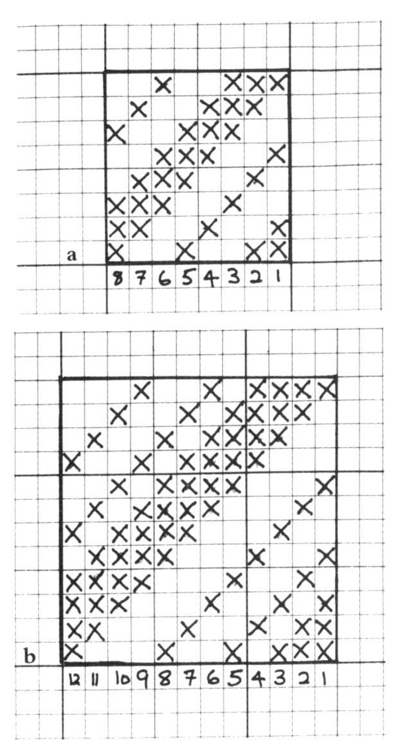

Diag 43 Multiple twill weaves a 3/2/1/2, b 4/1/1/2/1/3

3. Numerous colour and weave interlacings occur with 2/2 twill in particular, but others can be designed using the simple warp- and weft-faced twill weaves. These can be woven as an all over pattern or arranged in stripes and checks (see Chapter 8).

4. When the same colour, count and twist of yarn is used in both warp and weft, a distinct twill line is visible in the finished cloth. This line can be made to appear more developed and prominent if the warp and weft yarns are twisted in the opposite direction to the line of twill. For example, on a twill which runs from bottom left to top right ↗, the warp should be S twist and the weft Z twist. A subdued surface twill occurs if the warp and weft yarns are twisted in the same direction as the twill line.

For example, on a twill which runs from bottom left to top right ↗, the warp should be Z twist and the weft S twist.

Subtle stripe designs can be created if the warp includes Z and S twist yarns in striped sections and the weft in either Z or S twist yarns (Diagram 44a). A greater contrast in the stripes would occur if the warp was all S twist but the weave was composed of sections of twill to right and twill to left, and a Z twist weft used (Diagram 44b). A three-tone variation would result by combining both the above suggestions.

The main drawback with this type of designing is the necessity to carry stocks of both S and Z twist yarns.

Herringbone and Zig-zag Designs

The direction of all twill lines can be reversed. On point paper, the reversed twill is constructed by moving each consecutive end intersection one pick down and to the right instead of one pick up and to the right as in normal twill. A warp weave stripe results if twill to the right and twill to left are joined vertically, and a weft weave stripe results if they are joined horizontally. They can be joined by two methods. The herringbone join, or the point join. A more distinct pattern results if the warp and weft are two different colours.

HERRINGBONE JOIN

The same twill weave is used for both directions. One complete repeat of twill to right is joined to another complete repeat of twill to left. The reversing twills first end intersection is started on the clean cut of the previous weave, or in other words, by placing the warp floats of one weave against the

Diag 44 Twill weaves with S and Z twist yarns

Diag 45 Herringbone twills

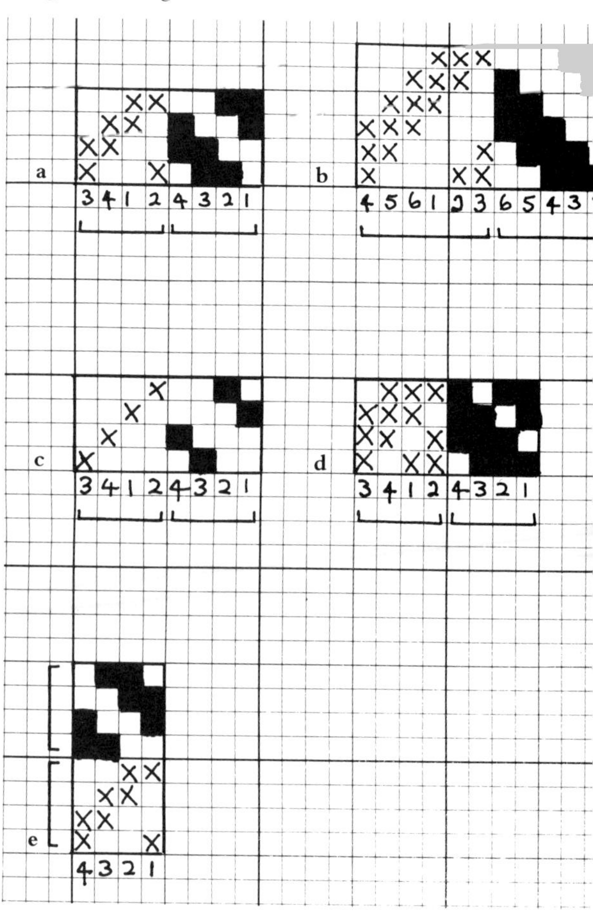

weft floats of the other so that the two adjoining ends are lifting in an exactly opposite order.

With the simple twills like 2/2 or 3/3 (Diagrams 45a, b), the clean cut join is obvious, but on warp-faced, weft-faced or multiple twills the exact herringbone join is not so clearly defined. In these cases the join must occur at a convenient place, perhaps where the long float of twill to right coincides with the short float of the reversing twill, and at a place which also ensures that there is no float at the join which is longer than any float in the basic weave. This is not always possible as in the cases of 1/3 and 3/1 twill (Diagrams 45c, d).

Because the same weave is being used in both directions, the end intersections are identical in both sections and the two effects can be drafted onto the same shafts. The drafting plan will indicate the different order of the end intersections in each stripe of the herringbone design. Each complete repeat unit in the design can be repeated numerous times to increase the width of each stripe, before the reversing twill begins. This is indicated on point paper by bracketing up each repeat unit of the weave as shown in Diagram 45. Figure 28 illustrates a herringbone 2/2 twill warp stripe and Figure 29, a herringbone 3/2/1/2 twill. A herringbone join in the weft is constructed on the same principle of joining on the clean cuts as in the warp (Diagram 45e). The draft remains the same as for basic twill, but the lifting plan is increased in length. The lifting plan can be bracketed up into repeats to enlarge the widths of the stripes in the design.

A broken zig-zag patterned cloth emerges from a herringbone join. The sett of the cloth is determined by the basic weave used.

DAMASK HERRINGBONE

If a warp-faced, weft-faced or multiple twill weave to the right is reversed, starting the join with clean cuts, the twill to left will not only show a reversal in direction but also be the complete opposite in surface pattern. For example, when 1/3 twill is reversed on its clean cuts, the reversed twill turns out to be 3/1 twill (Diagram 46a). This contrasting effect is called damask herringbone. 3/2/1/2 twill to right reversed on its clean cuts produces 2/1/2/3 twill to left as its damask (Diagram 46b), and (Figure 30).

When such a pattern is constructed as a warp stripe, the shaft requirements to weave the design

Fig 28 Herringbone 2/2 twill

Fig 29 Herringbone 3/2/1/2 twill

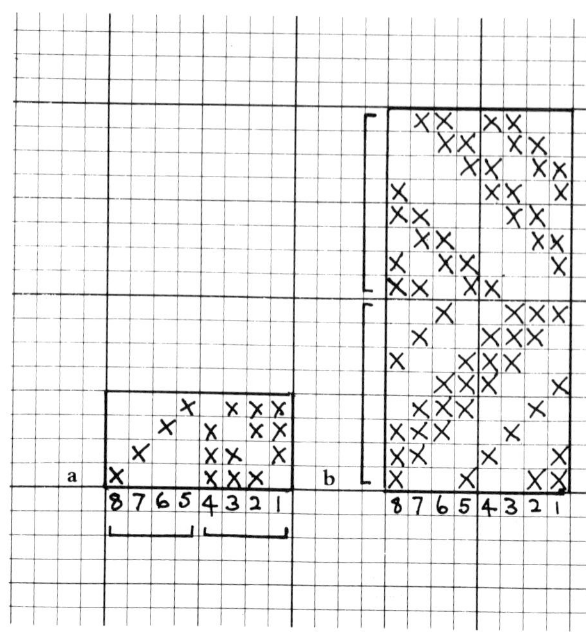

Diag 46 Damask herringbone twills

Fig 30 Damask herringbone 3/2/1/2 twill

are doubled. This is because the two sections of the design do not have identical end intersections. A weft damask herringbone, however, can be drafted onto the same shafts as the original weave, while the lifting plan will have twice as many lifting sequences.

POINT JOIN

Like the herringbone join the same weave is used in both directions, but with the point join the new direction is started by turning upon one end or pick of the weave. For example, 2/2 twill to right is sketched on point paper and twill to left is begun with the same intersection as the one but last lift of the previous weave (Diagram 47a). Long floats always occur at the joins by this method. The drafting plan of a point join warp stripe design forms a zig-zag arrangement which is known as a pointed draft (Diagram 47b). The actual fabric also has a zig-zag pattern as shown in Figure 31 which is a 2/2 twill point join fabric. If the twill is allowed to run twice as far in one direction as it travels in reverse, the zig-zag line gradually rises up and runs at a flattened angle across the cloth (Diagram 48). Figure 32 illustrates this phenomenon with a 3/2/1/2 twill.

The sett is based on the basic weave that is being used.

BROKEN TWILLS

As the name implies, these are twills in which diagonal lines are not continuous across a cloth, but are halted and a new twill line started from another point. They are constructed by completing two or more end or pick intersections of a basic twill on point paper, and then restarting the same twill in the same direction from the clean cuts available. For this reason they work best with simple twills such as 2/2, 3/3, 4/4 etc., but it is not essential to use these weaves, although clean cuts are usually not available with warp-faced, weft-faced or multiple twills.

The diagonal line can be broken and restarted at any point, at regular or irregular intervals, but a simple and very neat arrangement is to break it half way along the basic twill weave repeat. The woven effect is that of a small all-over pattern, when 2/2 twill weave is broken (Diagram 49a) while the larger twills produce much bolder designs (Diagram 49b). It should be noted that when twill to right is used and broken regularly, the resultant pattern has a distinct but flattened inclination to the left.

At the break, the twill can be reversed periodically if desired, giving the appearance of a herringboned twill stripe (Diagram 50).

It is very important when designing broken twills that a full repeat of a design is constructed before drafting begins. The start and finish of the weave

Fig 31 Point join 2/2 twill

Diag 48 Point join twill

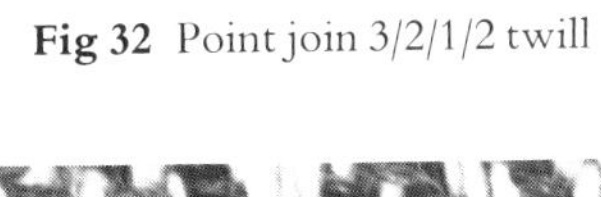

Fig 32 Point join 3/2/1/2 twill

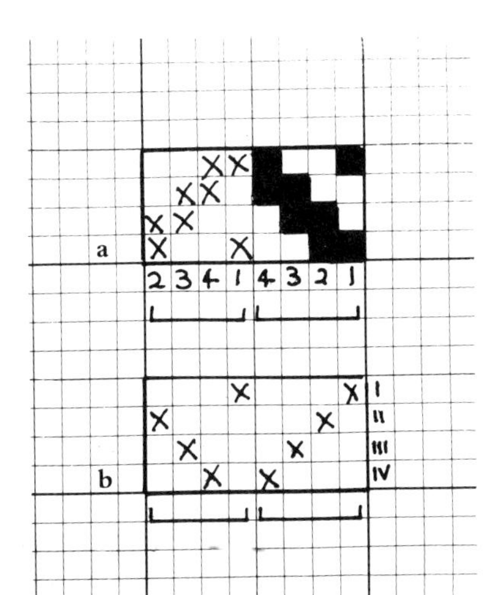

Diag 47 Point join twill and pointed drafting plan

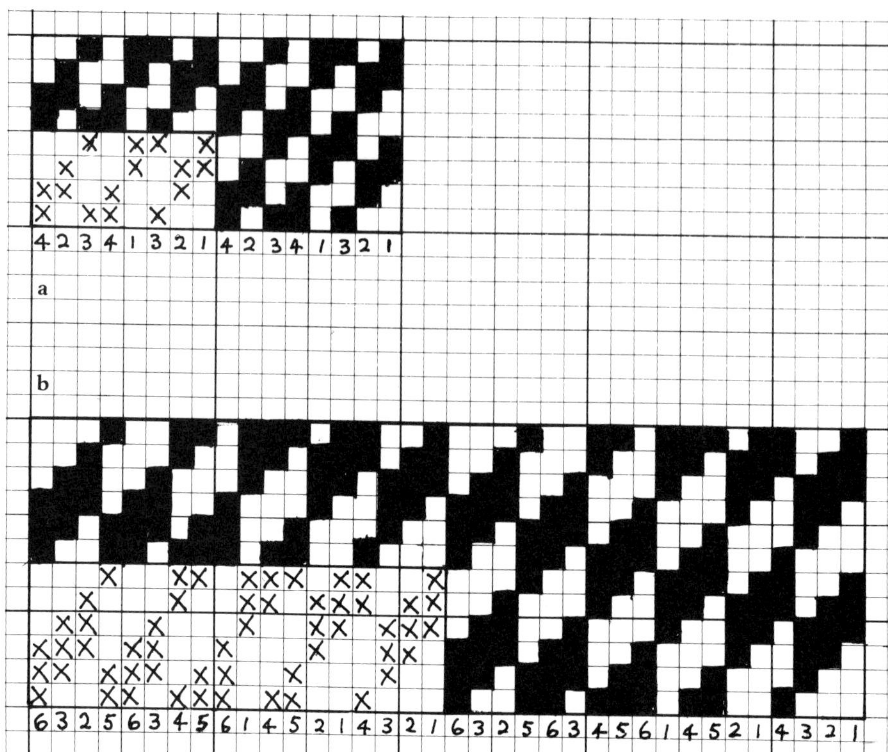

Diag 49 Broken twill weaves a 2/2, b 3/3

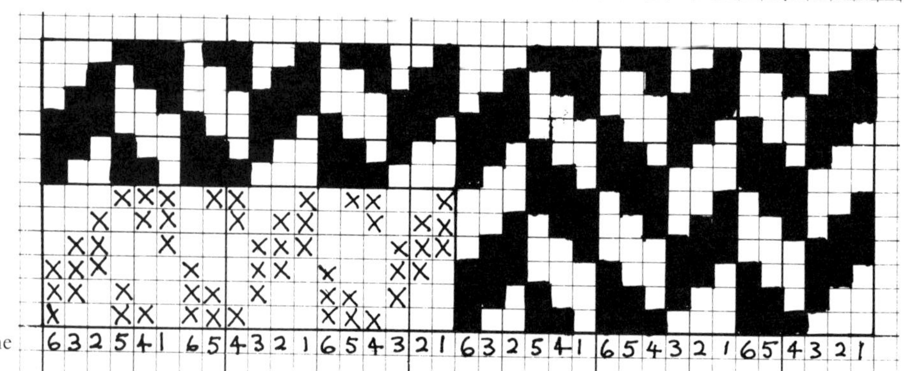

Diag 50 Herringbone 3/3 broken twill

must join up neatly to ensure that the design repeats correctly across the cloth. A 2/2 twill broken regularly every two ends repeats on 8 ends and 4 picks.

A similar principle for designing broken twills can be applied to the weft, with the pick intersections joining on clean cuts at regular or irregular intervals.

The sett of a broken twill design is based on the original twill weave which is being used.

UNDULATING AND WAVY TWILLS

Curved twills are constructed by following a normal twill weave's intersections but repeating any one lift, one, two or more times in succession before going onto the next end or pick, or even missing out one or two lifts before moving on to the next. Diagram 51a illustrates a 3/2/1/2 twill which has been modified in this way, and Figure 33 the woven fabric. Quite long warp and weft floats may emerge from this treatment of a basic twill, and a designer must be aware of the progressive deterioration of wearing qualities, and the instability of a fabric that will develop if this idea is taken to extremes. The direction of twill can be reversed at any time using a herringbone or point join, although with the point join very long floats might occur (Diagram 51b and Figure 34). A square sett is used which will be a fraction higher than the sett of the basic twill from which the design was constructed.

Fig 33 Undulating 3/2/1/2 twill

Fig 34 Point join undulating twill

Diag 51 Undulating twills

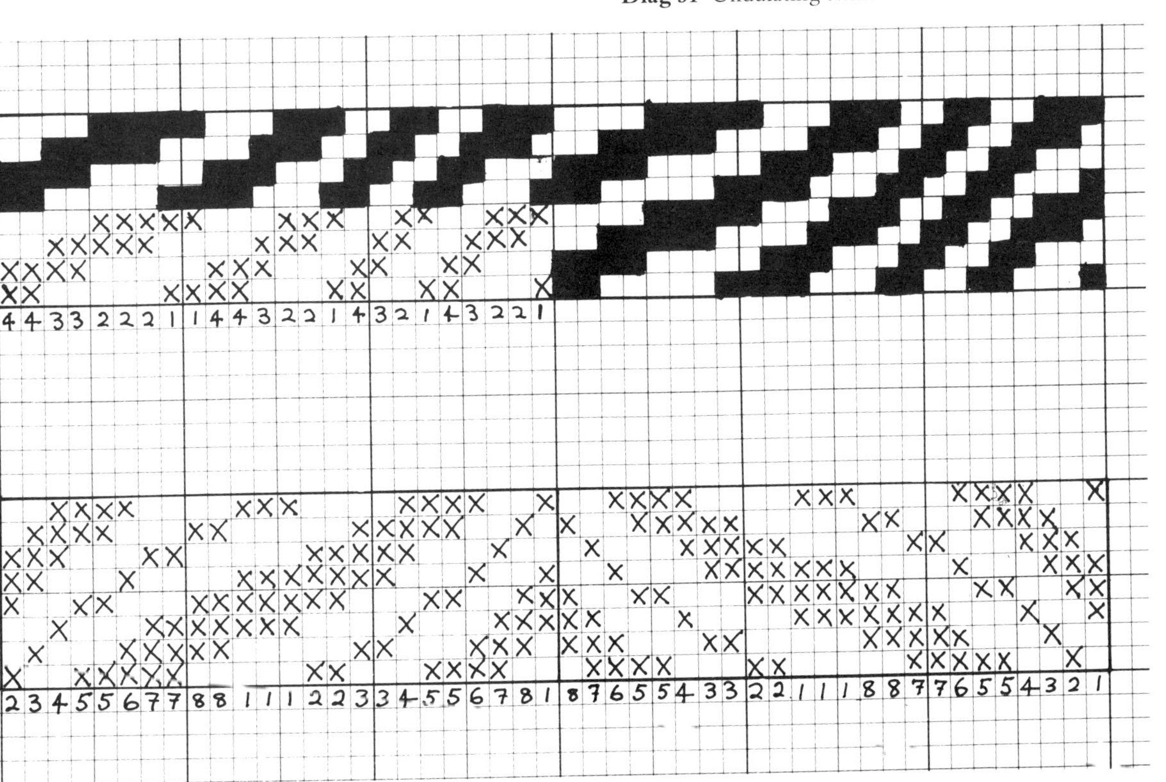

Undulating twills can also be created by weaving a basic twill in normal repeat, but gradually varying the sett of the warp across the width of the cloth. The gradual changes in sett are made while sleying the reed. For example, if 20 ends per inch are square sett and a 10's reed is being used, 4 ends per dent are sleyed in the oversett areas, gradually sleying becomes 3 per dent, then 2 per dent which is square sett, then one per dent as the sett falls below square to become 1 every other dent and perhaps 1 every second dent. This gradual sleying can then reverse in direction back through the different setts, or be started again abruptly with the oversett section.

When the cloth is oversett the angle of twill increases, while in the undersett areas the angle declines, thus producing the curved lines. In addition in the high sett areas, the warp yarn dominates and in the low sett areas the weft yarn dominates, so distinct coloured stripes result if the warp and weft are of two different colours (Figure 7). This type of undulating twill is only successful as a warp stripe, and will cause instability of the fabric in the low sett areas. It can be reversed in the weft with a point join if desired (Figure 35).

Fig 35 Point join spaced sleyed twill

The Angle of Twill

All basic twill weaves woven with a square sett produce a diagonal line which runs at an angle of 45° to the horizontal. The angle of twill can be made steeper or flatter than this if desired, by two methods:

1. *By altering the sett of the cloth.*

If the ends per cm/inch exceeds the picks per cm/inch, the angle of twill becomes steeper, and if the picks per cm/inch exceed the ends per cm/inch, the angle is flattened below 45°. This effect has been demonstrated in the undulating twill (Figure 7), which gradually varies its sett across the width of the cloth and goes steeper and flatter accordingly.

2. *By rearranging each end or pick intersections on the weave diagram.*

In a basic twill each end intersection starts one pick up for each end across the weave (Diagram 52a). If two picks upwards are counted before the next end intersection begins, an angle of 63° to the horizontal is produced (Diagram 52b). If three picks upwards are counted, an angle of 70° results (Diagram 52c). The angle gets progressively steeper if four or five picks are counted before the next intersection begins. A flattened line results if the pick intersections are started two, three or more ends across for one pick upwards (Diagrams 52e, f, g). The angle is exaggerated even more if the sett is unbalanced.

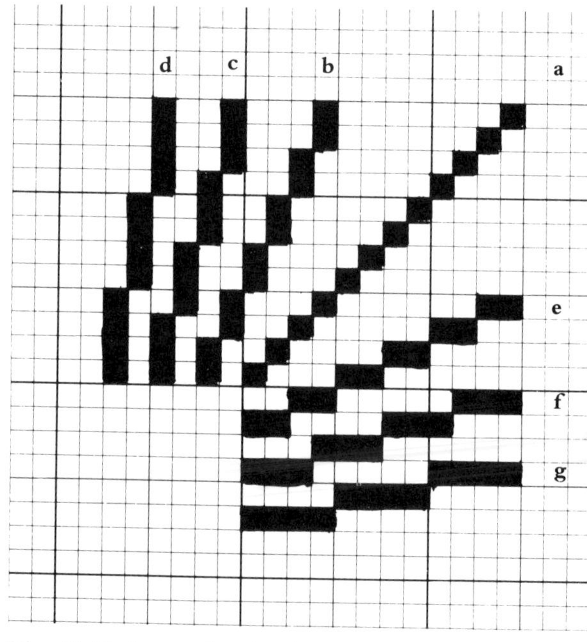

Diag 52 Various angles of twilled lines

Weaves known as whipcords are constructed on this basis and result in fabrics with diagonal cords separated by lines and cuts which vary in prominence.

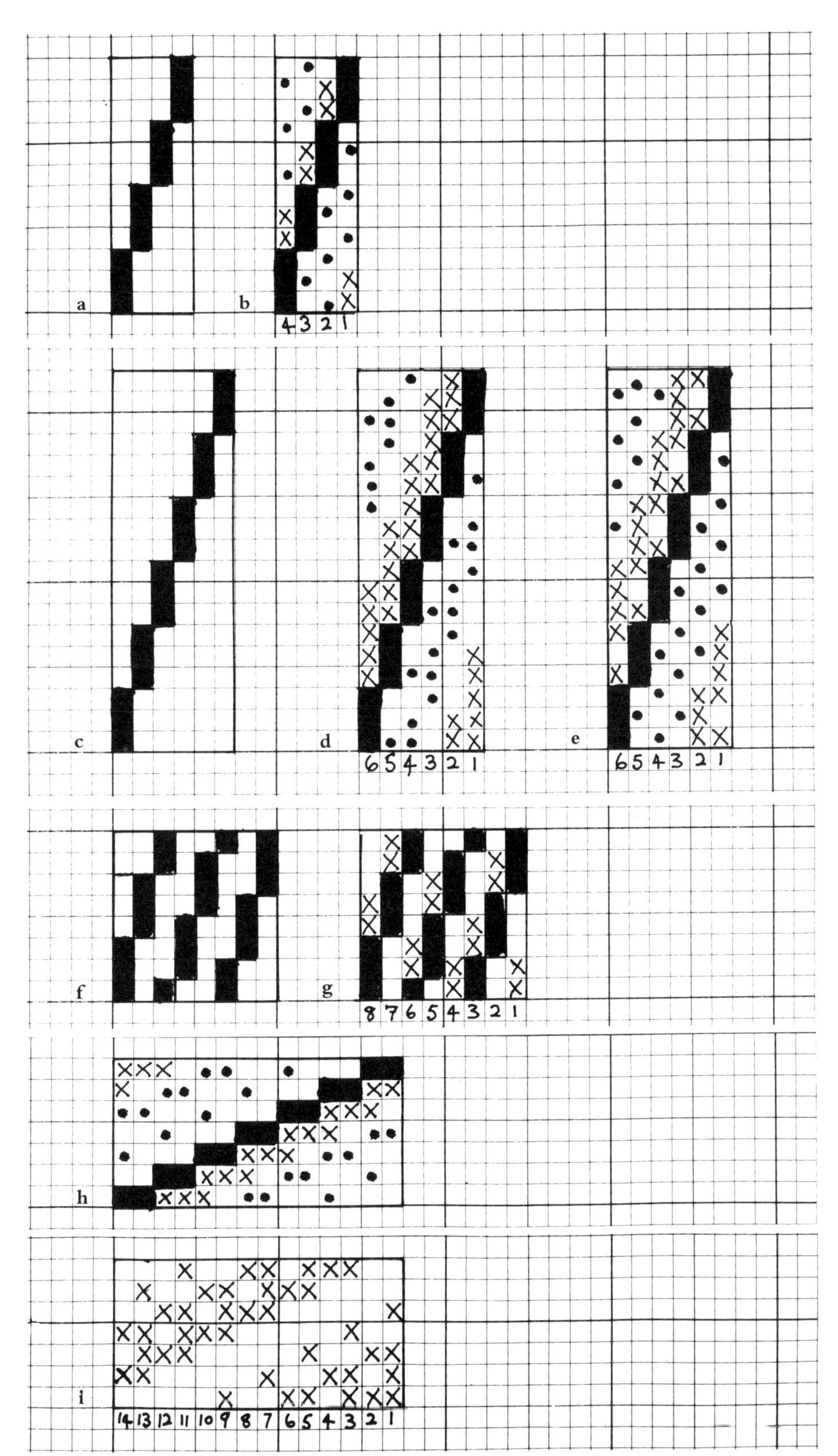

Diag 53 Whipcord weaves

CONSTRUCTING WHIPCORD WEAVES

A base line is run out at the angle required, and the repeat size is established. Additional marks are then inserted starting from each succeeding base mark to create long warp floats for a steep twill or long weft floats for a flattened twill with tight interlacings between these cords.

The correct angle can be determined by choosing one of the base lines illustrated in Diagram 52. This diagonal line can run to the right or to the left. The correct weave repeat size is determined by two methods:

Firstly, the base line can be halted after it has travelled as far across or up the point paper plan as required. It is essential that the final step of the base line has its full quota of marks inserted and is not left shorter than previous steps. The actual weave repeat size can now be indicated; it reaches to the end furthest to the right and the pick furthest upwards of the base line (Diagrams 53a, c). (*N.B.* A steep whipcord suitable for 4 shafts can only have four ends involved in the base line.)

Alternatively, the repeat size can have a predetermined height for a steep twill or a predetermined width for a flattened twill which is marked out on the point paper. Base line marks are then filled into this space, continuing them over and over again until a completely repeating unit of the base line is achieved. For example in Diagram 53f, a 3 up to 1 over base line for a steep twill which repeats on 8 picks requires the base line to be continued for three diagonals before a repeatable unit of the base line is produced covering 8 ends.

Additional marks must now be inserted lengthening each base line to a point not more than three-quarters of the repeat size. A firm interlacing is then inserted if space is available above these long floats to ensure a tightly constructed cloth. This can either be another short binding cord or a tightly interlacing weave such as 2/1 twill or plain weave (Diagrams 53b, d, e, g).

With steep twills the marks in the weave diagram represent the normal warp-up marks and indicate long warp floats. On a flattened twill, however, long weft floats on the surface are required and therefore care needs to be taken when designing flattened whipcords ensuring that a weave, as constructed above (Diagram 53h), is rewritten, changing all the marks into blanks and the blanks into marks. The new diagram will now show long weft floats separated by tight interlacings (Diagram 53i).

These weaves are most effective either self-coloured or with a plain coloured warp crossed by another plain coloured weft.

The sett of whipcords should be slightly higher in the warp for steep twills and vice versa for flattened twills. For example, on a yarn which has a diameter of 60: the weave firmness formula applied to the weave shown in Diagram 53g gives a reduction of diameters in the warp of $\frac{8}{8+2} = \frac{8}{10} \times 60 = 48$ ends per cm/inch maximum sett, and a reduction in diameters in the weft of $\frac{8}{8+6} = \frac{8}{14} \times 60 = 34$ picks per cm/inch maximum sett.

CONSTRUCTING ELONGATED TWILLS FROM BASIC TWILLS

Steep and flattened twills can be constructed by selecting and/or rearranging the position of end and pick intersections of basic twills.

Choose a basic twill which repeats on an odd number of ends and picks, and which includes at least one quite long warp float (Diagram 54a). If every alternate end is placed adjacent to each other and then those ends which were missed out before are continued onto the first group, a steep twill is produced (Diagram 54b). A steeper angle will be designed if every third (Diagram 54c) or fourth end is transposed. In these cases the original weave will have to be rescanned three or four times respectively for all the intersections to be allocated new positions, and a repeating twill weave completed.

By the above method all the ends of the original weave are still present in the new steep twill arrangement, and therefore the two weaves can be drafted on to the same shafts. For this reason weave stripe patterns can be designed easily. The steep twill stripes can be sett slightly higher in the warp than

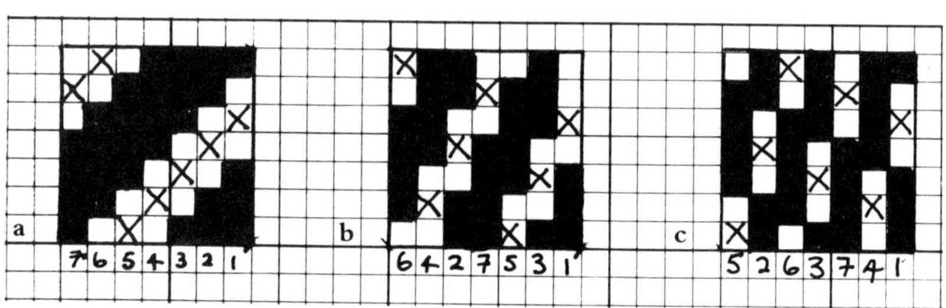

Diag 54 Elongated twills using an odd numbered repeat

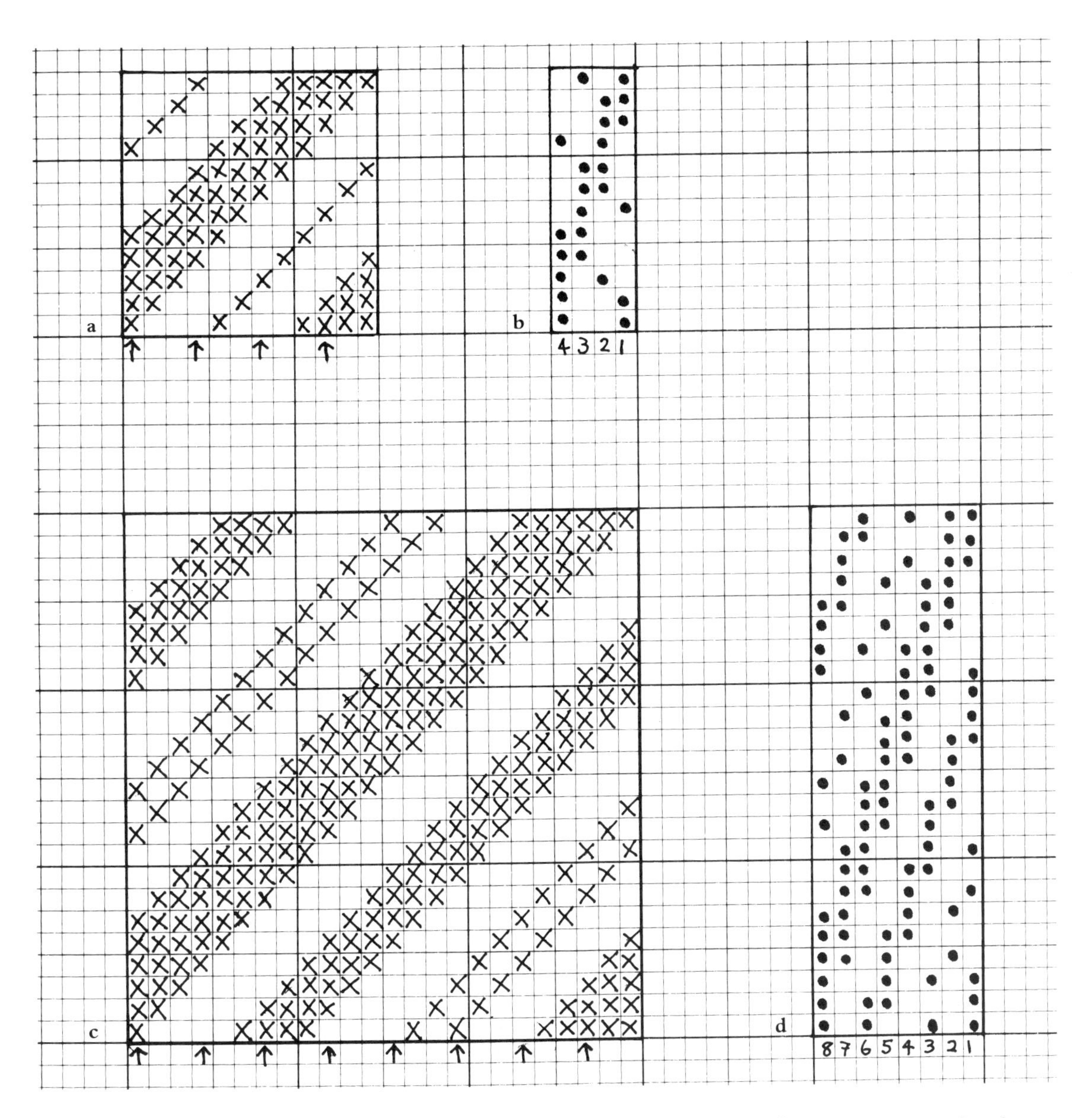

the basic twill in order to emphasise the contrast in weaves.

If a twill is chosen with an even number of ends and picks per repeat (Diagram 55a, c), a similar selection of every second, third or fourth end or pick can be done, but it is only necessary to scan the basic weave once to obtain a repeating twill line. The proportion of ends or picks selected must divide equally into the original repeat size of the basic weave. For example, a twill which normally repeats on 24 by 24 with every third end selected, will now produce a steep twill which repeats of 8 ends and 24 picks (Diagram 55d). If a four shaft loom is to be used, a twill which normally repeats on 12 ends can be woven as a steep twill on four

Diag 55 Elongated twills using an even numbered repeat

shafts if every third end is extracted (Diagram 55b). Figure 36 illustrates a cloth woven as Diagram 55b.

Flattened twills must be rewritten to exchange warp marks into long weft floats, as suggested with traditional whipcord weaves above.

All steep or flattened twills may be reversed with a point join if desired, taking care that very long floats do not occur at the joins.

Fig 36 Elongated twill on 4 shafts

Fig 37 2/2 twill diamond (below)

Fig 38 Oval shaped diamonds (right)

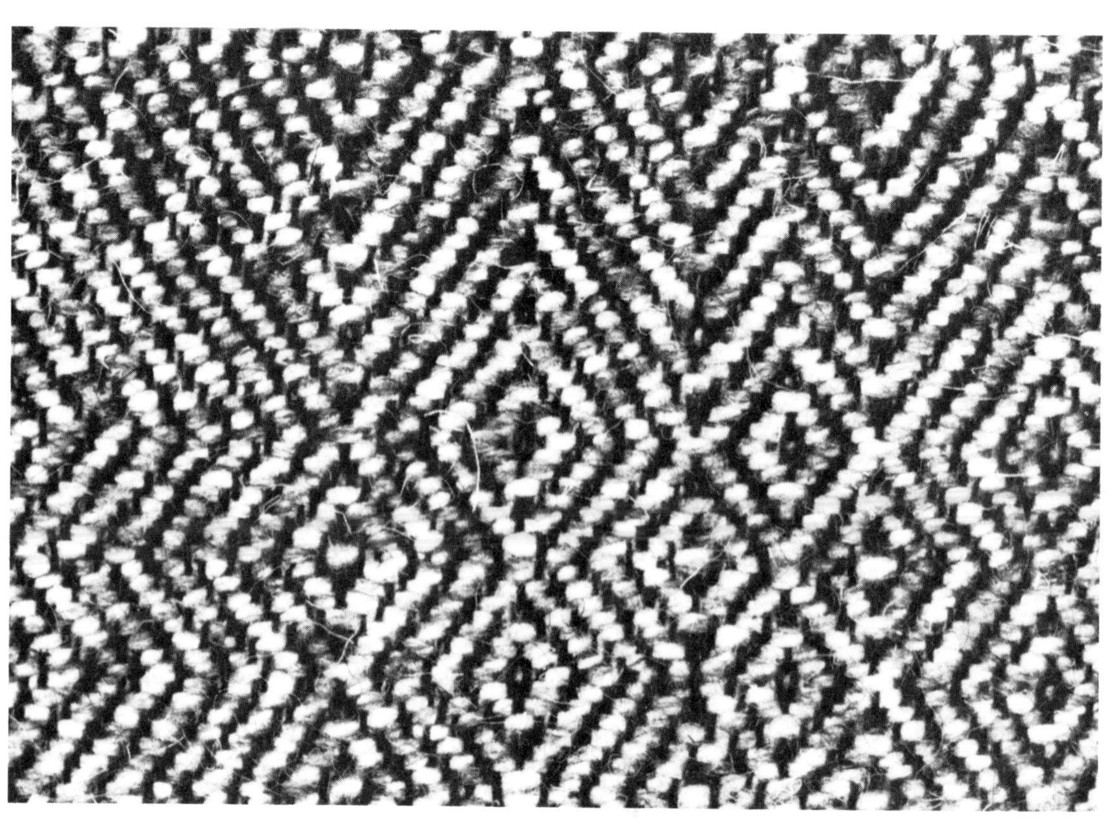

Diag 56 Diamond shaped twills

Diamond Designs

If any twill is reversed with a point join vertically and horizontally simultaneously, the resulting pattern will be diamond-shaped (Diagram 56a and Figure 37). When wavy twills are treated in a similar manner, oval shapes occur (Diagram 56b and Figure 38), while steep twills become elongated diamonds (Diagram 56c).

In all cases, some of the floats at the joins will be longer than any float in the original weave, especially with wavy twills, and these can show as ugly marks in the woven cloth.

When a point join, zig-zag warp-stripe design, with varying widths of stripe, is reversed, diamonds of different sizes emerge. These can become quite ornate patterns, if each turn in direction up the weft occurs after either one, two or more complete repeat units of the basic twill. A diamond weave will always be able to be drafted onto the same shafts as the basic weave that is being manipulated. This fact enables innumerable stripe and check patterns to be woven by combining sections of straight twill with sections of a diamond twill (Figure 37).

CONSTRUCTION OF LARGE DIAMOND PATTERN

1. Choose a basic twill to manipulate, one that can be woven on the shafts available on your loom. Diagram 57a illustrates a 2/2 twill and Diagram 57b illustrates a 3/2/1/2 twill.

2. Construct a warp-striped zig-zag design, with each point join reverse starting after either half a repeat or at least one complete repeat unit of the original weave. The height of the initial warp stripe is one repeat of the basic weave chosen. (See bracketed sections in Diagram 57.)

3. Lightly indicate with fine lines the point at which each reverse occurs, continuing these lines a fair distance up the point paper.

4. Reverse each individual twill stripe of the zig-zag base pattern up the weft, completing one, two or more repeat units, as desired.

5. Reverse the twill lines back again in each warp stripe section in a similar manner to above.

6. Continue zig-zagging back and forth until an attractive design is constructed. It is of course essential that the weave diagrams of these large diamond designs repeat accurately, with a point join, from side to side as well as from top to bottom before any drafting can begin. (*N.B.* While constructing the weave diagram, it may be clearer to see the reversing points of the weave, in both warp and weft direction, if each reversing section uses different warp-up notation marks as shown in Diagram 57.) If desired, after the weave diagram is complete, all warp-up marks can be filled in as solid squares in order to allow the actual diamond shapes that will emerge on the cloth to be seen clearly. The back jacket illustrates a tablecloth based on the design shown in Diagram 57b.

A similar treatment can be applied to a herring-bone zig-zag, which will result in a more broken diamond shape. Unusual but attractive disjointed diamond designs can be constructed by combining point join and herringbone join reversing in the same weave. Diagram 58a illustrates a design using 2/2 twill and herringbone joins in the warp with point join reversings in the weft. 1/3 twill, 3/1 twill and multiple twills can be given a similar treatment (Diagram 58b).

Additional designing with diamond designs can involve superimposing coloured stripes and checks over the patterns.

The sett of the cloth is based on the normal sett of the original weave chosen.

Diag 57 Construction of large diamond patterns

1 Ornamental repp

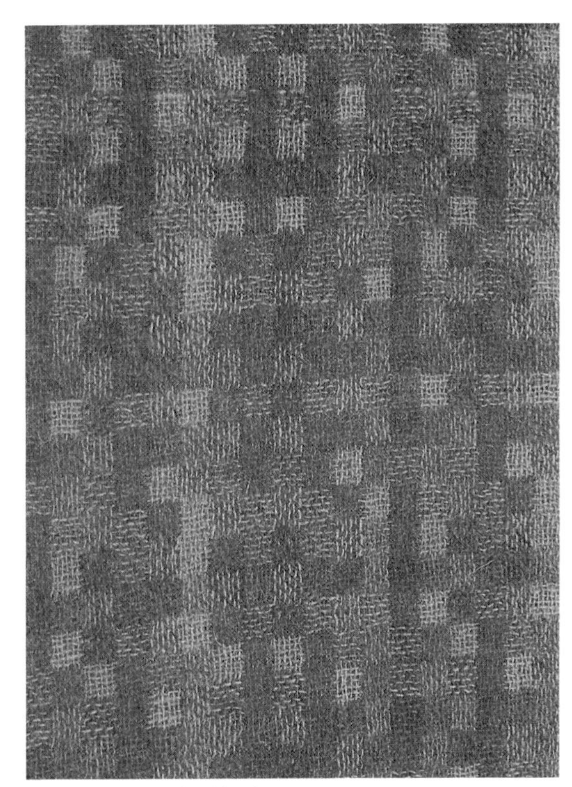
2 Interchanging double plain

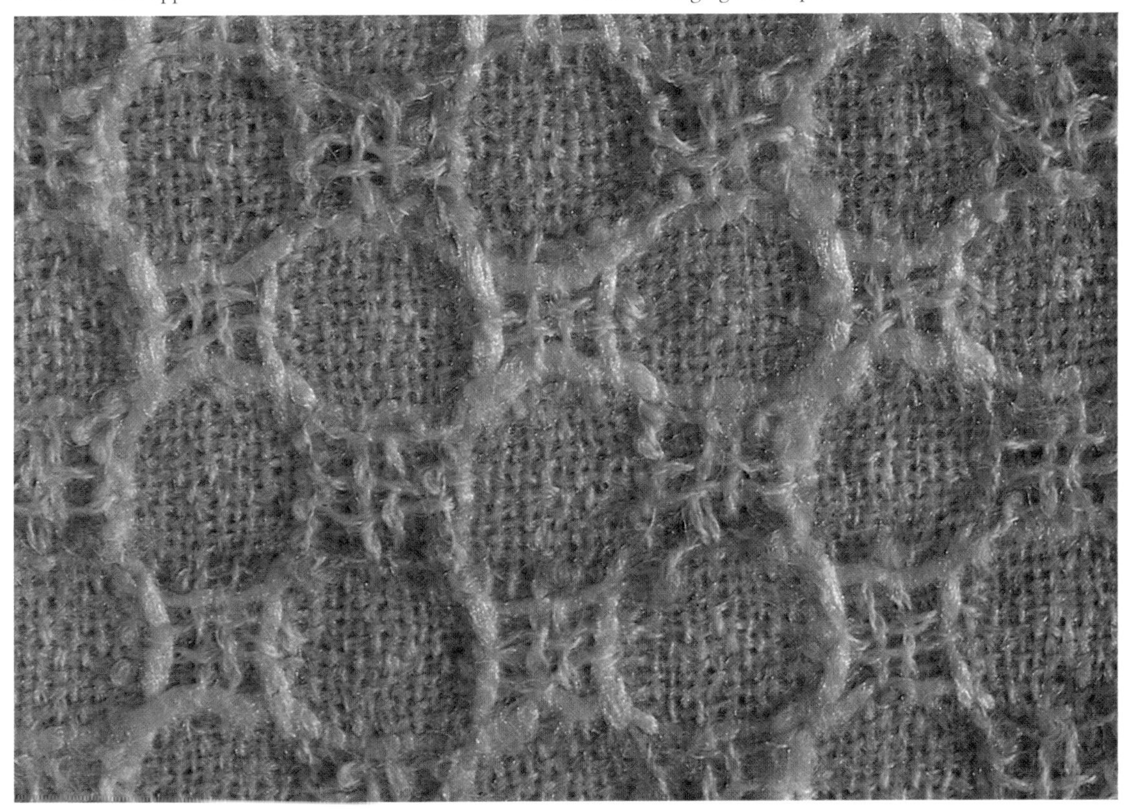
3 Double plain and plain weave

4 4 end satin and sateen

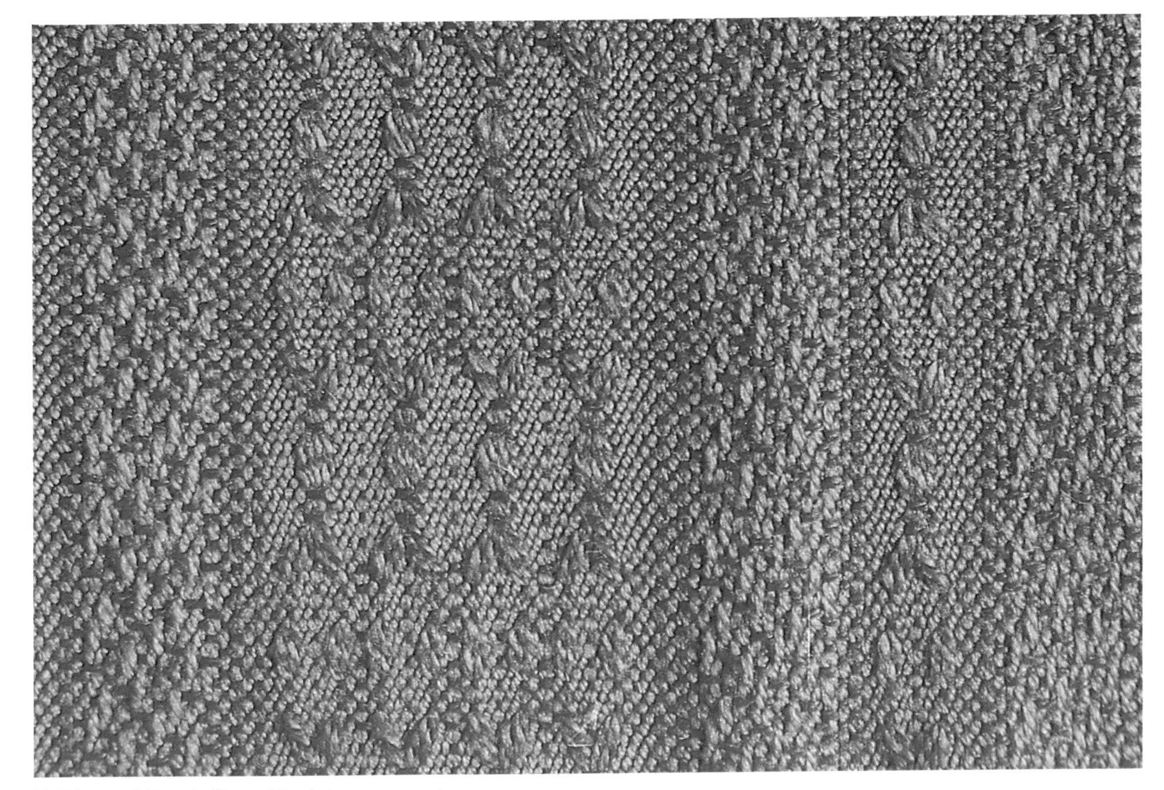

5 Distorted thread effect with plain weave

6 Honeycomb and plain weave

7 Summer and winter weave

8 Warp rib man motif design

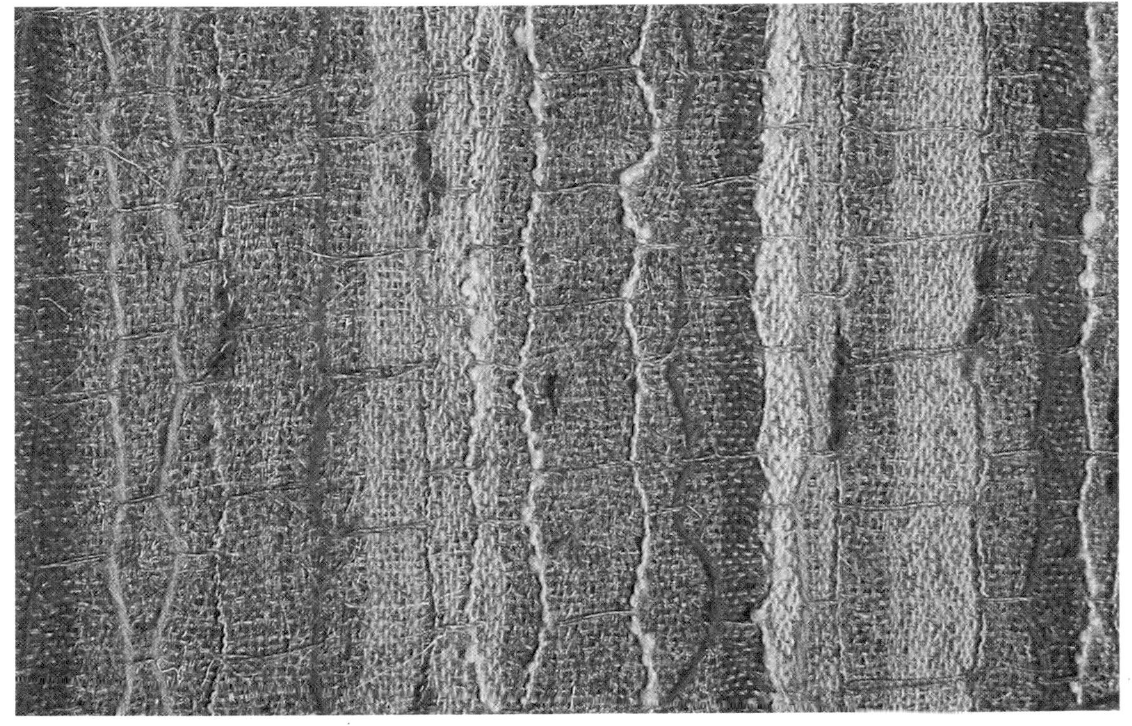
9 Distorted thread effect on striped ground cloth

10 Mock leno and plain weave linen table mats

11 Double plain and bold colour and weave effect suit fabric

12 3/1 twill and 4 end sateen striped cushion

13 Repp weave jacket

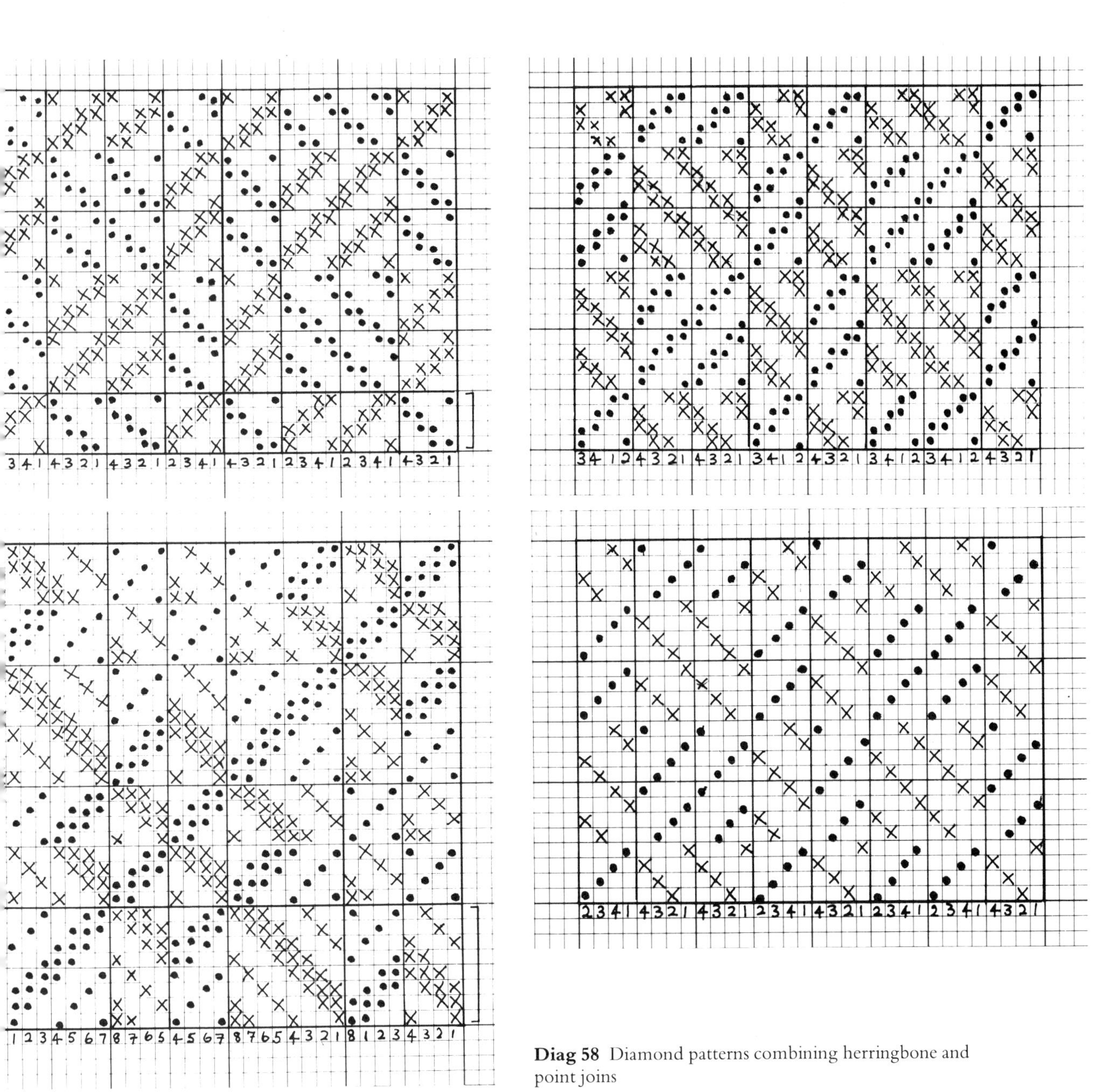

Diag 58 Diamond patterns combining herringbone and point joins

COLOUR AND WEAVE EFFECT

There are a great variety of small repeating patterns that are produced by the interaction of simple two-colour warping and wefting plans on the standard interlacings of plain weave, 2/2 hopsack and 2/2 twill, 4 end satinette, 1/3 twill, 3/1 twill and some dice weaves. In most cases the characteristics of the basic weave is hidden by the new coloured patterns that are formed.

These patterns create a huge library for designing all-over designs, stripes and checks. They are traditionally used in tweeds, but are effective in all fibres and weights of fabrics and in combination with other weaves. Many of them have traditional names by which they are referred to.

Usually the same two colours are involved in both the warping and wefting plans, in proportions of 1 and 1, 2 and 2 or 4 and 4. 'True' colourings are produced when a warping plan is crossed by an identical wefting plan, and it is these true colourings which have traditional names. There are, however, many other patterns resulting from crossing different colour plans with each other and these are called cross colourings. The patterns are more distinctive if sharply contrasting colours are used.

The best way of seeing the many true colourings and cross colourings that are possible is to weave a sampler. Make a warp of at least four sections of about 10 cm (4 ins) each. The first section should be self-coloured, the second 1 light and 1 dark, the third 2 light and 2 dark, and the fourth section 4 light and 4 dark. If space is available, other sections can be made with warping plans such as 2 light and 1 dark, 3 light and 1 dark, 3 light and 2 dark, etc.

Dress the loom in the normal manner to weave plain weave. Weave a 10 cm (4 in) strip for each section of the warp using the identical wefting plans as warping plans. For each weft strip, one true colouring will result with many cross colourings.

A similar sampler can be woven for 2/2 hopsack and 2/2 twill, which can be combined on the same warp as the setts are identical.

Figures 39 to 50 illustrate some of the patterns possible in these weaves.

Figure 39 illustrates vertical hairline pattern, woven using plain weave (Diagram 59a) with a warping plan repeat of 1 light, 1 dark and the wefting plan repeat coloured 1 light, 1 dark. (See also Diagram 59c.)

Figure 40 illustrates four point star pattern, woven using plain weave (Diagram 59a), with a warp coloured 2 dark, 2 light and the weft coloured 2 dark, 2 light. (See also Diagram 59g.)

Figure 41 illustrates a cross-colouring pattern, woven using plain weave (Diagram 59a) with a warp coloured 3 light, 1 dark and a weft coloured 1 light, 2 dark.

Figure 42 illustrates a cross-colouring pattern, woven using plain weave (Diagram 59a) with a warp coloured 2 light, 1 dark and the weft coloured 1 light, 2 dark.

Figure 43 illustrates horizontal hairline, woven using 2/2 hopsack weave (Diagram 35b) with a warp coloured 2 dark, 2 light and a weft coloured 2 light, 2 dark.

Figure 44 illustrates step effect, woven using 2/2 hopsack weave (Diagram 35b) and a warp coloured 1 light, 1 dark and the weft coloured 1 dark, 1 light.

Figure 45 illustrates a large four point star pattern woven using 2/2 hopsack weave (Diagram 35b) and a warp coloured 4 dark, 4 light and the weft coloured 4 dark, 4 light.

A small four-point-star pattern similar to that illustrated in Figure 40 can be woven using 2/2 hopsack weave (Diagram 35b) and a warping plan repeat coloured 1 light, 2 dark 1 light, and the wefting plan repeat coloured 1 light, 2 dark, 1 light.

Figure 46 illustrates step effect woven with 2/2 twill weave (Diagram 40a), and a warp coloured 1 dark, 1 light and the weft coloured 1 dark, 1 light. (See also Diagram 59h.)

Figure 47 illustrates horizontal hairline woven using 2/2 twill (Diagram 40a) and a warp coloured 2 light, 2 dark and the weft coloured 2 dark, 2 light.

Figure 48 illustrates birds eye effect, a cross colouring woven using 2/2 twill weave (Diagram 40a) with a warp coloured 1 light, 1 dark and the weft coloured 2 light, 2 dark.

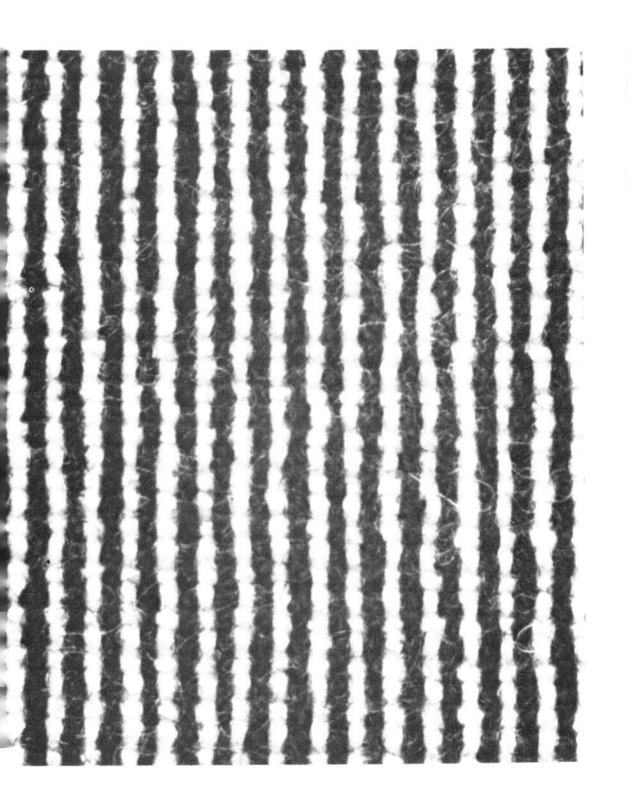

Fig 39 Vertical hairline on plain weave

Fig 41 Cross colouring on plain weave

Fig 40 Four point star pattern on plain weave

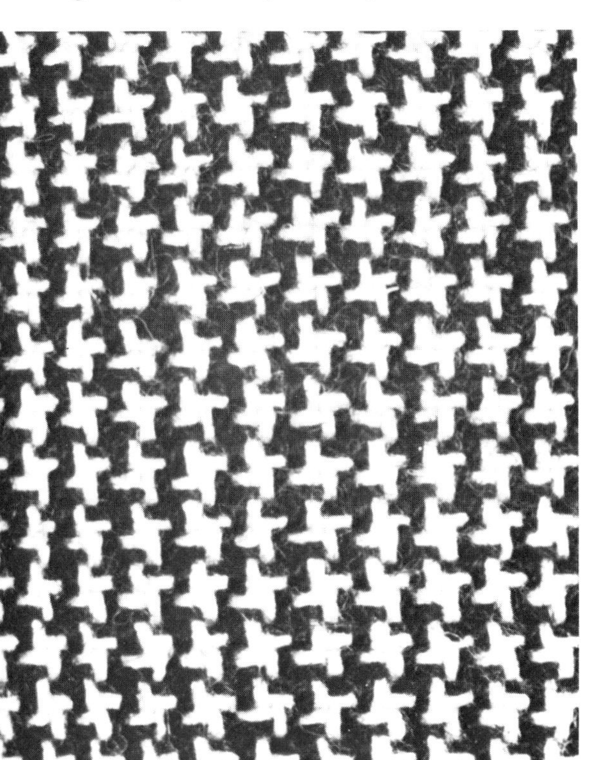

Fig 42 Cross colouring on plain weave

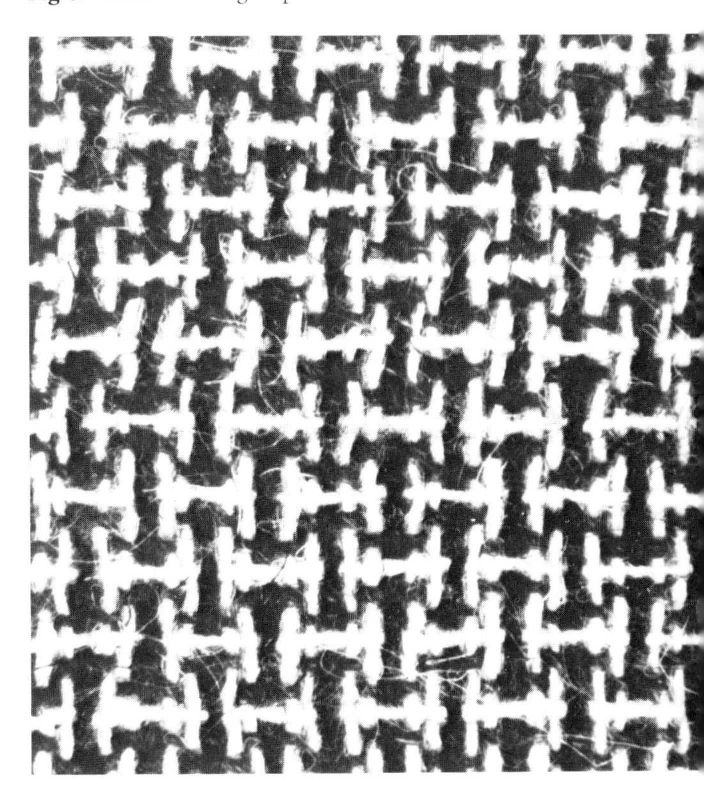

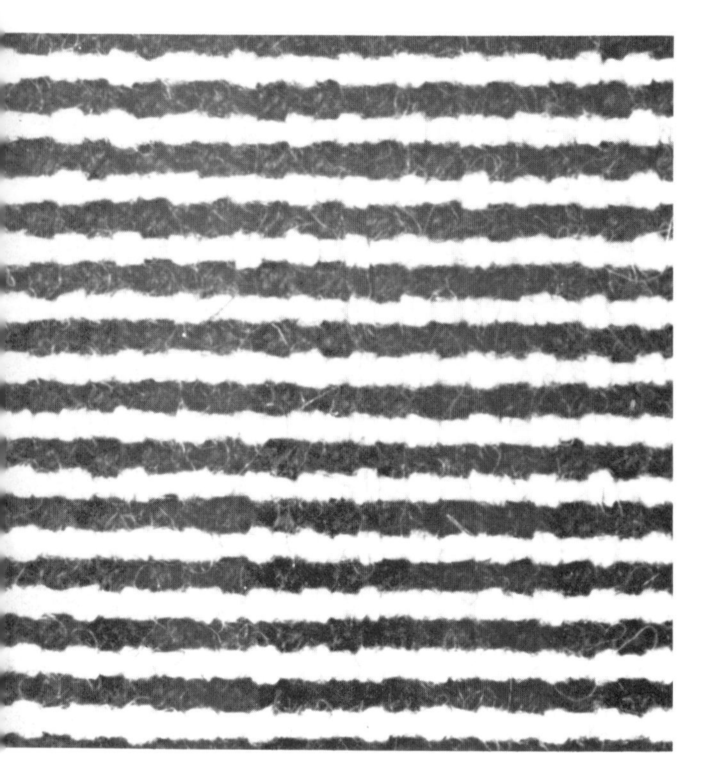

Fig 43 Horizontal hairline on 2/2 hopsack

Fig 45 Four point star on 2/2 hopsack

Fig 44 Step effect on 2/2 hopsack

Fig 46 Step effect on 2/2 twill

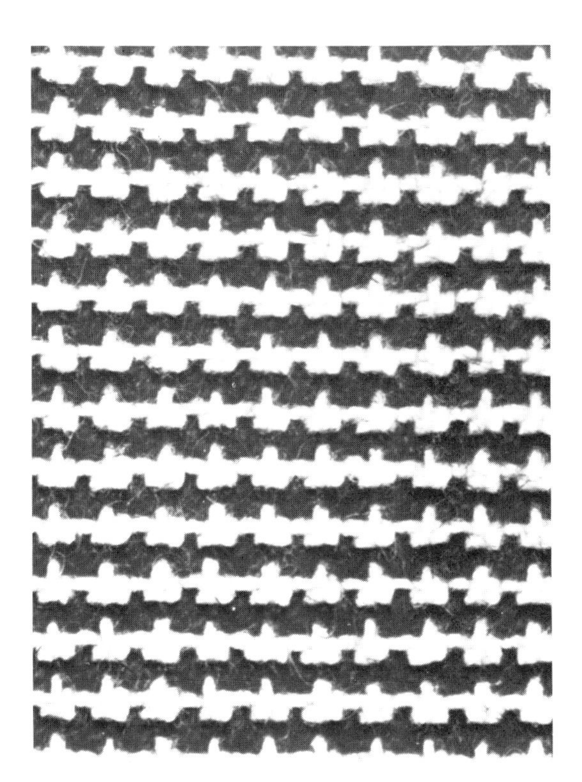

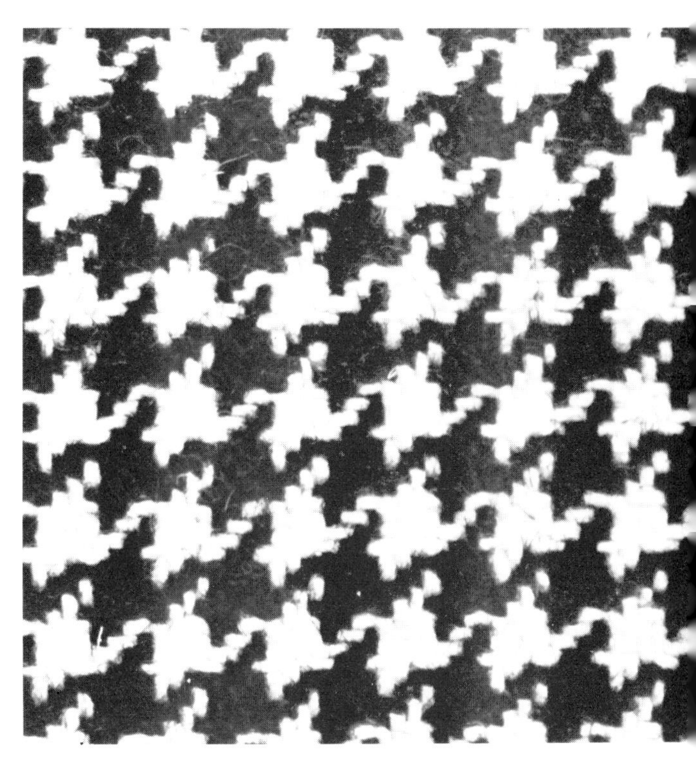

Fig 47 Horizontal hairline on 2/2 twill

Fig 49 Dog tooth check on 2/2 twill

Fig 48 Birds eye effect on 2/2 twill

Fig 50 Shepherds check on 2/2 twill

Figure 49 illustrates dog tooth check, woven using 2/2 twill (Diagram 40a) with a warp coloured 4 dark, 4 light and the wefting plan repeat coloured 2 dark, 4 light, 2 dark.

Figure 50 illustrates shepherds check, woven using 2/2 twill (Diagram 40a) with a warp coloured 6 dark, 6 light and the weft coloured 6 dark, 6 light.

The same patterns can be easily interpreted on point paper, which enables designing off the loom to take place.

METHOD OF SKETCHING COLOUR AND WEAVE EFFECTS ON POINT PAPER USING GREY AND WHITE YARNS IN BOTH WARP AND WEFT (Diagram 59)

1. Determine one repeat size by finding the lowest common multiple of the colouring plan and the weave. For example, a warping and wefting plan of 2 light, 2 dark combined with 2/2 twill needs a repeat size of 4 ends and picks. A warping and wefting plan of 3 light and 2 dark combined with 2/2 twill, needs a minimum repeat size of 20 ends and 20 picks.

2. Run out the normal interlacing of the chosen weave within this repeat. Mark off the warping and wefting plans below and to the side of the repeat using the initials of the colours or dashes and blanks. (Dashes represent grey and blanks white in Diagram 59a.)

3. Shade in all the warp-up marks along each grey end. (Because a mark on point paper means warp showing on surface of the cloth, the grey ends will dominate on the surface of the cloth where the warp-up marks are.) (Diagram 59b.)

4. Shade in all the blanks along each grey pick. (Because a blank on point paper means weft showing, the grey picks will dominate the surface of the cloth where the blanks are.) (Diagram 59c.)

5. The shape now obvious on the paper represents the pattern that will be woven using the weave and colouring plans used. Diagram 59c illustrates vertical hairline.

N.B. It is crucial to maintain the relationship between weave and colouring, as indicated on the weave diagram, when warping and weaving the cloth, otherwise the pattern produced may be different from that which is desired. For example, Diagram 59d shows the same warping and wefting plans as Diagram 59a, but the plain weave lifts are starting on the opposite ends and picks. Horizontal hairline is produced instead of vertical hairline (Diagram 59f). Diagram 59g shows a 2 grey, 2 white colouring in warp and weft combined with plain weave, which results in the four point star pattern. Diagram 59h shows a 1 grey, 1 white colouring in warp and weft combined with 2/2 twill which results in step effect pattern.

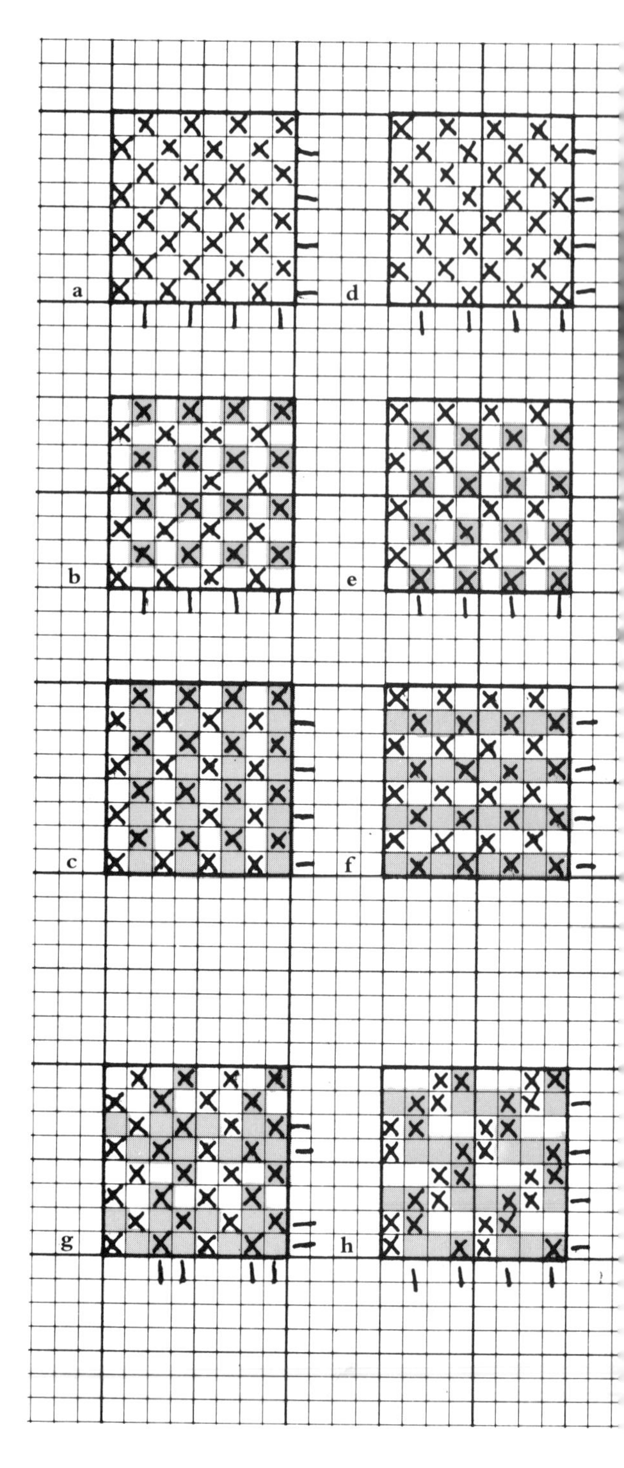

Diag 59 Simple colour and weave effects

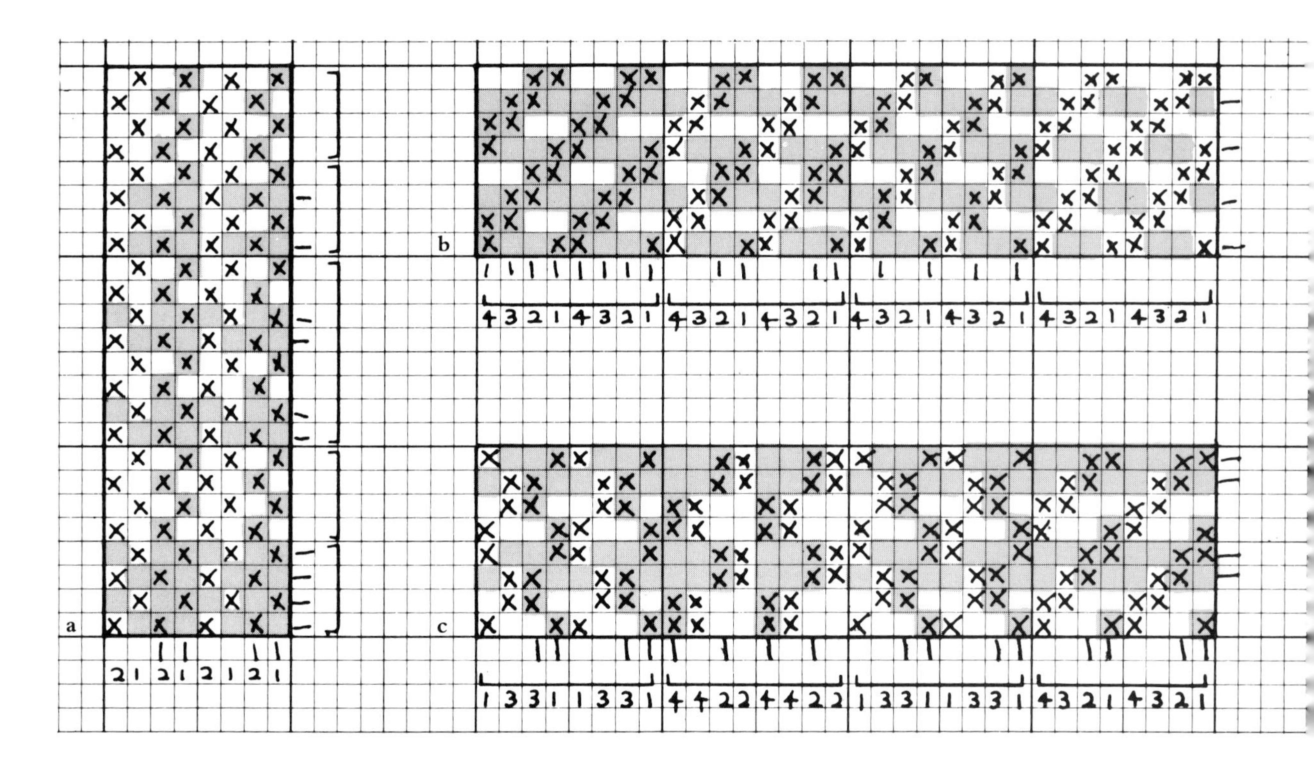

Diag 60 Colour and weave effect stripes

Colour and Weave Effect Stripes and Checks

Horizontal stripe patterns of different colour and weave patterns can be woven if a common warp colouring plan is crossed by a variety of weft colouring plans. A design is constructed in the following manner:

CONSTRUCTING A WEFT STRIPE, A WARP STRIPE AND CHECK DESIGNS

Choose the weave and the warp colouring plan to be used. Run out on point paper at least two repeats of the weave, one above the other. Indicate the warp colouring plan underneath the weave diagram. For each weave repeat in the design an alternative weft colouring plan is used, which when it interlaces with the warp, produces differently patterned stripes. These stripes can be of various widths depending on the number of times each wefting plan is repeated (Diagram 60a).

Vertical stripe patterns can be designed in a similar manner. Different warp colouring plans are warped in succession and a common weft colouring plan is sent across (Diagram 60b).

In both cases, normally the same weave is used throughout the fabric, but there is no reason why, for example, 2/2 twill and 2/2 hopsack, which have similar setts, cannot be combined in a horizontal or vertical stripe to produce a wider choice of patterns to design with. Diagram 60c illustrates the weave diagram of a vertical stripe pattern combining 2/2 twill and 2/2 hopsack and a weft colouring plan of 2 white, 2 grey crossing different warp colouring plans.

Checked patterns are designed by crossing two warp colouring plans by the same or different weft colouring plans. If identical plans are used in warp and weft, true colouring will occur in diagonally opposing squares, and cross colourings in the other shapes. Ornate and attractive designs can be created this way which can still be woven on few shafts. Diagrams 61a, b and c illustrate checks constructed in this way. Diagram 61a is known as the basket weave or log cabin and Figure 51 shows it woven into a cloth. Figure 52 illustrates cloth woven as Diagram 61b. This idea can be extended to design larger checkerboard type checks by combining three or more different colouring plans in warp and weft (Diagram 61c). Figure 53 illustrates an attractive silk fabric woven as a large checkerboard design.

Additional interest can be designed by allowing coloured threads to form an overcheck.

Shadow Weaves

The basket-weave effect illustrated in Diagram 61a

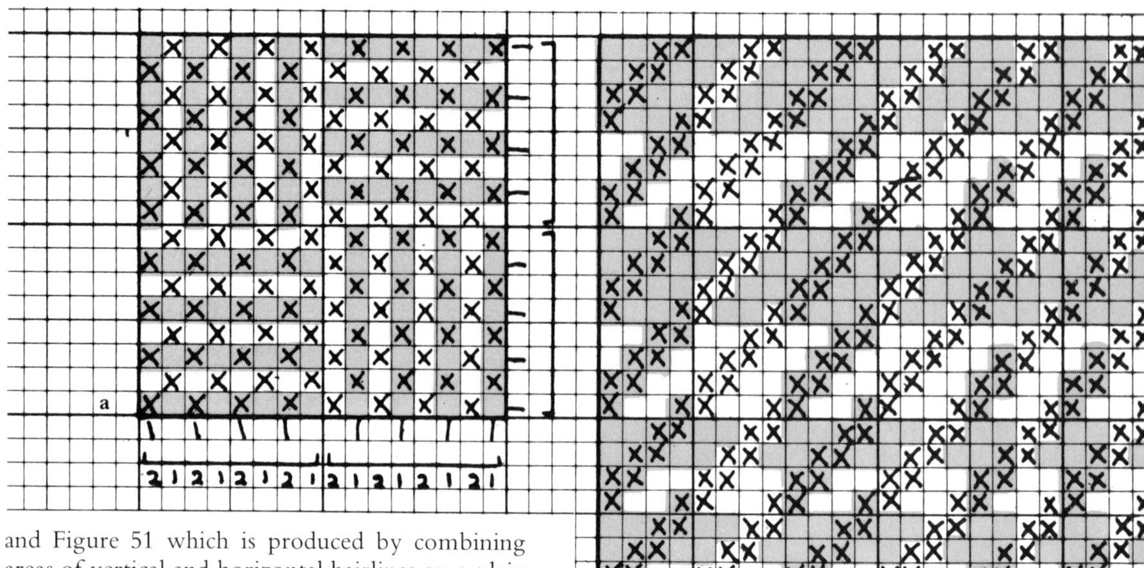

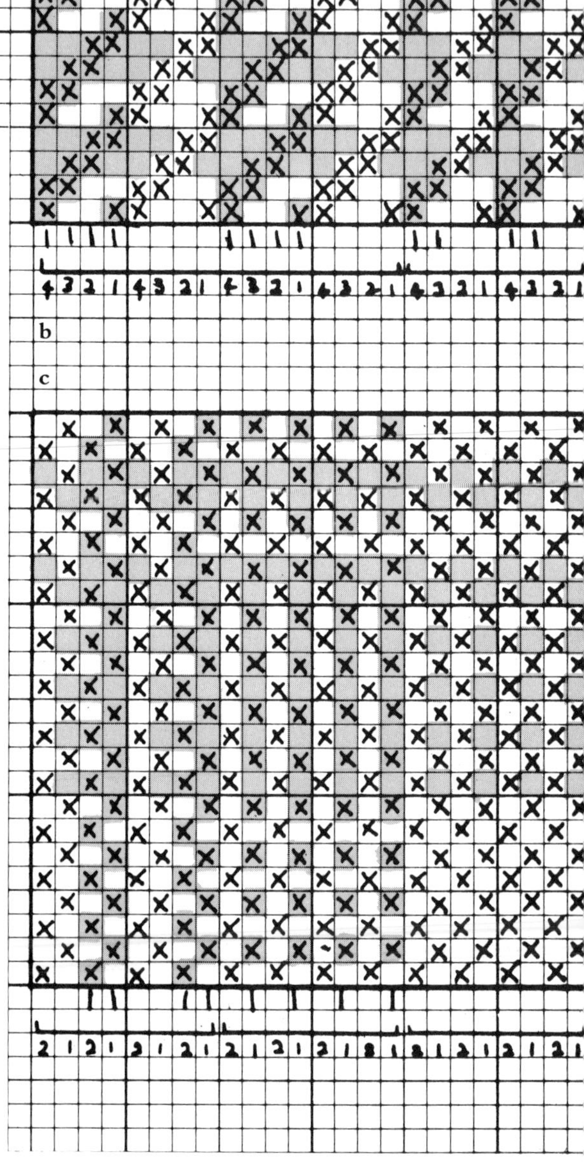

Diag 61 Colour and weave effect checks

and Figure 51 which is produced by combining areas of vertical and horizontal hairlines on a plain weave ground cloth, can be applied to the motif designing concept described in Chapter 12. The attractive and unusual patterns which result, particularly when diamond-shaped motifs are used, are known as shadow weaves.

A diamond-shaped motif is designed as illustrated in Diagrams 62a, 63a and 64a. Each square of the motif is normally allocated a 4 × 4 section of point paper in the weave diagram, although a more striking shadow pattern results if the blocks occurring at the reverse of the diamond shape is made up of an uneven number of ends and picks, as illustrated in Diagrams 62b and 64b. The total weave diagram must repeat on an even number of ends and picks. The motif shape can now be transposed onto the weave diagram. The dark areas are filled in with plain weave as illustrated by the dots in Diagram 62b, while the light areas are filled in placing the first plain weave lifts in the identical position to the previous marks. (Crosses in diagram.) The two ends and picks which adjoin the dark and light areas will thus be lifting in an identical order.

A warping plan of 1 light, 1 dark is used throughout, with a similarly coloured wefting plan. When the colours interlace the horizontal and vertical lines emerge. Diagram 62b illustrates the weave diagram for the fabric shown in Figure 54, while Diagrams 62c and d illustrate its drafting and lifting plans respectively. The design can be increased in size by repeating the sections shown in brackets. When designing your own weave diagrams, it is easier if drafting and lifting plans are worked out before superimposing the colouring plans.

Fig 51 Basket weave effect on plain weave

Fig 52 Glen check on 2/2 twill (right)

Fig 53 Colour and weave effect check

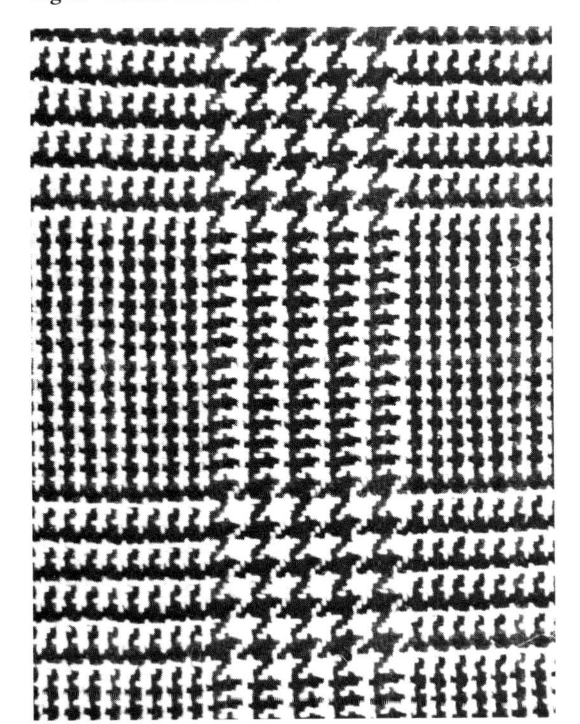

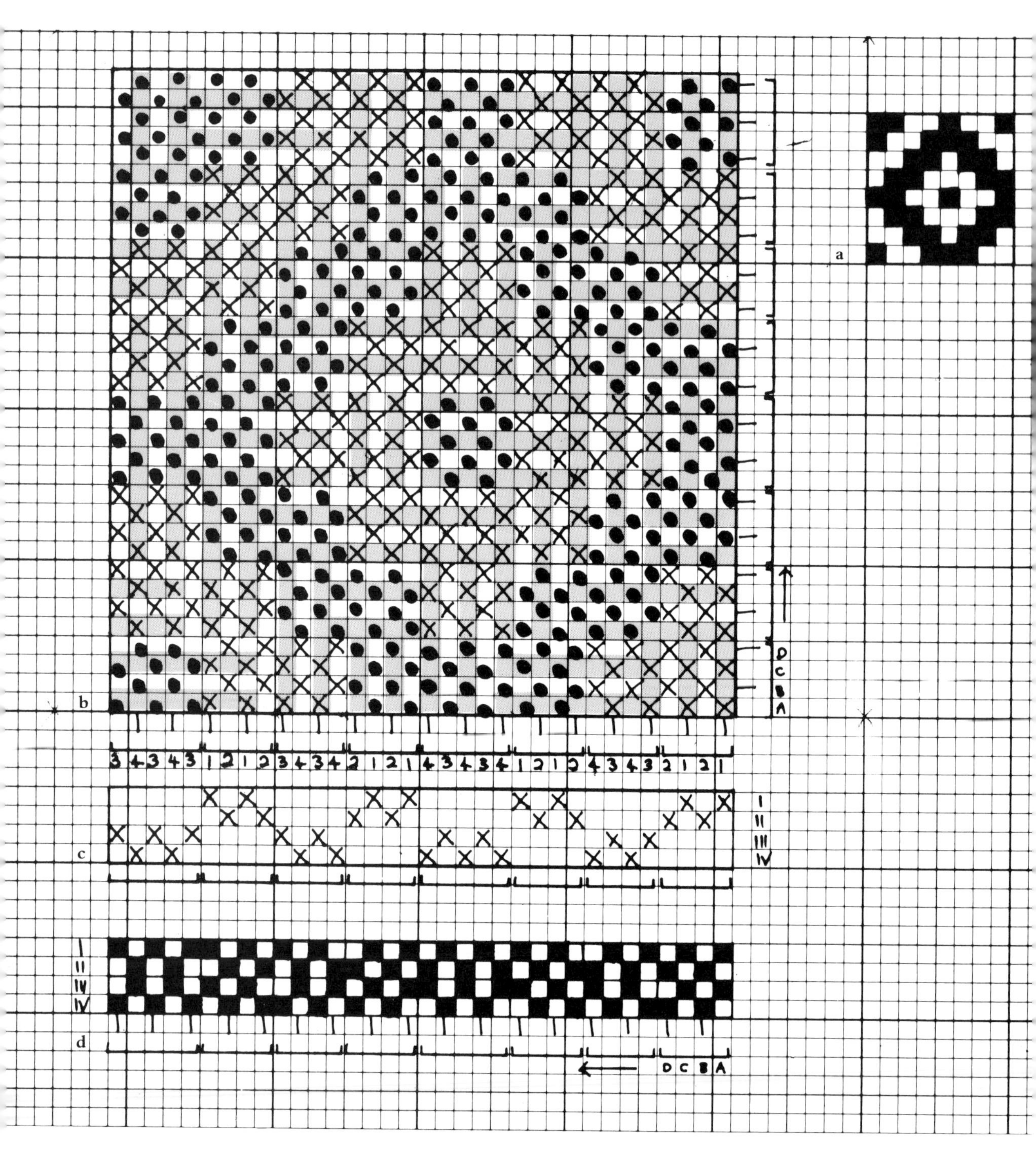

Diag 62 Shadow weave

Either 1 or 2 shafts per vertical block of a motif will be needed depending on the design although diamond shaped and clean cut motifs (Diagrams 93a, b) usually only need one shaft per vertical block of the motif. A four-shaft loom can thus weave designs composed of 4 blocks.

Diagrams 63 and 64 illustrate two shadow weave patterns with their drafting and lifting plans, which result if the above procedure is applied to the motifs illustrated. They both require six shafts.

Fig 54 Shadow weave

a

b

c

d

Diag 63 Shadow weave

Diag 64 Shadow weave (overleaf)

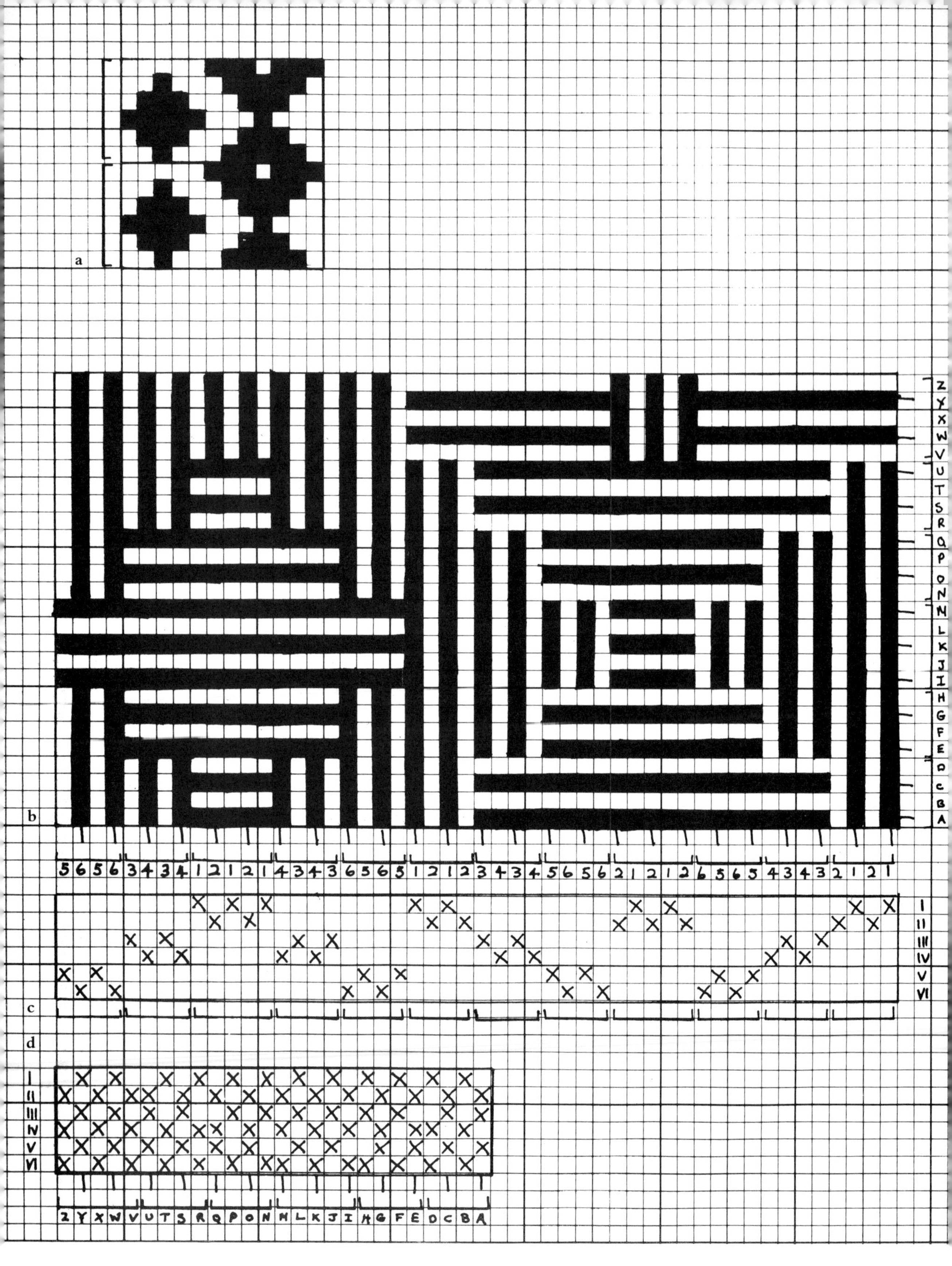
a
b
Z Y X W V U T S R Q P O N M L K J I H G F E D C B A
5 6 5 6 3 4 3 4 1 2 1 2 1 4 3 4 3 6 5 6 5 1 2 1 2 3 4 3 4 5 6 5 6 2 1 2 1 2 6 5 6 5 4 3 4 3 2 1 2 1
I II III IV V VI
c
d
I II III IV V VI
Z Y X W V U T S R Q P O N M L K J I H G F E D C B A

SATIN AND SATEEN WEAVES

Satins are warp-faced weaves and sateens are weft-faced weaves. They both produce very smooth, soft handling cloths and in their best constructions have no definite surface directions or patterns. Lustrous yarns are particularly effective when used in the direction of the floating threads.

All satins and sateens repeat on the same number of ends as picks. Each end in the weave requires its own shaft on the loom. In satins, each end floats over all but one of the picks per repeat, and in sateens, each pick floats over all but one of the ends per repeat. The point where the ends and picks interlace is called the stitching point. These stitching points should be equally distributed over the repeat area.

Sateens being weft-faced, have very few marks on the point paper weave diagram compared to satins, and as a result appear to have a clearer and less complicated construction. In fact they are constructed in exactly the same way. It should be noted also that sateens are considerably lighter and easier to weave than satins, particularly on looms which create a rising shed. This is because only one shaft needs to be moved for each pick instead of all but one for satins. For this reason, satin fabrics are often woven 'back up', i.e. as a sateen weave.

Satin and sateen weaves fall into two main groups, regular or irregular.

Regular Satin and Sateen Weaves

Regular weaves are constructed by a systematic counting known as the stitching step, of the stitching points. In most cases a faint twill line does develop in the weave. If the direction of twist in the yarn is the same as the direction of this faint twill line, an almost untwilled cloth surface can be produced.

METHOD FOR DETERMINING THE STITCHING STEP:

1. Determine number of ends in weave repeat.

2. Write down all the numbers from 1 to x (x equals ends in repeat).

3. Cross out first, and last two numbers.

4. Cross out any number that divides into x, or any multiple of such a number.

5. Any remaining numbers give possible stitching steps for regular satin and sateen weaves.

For example, on a repeat size of 8 ends and picks, a stitching step of 3 or 5 should be used to construct the weave diagram.

~~1~~ ~~2~~ 3 ~~4~~ 5 ~~6~~ ~~7~~ ~~8~~

N.B. No regular satin or sateen weave can be constructed on a repeat size of 4×4 or 6×6.

Construction of regular sateen weave on point paper:

1. Mark off repeat size.

2. Place first stitching point in bottom left hand corner.

3. Count each pick above this mark for the calculated stitching step. Place a stitching point on that pick, but on the adjacent end to the right.

4. Continue counting stitching steps from this point as above, following through the weave repeat, until each end and pick has one stitching point on it.

N.B. In Diagram 65a the stitching points have been indicated as numbers to show the order that they are placed on the weave diagram.

Satin weaves are constructed in a similar manner except that the stitching points remain as blank squares on the weave diagram, and all other points have warp-up marks indicated (Diagram 65b).

IRREGULAR SATIN AND SATEEN WEAVES

The stiching points for irregular satin and sateen weaves are determined by the following method:

1. Determine a stitching point for a regular satin or sateen in the normal manner.

2. Run out this weave on the point paper diagram, covering half the repeat.

3. The next stitching point is placed after a counting step which is equal to half the number of ends in the weave repeat

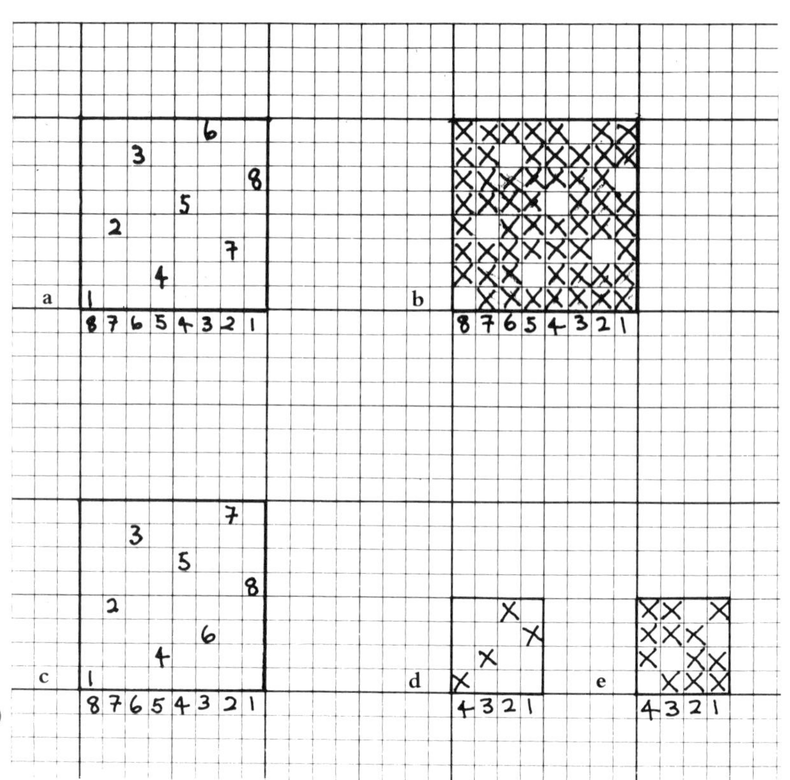

Diag 65 Satin and sateen weaves

Fig 55 4-end mock sateen (below)

Fig 56 8-end satin stripe

4. The original stitching step is then adhered to, but counting is done in the reverse direction.

Diagram 65c illustrates an irregular sateen on eight ends and picks. The completed weave will not have a prominent twill line on its face.

Alternatively, the stitching points on irregular weaves are placed at random on point paper ensuring that none lie adjacent to each other, or produce a prominent twill line, and that each end and pick has only one stitching point.

A true satin or sateen is impossible to construct on a repeat size of 4 ends and picks. Diagram 65d and Figure 55 shows a 4-end satinette or mock sateen weave, which is the best compromise. In fact on close inspection it will be seen that it is a broken twill of 1/3 twill. The mock satin (Diagram 65e), is a broken twill of 3/1 twill.

Sett

The sett of both regular and irregular satin and sateen can be balanced, but a better fabric is produced if the face threads have a slightly higher sett than the back threads. The weave-firmness formula should be used to determine the amount by which the number of diameters per cm/inch need to be reduced to obtain maximum sett.

Designing with Satin and Sateens

Because of their smooth, uncluttered surface-appearance satin and sateens lend themselves to coloured stripe patterns, a warp stripe with satins and a weft stripe with sateens. Figure 56 illustrates a regular 8-end satin stripe and Figure 57 the same stripe in 4-end satin. Card wind colour trials weave up to almost exact replicas of themselves. Textured yarns and lustrous yarns can be shown off to good advantage. Because of their opposing surface effects they can be used for motif and block designs. (See Chapter 12.)

Fig 57 4-end satin stripe

COMBINING SATIN AND SATEEN AND WARP- AND WEFT-FACED TWILLS

The distinct contrast between the surface appearances of satin and sateen weaves can be used for design effect. If two comparative weaves such as 5-end satin and 5-end sateen are joined horizontally (Diagram 66a), the number of shafts required is limited to the same five shafts. The picking sequence is, of course, increased in length. The resulting design on a cloth would show as a subtle horizontal stripe relying on light and shade reflection, if the

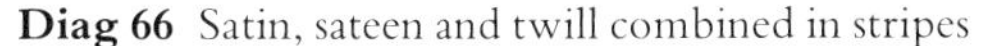

Diag 66 Satin, sateen and twill combined in stripes

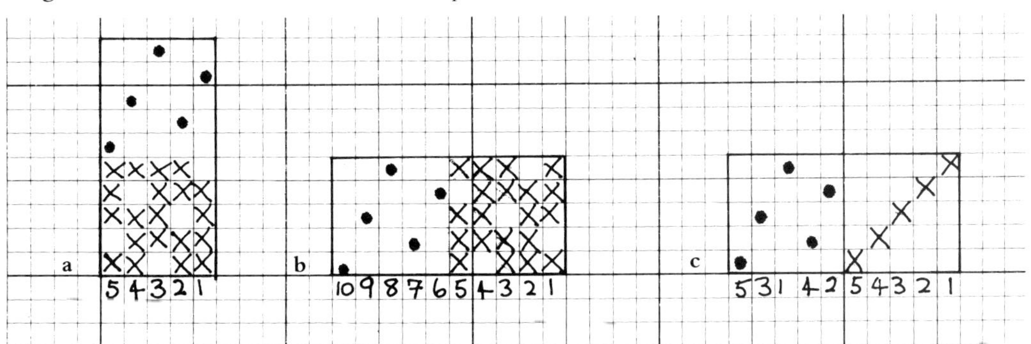

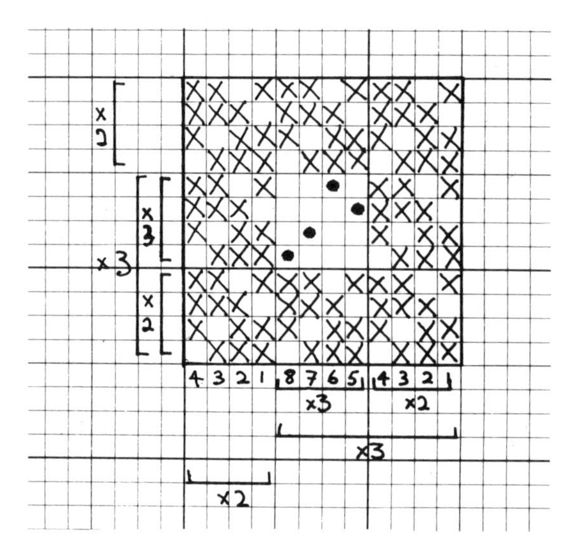

Diag 67 4-end satin and sateen guard check design

same colour was used in warp and weft. The satin stripe will appear to stand above the sateen stripe, creating a subtle texture also. The same weave-diagram with a coloured striped warp would show as areas of vertical stripe in the satin weave, crossed by bold horizontal lines when a self-coloured weft is used and the sateen weave, similar to the cushion in Plate 12 which has 1/3 twill as the warp stripe crossed by a white weft in 4-end sateen.

If the same two weaves were joined vertically, the shaft requirements on the loom are immediately doubled (Diagram 66b). If, however, a basic sateen weave such as 5-end sateen is combined with its partner in the twills, i.e. 1/4 twill, two distinct weaves can be combined in a vertical stripe using the same shafts (Diagram 66c).

Satin and sateens will combine with any other weave as long as the setts are similar. 4-end satin will, therefore, combine comfortably with 2/2 twill. Plate 4 illustrates 4-end satin and sateen in a guard check arrangement with a coloured over-check. Note the subtle check pattern emerging in the self-coloured areas due to the satin areas standing above the sateen areas. Diagram 67 shows the weave diagram.

Shadow Stripes

Shadow stripes are constructed by gradually moving from a weft-faced weave through to a warp-faced weave. Satin and sateen weaves and twill weaves can be treated in this way. Using this technique, a light-coloured warp crossed by a dark-coloured weft will produce a fabric which graduates from the light colour to the dark colour. The larger

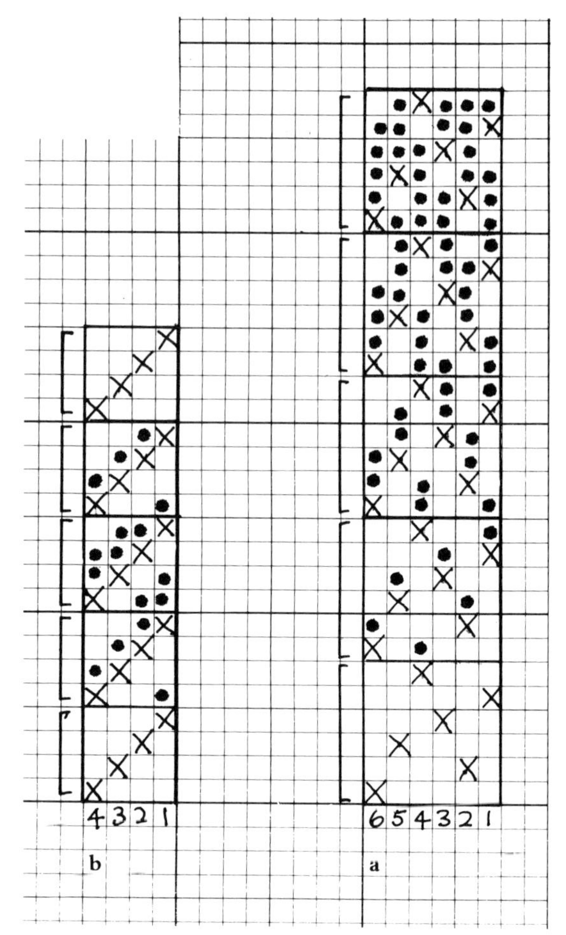

Diag 68 Shadow stripes

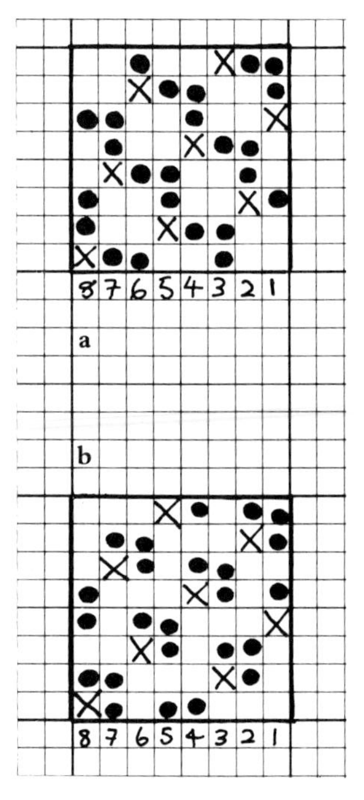

Diag 69 Barathea and twilled hopsack

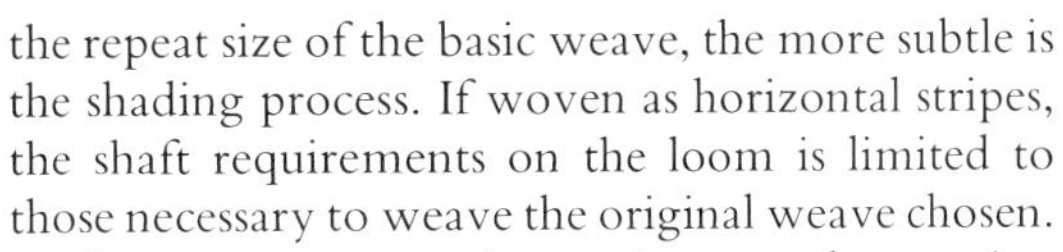

the repeat size of the basic weave, the more subtle is the shading process. If woven as horizontal stripes, the shaft requirements on the loom is limited to those necessary to weave the original weave chosen.

They are constructed on point paper by running out one repeat of either a weft-faced twill or sateen weave. Another repeat is then run out above the first, but this time an additional warp-up mark is indicated on each end immediately above the first mark. A third repeat of the original weave is now drawn out above. This time two warp-up marks are added to the original end intersections. The fourth repeat has three additional marks indicated and the process is continued until the warp-faced partner of the original weave is arrived at (Diagram 68). Each separate repeating section of the shadow design can be bracketed up to increase the width of any particular stripe. Diagram 68b illustrates a reversing shadow twill stripe and Figure 58 a cloth woven in this manner.

Barathea and Twilled Hopsack

Two traditional weaves, barathea and twilled hopsack, base their construction on placing identical warp-up marks on every end above the stitching point of a regular 8-end sateen, barathea using a stitching step of 3 and twilled hopsack a stitching step of 5. Diagram 69a illustrates the weave diagram for barathea and Diagram 69b the twilled hopsack. Figures 59 and 60 illustrate the two weaves woven into cloth.

Fig 58 Shadow twill stripe

Fig 59 Barathea (below)

Fig 60 Twilled hopsack

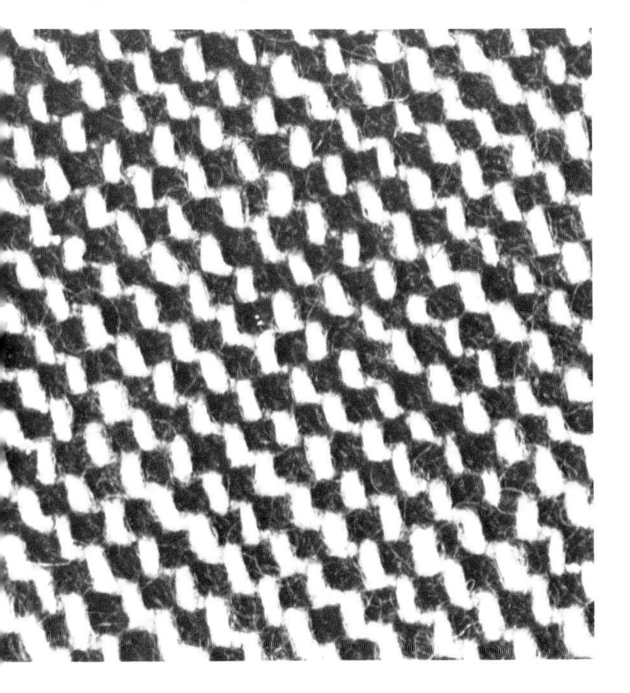

10 DESIGNING STRIPES AND CHECKS

Stripes and checks are the most obvious form of design in woven textiles. The ends and picks interlacing at right angles to each other lend themselves to this type of pattern. Stripes and checks can be achieved by the use of colour, yarn, weave or a combination of these.

Stripes using Colour and/or Yarns

Horizontal stripes across the width of a fabric are perhaps the easiest to tackle. A plain-coloured warp can be set up on the loom and picks of different colour or texture in varying proportions can be inserted. Changes in the proportions and arrangements of the stripes can be made quite freely and designing on the loom is tempting. It is, however, well worth while to pre-plan stripe patterns before weaving to ensure an attractive selection of colour and proportion, which can be difficult to visualise once weaving begins and the cloth is wound around the front beam.

With vertical stripes it is essential to pre-plan. The stripes are made during warping and unless the designer is clear about the order of the yarn, it is impossible to continue. Also, once the loom is dressed, it is difficult, time-consuming and wasteful of materials to make changes.

Pre-planning can take the form of drawing stripes out with coloured crayons or by making card winds.

CARD WINDS

Use a piece of stiff card about 5 cm wide (about 2 inches) and several centimetres long. Select the colours and yarns to be used and wind these around the card one at a time, evenly and close together in various combinations of widths. The stripes can be only one strand wide or several centimetres wide, and can represent a small repeating pattern to be duplicated several times across the fabric or a large free-flowing arrangement more suitable for a border design (Figure 61).

When a new colour is to be introduced, it can either be tied to the last end and the knot placed on the back of the card, or adhesive tape can be used to keep the ends in place.

The finished card wind is a permanent record of a stripe pattern and several should be made before selecting the one that is the most pleasing on the eye, to be woven. The pattern should be followed rigidly when weaving, remembering that it is the width of each stripe that is the important factor, rather than the number of threads producing the width, because the weave being used and the sett of the cloth can alter these figures.

THE WEAVE TO CHOOSE

The card wind produces a clean-coloured stripe, but only weaves like sateen for a weft stripe, or satin and warp rib for a warp stripe will produce a cloth of the same colour intensity (Figures 11, 13, 25, 56 and 57).

All single square-sett weaves like plain weave, twills and crepe weaves will subdue the colour intensity, because the self-coloured warp or weft combines with the coloured stripes causing colour mixing to take place which can drastically alter the stripe colour. As long as this is understood, the finished cloth can be visualised (Figures 12 and 27).

Fig 61 Card wind

Weaves which combine well with coloured stripes include plain weave, 2/2 twill and other small twills, 2/2 hopsack, satin and sateens, warp and weft rib, crepe weaves, huckaback and mock leno and bedford cord.

If a warp stripe design needs to be woven as a sample, it is easier to experiment if the sample is woven as a weft stripe and then turned a quarter turn to see the warp stripe effect.

Weave stripes

These are created by combining weaves of different texture and pattern into a stripe. A self-coloured warp with a weft of the same or contrasting colour is used.

The proportions of stripe widths is very important and can best be envisaged by sketching and shading stripes on paper. Point paper is useful for this. A card wind in neutral colours, with one colour for each weave, can also be used. The variety of widths should be limited, as too many can conflict with the variety of surface patterns of the individual weaves. Two or three different weaves is usually sufficient for an interesting design.

One repeat of any simple weave constitutes the narrowest possible stripe. The number of times this repeat needs to be duplicated to create a wider stripe is determined by the sett of the cloth. Only weaves with a similar sett and shrinkage should be combined and they must join neatly. (See Chapter 4.) If weaves with different take-up are combined in a warp stripe, a separate warp beam is required for each weave.

When combining different weaves in a vertical direction, the number of shafts that your loom can accommodate must be considered, and in some cases will dictate the weaves that can be combined. Only weaves that can be drafted onto the same shafts can be used, unless a high number of shafts are available.

A herringbone or pointed twill design produces a simple weave stripe. If any of these weaves' end-intersections are repeated not only in reverse, but consecutively, or arranged in an irregular order, other weave patterns result. Because the same end-intersections are being transposed, the new design will be able to be drafted onto the same shafts.

For example, examine the basic weave 2/2 twill to right. The ends intersecting 2 up, 2 down, when repeated two or three times, and then followed by 2 down, 2 up two or three times, produce hopsack weave. Bell celtic design (Diagram 70), is composed of an irregular arrangement of the basic 2/2 twill intersections. The herringbone or point join reverse need not begin after a complete repeat of the basic weave but at any point along the repeat. A combination of some or all of these ideas in a warp stripe produces interesting weave patterns. The drafting plan for this design will be quite long and complicated, but the lifting plan will be short (Diagram 71). Figure 62 illustrates this design woven.

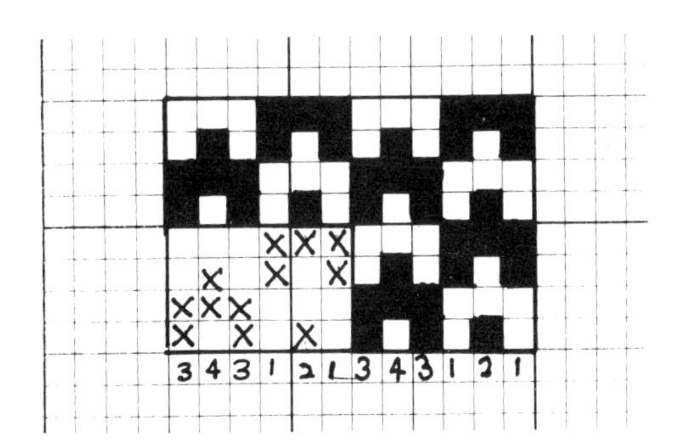

Diag 70 Bell celtic weave

Weaves with identical setts and drafting plans can be combined to form horizontal stripes. The lifting plan will change for each new weave, and each repeat can be bracketed up to increase its width. The variety of weaves that can be combined in a weft stripe is much greater than for warp stripes. Most weaves that repeat on the same number of ends as each other can be combined, especially if they also can be drafted onto a straight draft. Problems will only occur with countermarche looms which do not have enough pedals to cope with the variety of different lifts in each weave. A four-shaft countermarche loom will need eight pedals and the universal tie-up, to weave more than six different lifting orders.

If desired, additional coloured stripes can be introduced into a weave stripe. Weaves which combine well in warp or weft weave stripes include:

1. 2/2 twill; 2/2 hopsack; broken twill; bell celtic (Diagram 71 and Figure 62).

2. Satin and sateen and twills with similar lifts (Diagram 66 and Figure 58).

3. Interchanging double plain and 2/2 twill (Diagram 120).

4. Honeycomb and plain weave (Diagram 87 and Plate 6).

5. Bedford cord and plain weave (Figure 70).

6. Mock leno or huckaback and plain weave (Plate 10).

7. Distorted thread effect and plain weave (Diagram 91).

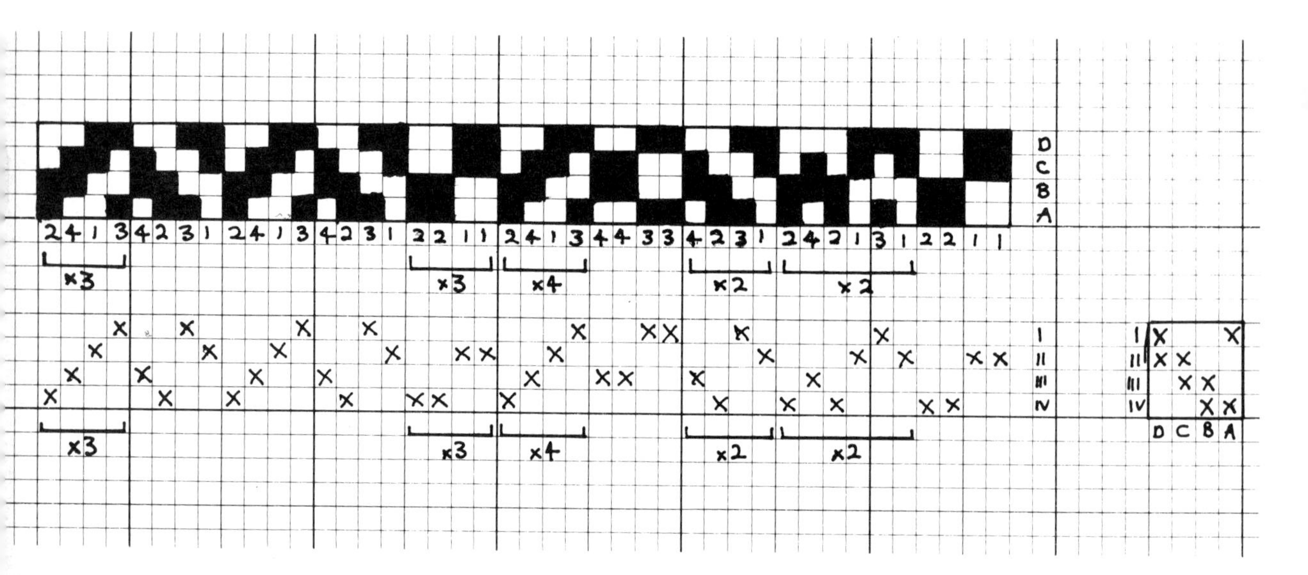

Diag 71 Weave stripe based on 2/2 twill with drafting and lifting plans

Fig 62 Weave stripe based on 2/2 twill

8. Weft figuring and plain weave (Figure 86).

9. Straight twills and undulating twills (Diagram 51).

10. Shadow stripes (Diagram 68).

Checks

Checks are probably the most difficult of fabrics to design and weave successfully. They can easily look drab and uninteresting if the colours and proportions are not chosen with care, and they require a consistently even beat up during weaving, otherwise they will look very ugly. Checks can either be formed by the use of colour only, weave only or a combination of the two.

COLOURED CHECKS

Coloured checks are a combination of a striped warp and a striped weft, of different colours and/or yarns, woven with a simple weave. Usually the warping and wefting plans are identical but this need not be the case.

Initially, designing checks should involve simple proportions with limited colours. Only with practice and sample weaving should large and complicated designs using numerous sizes of checks and colours be woven.

Figures 63 to 68 illustrate six different coloured checks using rough spun linen and plain weave.

WEAVE CHECKS

Most of the weaves that combine well in stripe form can be combined in a check arrangement. There are basically two check arrangements with which to construct weave check designs.

Fig 63 Checkerboard check

Fig 65 Multicoloured check

Fig 64 Checkerboard check with overcheck

Fig 66 Guard check

Fig 67 Guard check with overcheck

Fig 68 Checkerboard check

1. *Checkerboard Check*
Four blocks of weave are combined to form a checkerboard arrangement. Similar block sizes create a regular checkerboard, while uneven block sizes create three different shapes. Diagrams 72a and b illustrate several repeats of two simple checkerboard arrangements with regular and uneven block sizes.

Each square or rectangle of the arrangement can be allocated a different weave. Usually a regular

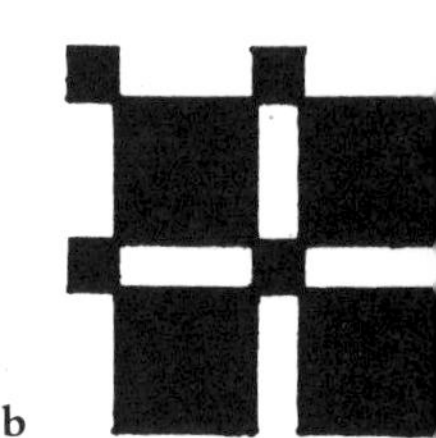

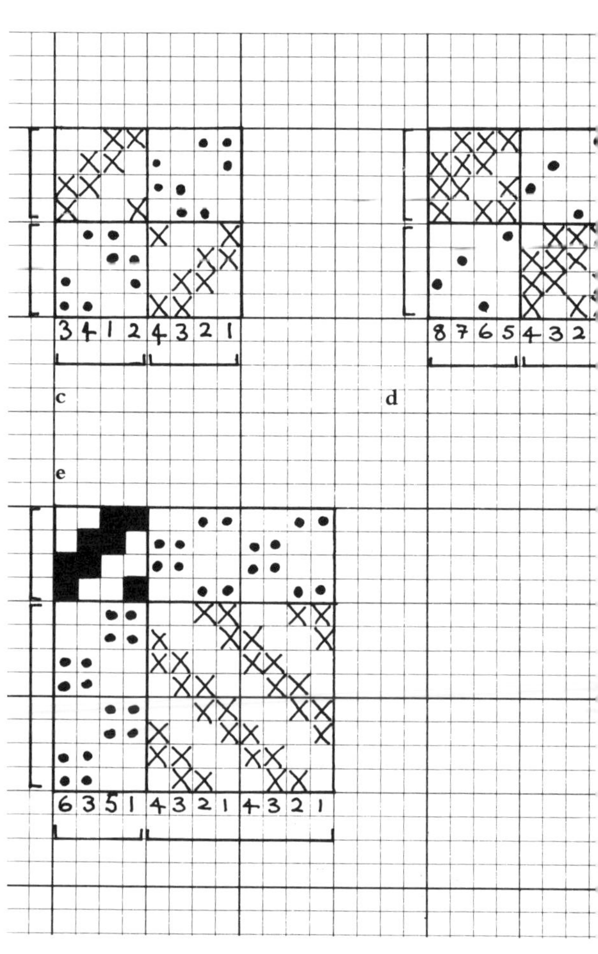

Diag 72 Checkerboard checks

checkerboard arrangement combines two weaves, diagonally opposed. For example, 2/2 twill to right and left (Diagram 72c), or 3/1 twill and 4-end sateen (Diagram 72d).

With an irregular checkerboard check, the two squares might be of different weaves and the two rectangles of the same weave. For example, 2/2 twill to right and left and 2/2 hopsack (Diagram 72e). Both the warp and weft are self-coloured, usually the warp lighter in colour than the weft, leaving the individual patterns of the different weaves to create the interest within the design.

On point paper, each weave repeat can be bracketed up to increase the block size in either warp or weft. Drafting takes place in the normal manner to establish the drafting plan and lifting plan. Usually each warp block in the design will require its own set of shafts. Combining twill to right with twill to left in opposite corners can usually be drafted onto the same shafts as the basic twill weave (Diagram 72c). These designs result in simple diamond patterns.

2. *Guard Checks*
This arrangement consists of a square or a rectangle being totally surrounded by another. Diagram 73a illustrates a motif of a simple guard check. Each shape in the weave diagram is made up of a different weave. Diagram 73b illustrates a guard check weave diagram combining 1/3 and 3/1 twill. Plate 4 illustrates a guard check using 4-end satin and sateen.

OVERCHECKS
A checkerboard check or a guard check can incorporate coloured checks woven upon them. These coloured checks are called overchecks. Especially on large guard checks, an overcheck can create considerable additional interest. Alternatively, a guard check formed from two contrasting weave effects can use a third weave to form a patterned overcheck. Diagram 74 illustrates a motif of a guard check with overcheck.

Colour and Weave Effect Stripes and Checks

The numerous patterns that can be formed by the colour and weave effect interlacings lend themselves to stripe and check arrangements. They can be sketched out and designed on point paper in the normal manner. Usually only one weave is chosen throughout, but more complicated designs can be created by combining different weaves and colouring orders. (See Chapter 8.) Figure 53 illustrates a colour and weave effect check.

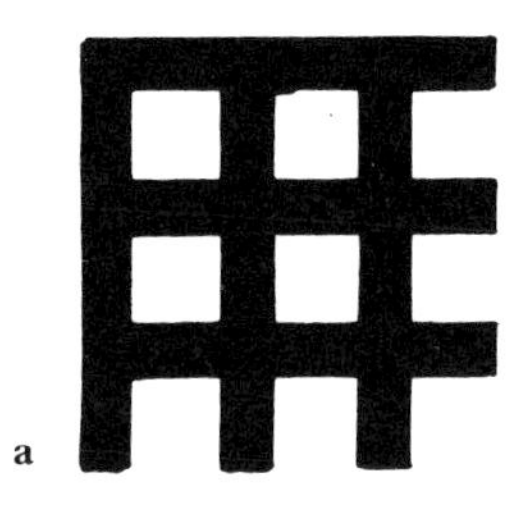

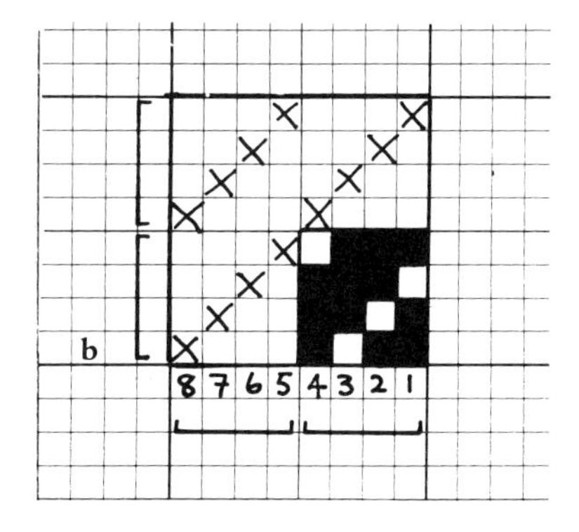

Diag 73 Guard checks

Diag 74 Motif of guard check with overcheck

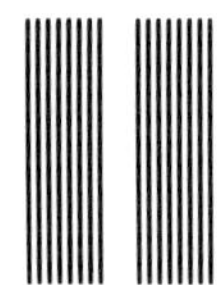

MORE TRADITIONAL WEAVES

Nearly all the other traditional weaves available to the handweaver are developments of the four basic weaves, plain, twill and satin and sateen, which were discussed in the previous chapters.

Bedford Cord Weave

Normally bedford cord fabrics have fine cords running in a warp direction, but they can just as easily be constructed to create horizontal cords. These have the advantage of being able to be woven on four shafts compared to the six or eight required for a warp cord.

The cord effect is achieved by the difference in shrinkage that occurs between a tightly interlacing weave and floating ends or picks. The face of each cord interlaces in plain weave or perhaps 2/1 twill. The back of each cord has long floats stretching across its full width. These floating ends or picks shrink more than the face cloth, forcing the face to arch and form a cord on relaxation and finishing. Plain weave is also woven between each cord to create deep cutting lines.

CONSTRUCTION OF WARP BEFORD CORD WITH PLAIN WEAVE FACE (Diagrams 75a and b)
One repeat of the weave includes two cords. Each cord can be of any width, but must be a multiple of the face weave repeat. (For plain weave, a multiple of two.) Plain weave is inserted along the cutting ends, which are running on either side of each cord. (Dots in diagram.) Next, the face weave is inserted on a pair of picks in the first cord and on the alternate pair of picks in the second cord. (Solid squares in diagram.) The floating picks are then allowed to lie along the back of the cord. In a warp cord this means that all the ends in the cord must lift up. Warp-up marks are, therefore, indicated on remaining picks in each cord. (Crosses in diagram.)

The basic bedford cord weave is complete. It should be noted that the picks are working in pairs, plain weave on the surface of one and then becoming the floating picks in the second cord. Each cord can be increased in size by repeating it several times, as can the cutting ends. The cords can be given extra body if desired by inserting extra wadding ends which lie between the floating picks and the face of the cord. (The dashes and the 'W' marks in Diagram 75b indicate the wadding ends.) In a warp cord these wadding ends require an additional shaft and should run from a separate beam. During sleying they should be regarded as extra in the reed. Ideally, the cutting ends should be allocated the front two shafts of the loom. A plain weave selvage can be employed. Shrinkage will be considerably higher in the width than the length.

Diagram 75c shows a bedford cord constructed with a 2/1 twill face. In this example, alternate picks are forming each cord instead of them working in pairs.

Sett
In order to accentuate the sunken lines and raised cords, it is usual to sley the plain weave cutting ends of a warp bedford cord two per dent and the cord ends three or four per dent. This in fact means that the cord sections are sett twice as high as the cutting ends. If the same yarn is being used throughout, a basic sett is worked out using the normal procedure for a plain weave cloth, but the cord sections are sett tighter.

Alternatively, a strong finer yarn can be used for the cutting ends and a plain weave sett determined from its count. The cord sections then use a slightly thicker yarn and all the ends are sleyed 2 per dent in the reed.

Weft Bedford Cord

The weft bedford cord is constructed on the same principles as the warp cord. Diagram 75d shows a plain weave weft cord with wadding picks inserted. A floating selvage is necessary to maintain a neat edge.

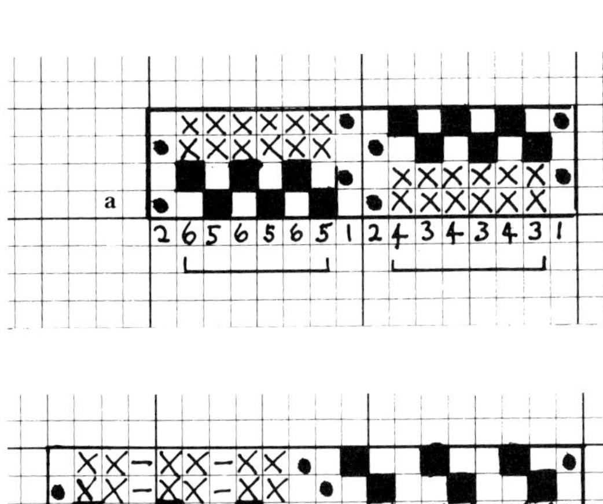

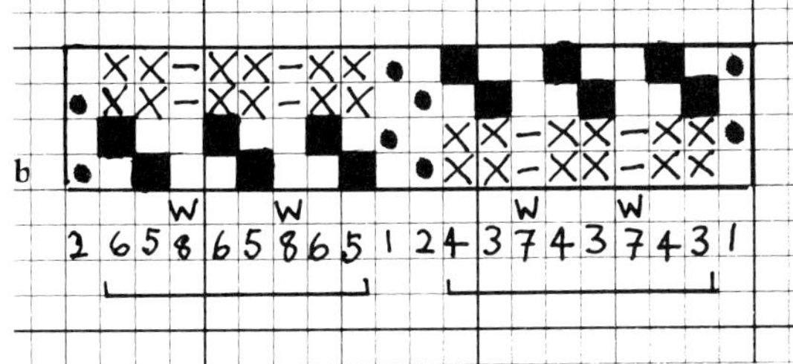

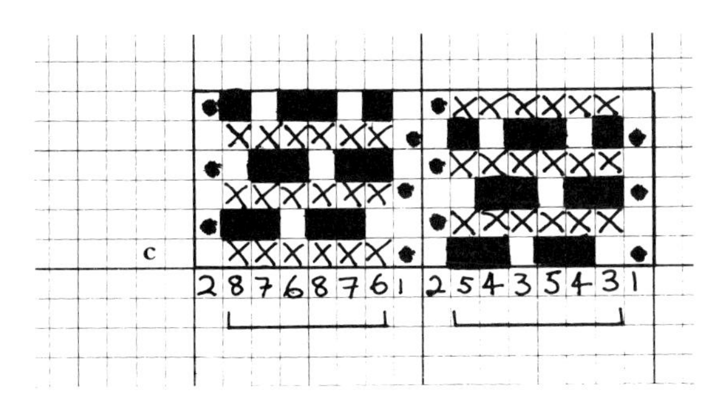

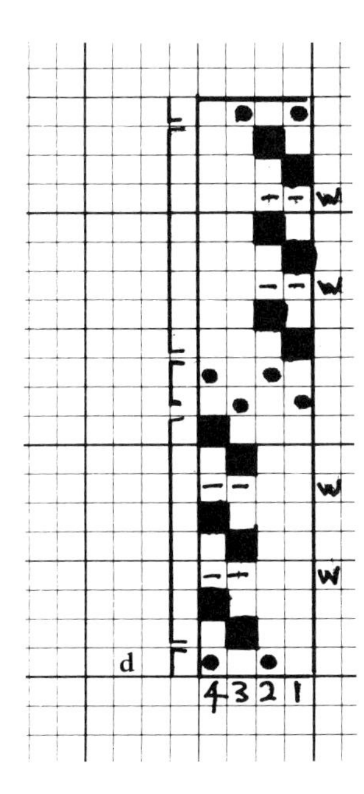

Diag 75 Bedford cord weaves

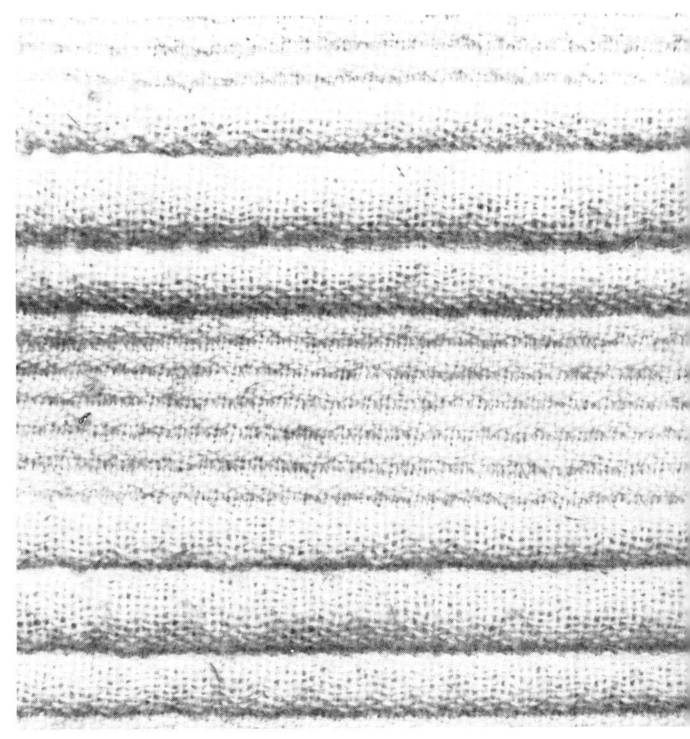

Fig 69 Weft bedford cord, plain and wadded

Fig 70 Bedford cord with fancy yarns

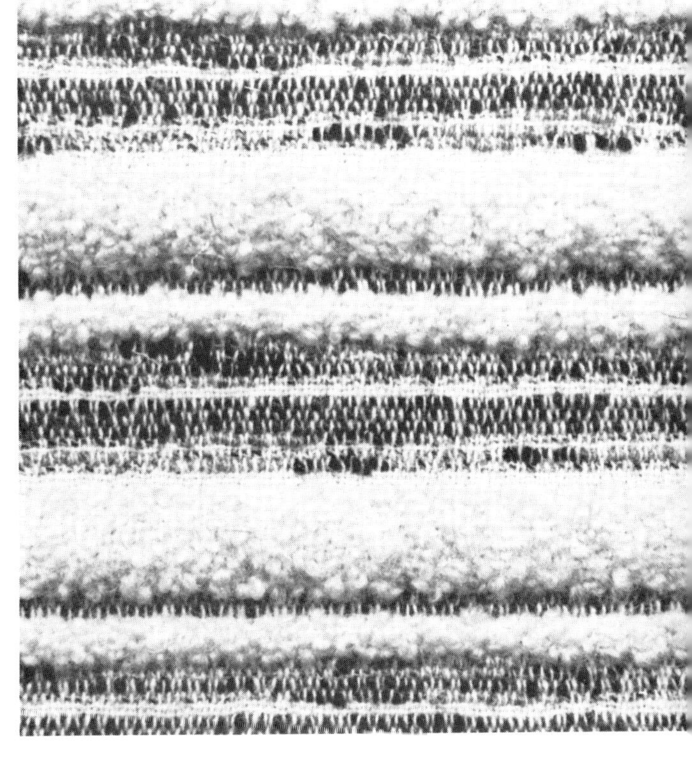

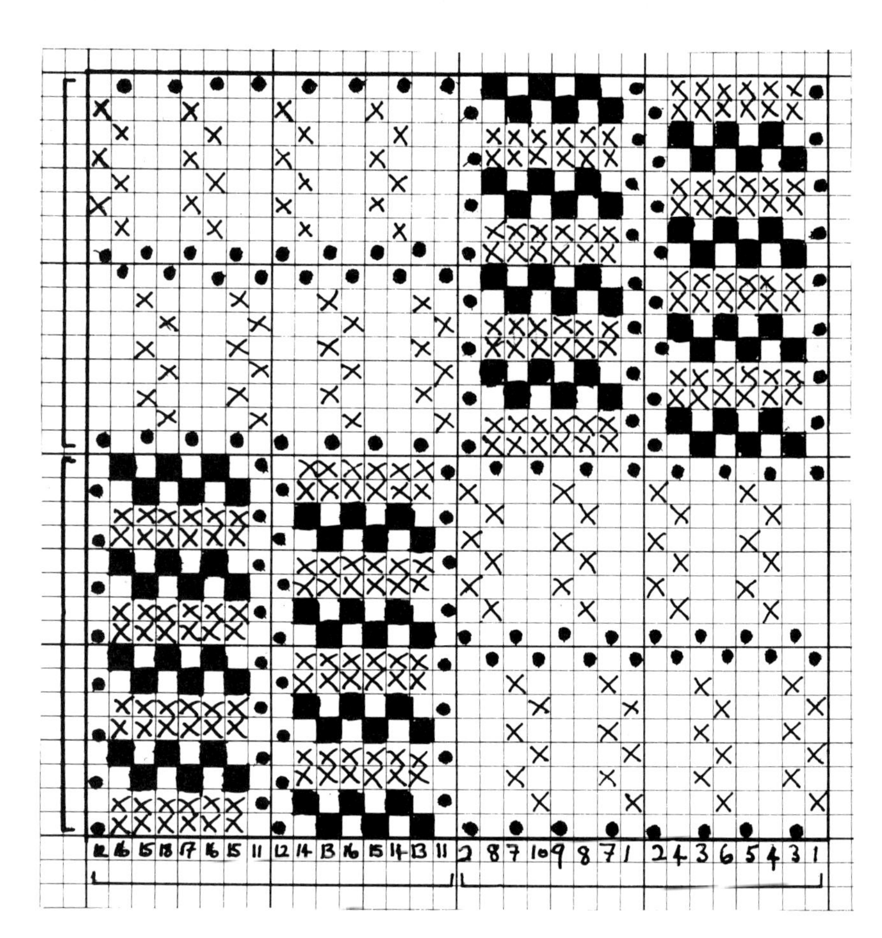

Diag 76 Warp and weft bedford cord combined

Fig 71 Bedford cord and colour and weave effect

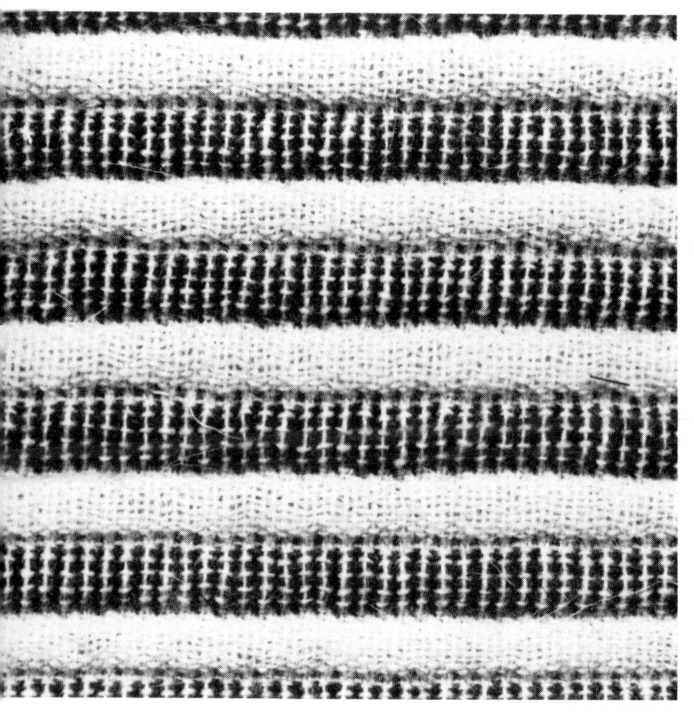

DESIGNING WITH BEDFORD CORDS

With fine yarns, both warp and weft bedford cord result in crisp neat fabrics suitable for clothing and furnishings. A simple variation is to weave each individual cord with a different width (Figure 69). This involves repeating the cord sections of the draft in a warp cord or the cord sections of the lifting plan in a weft cord, as indicated by the brackets in the weave diagrams. The weft cord in particular lends itself to the use of thick chunky yarns to make very textured cords (Figure 70). Both weaves combine well with stripes of plain weave without increasing the shaft requirements. Warp and weft bedford cords can be combined together to produce checkerboard ribs as shown in Diagram 76. No wadding ends or picks, however, can be used.

On cords with a plain weave face, the traditional colour and weave effect designs can be superimposed on the cords if desired. For example, Figure 71 shows a weft cord as designed in Diagram 75d, which has a warp colouring plan of 3 light, 1 dark. The weft is 1 dark, 1 light in the first cord and all light in the second cord resulting in alternate cords of white or vertical hairline. Similarly a warp

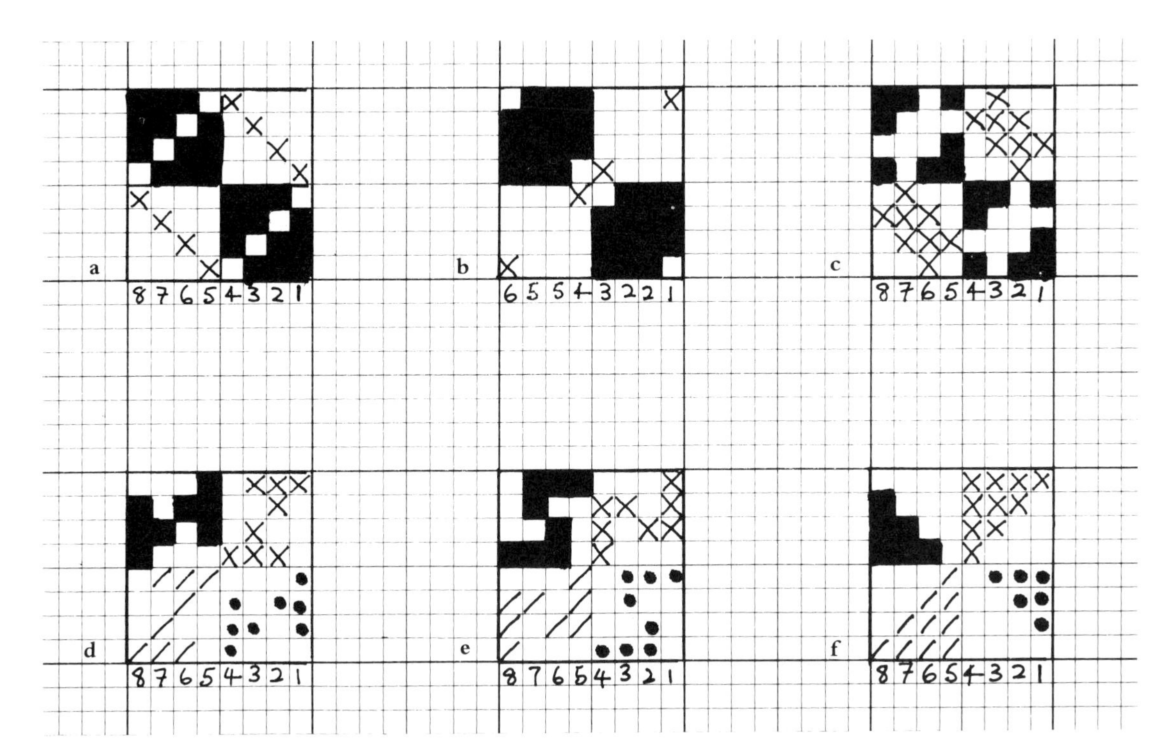

Diag 77 Dice weaves

coloured 2 light, 2 dark will produce cords of two different colours, if each colour is sent across as weft for alternate cords.

Dice Weaves

Dice weaves are small repeating patterns that are constructed on a checkerboard arrangement whereby two opposing squares on a weave diagram are identical to each other and the other two are a damask of the first.

They repeat on the same number of ends as picks, and in theory can be of any size, although a very large repeat begins to lose the typical intricate dice weave patterning. Usually a repeat size of 8 × 8 is ideal. They can be constructed by two main methods:

1. Take a 4 × 4 regular hopsack and transpose some of the marks from the warp-faced section into the weft-faced section retaining clean cuts (Diagrams 77a, b and c).

2. Run out a motif in one quarter, and damask each other quarter all the way around the repeat (Diagrams 77d, e and f).

Many of the most popular dice weaves have individual names. For example, 8-end barleycorn (Diagram 77a and Figure 72); birds eye (Diagram 77d and Figure 73); damask crepe (Diagram 77c). Drafting and lifting plans are constructed in the

Fig 72 8-end barleycorn dice weave

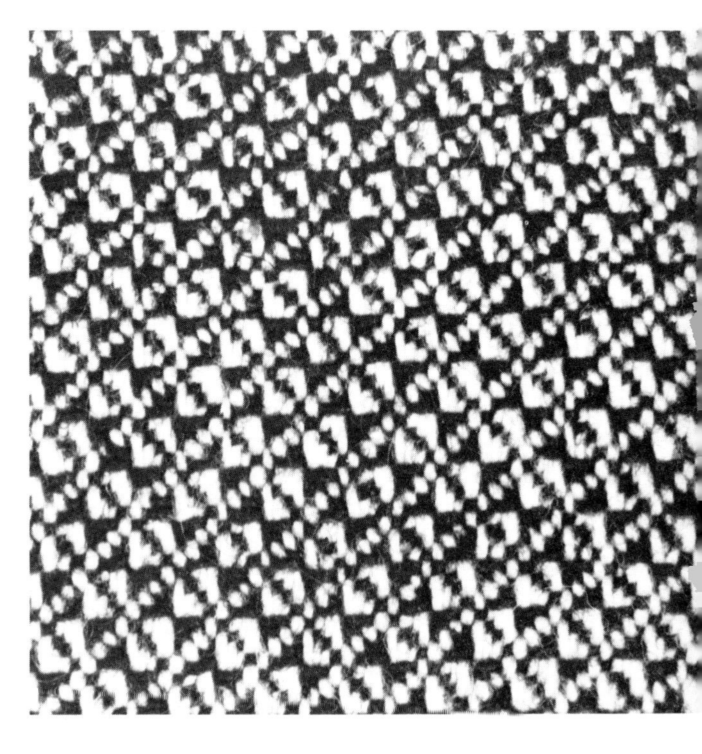

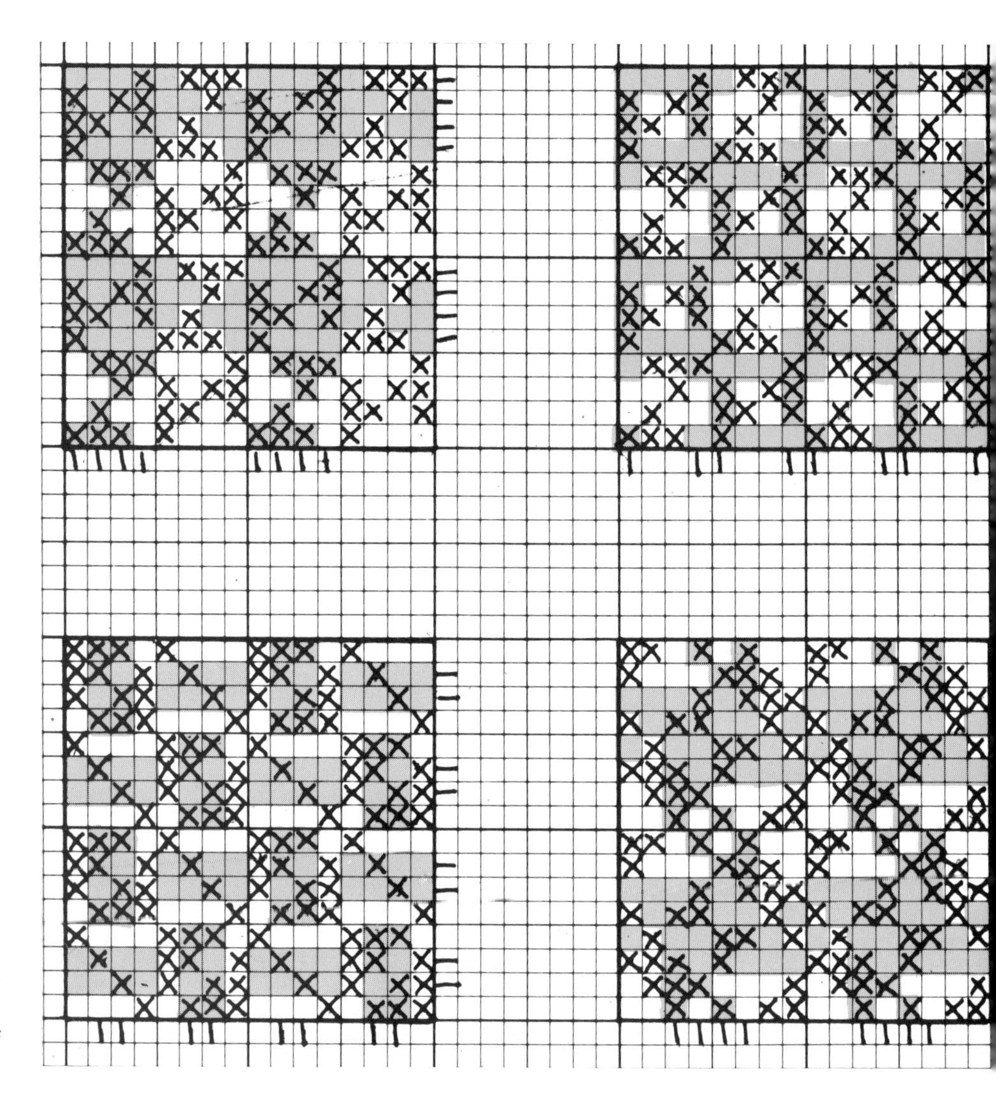

Diag 78 Colour and weave effect with dice weaves

Fig 73 Birds eye dice weave

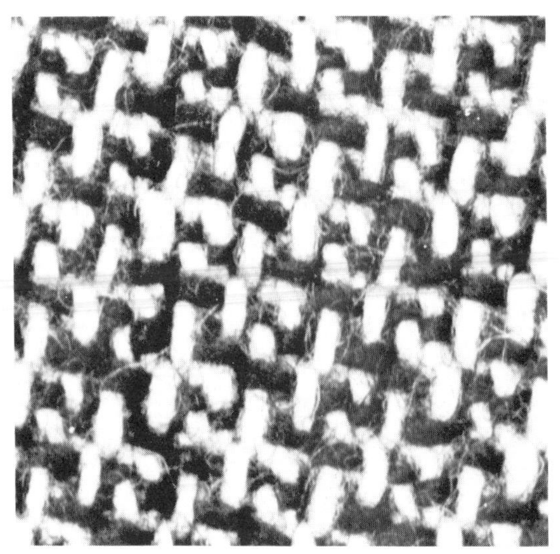

normal manner. Usually each end in the weave requires its own shaft. They are woven with a square sett, which with an average 8 × 8 repeating weave is the same as 2/2 twill, i.e. $\frac{2}{3}$ of diameters, but if there is any doubt the weave firmness formula should be employed.

DESIGNING WITH DICE WEAVE

Pretty, small repeating designs result if the basic weaves are woven with a contrasting colour in warp and weft. Colour and weave interlacings combine to produce traditional and striking patterns. Woven with wool they look very tweedy, and in cotton or linen make very crisp-looking fabrics.

Figures 74 to 77 illustrate these patterns and Diagram 78 gives the weaves and warp and weft colouring plans necessary to create them.

As dice weaves have the same sett as 2/2 twill, 3/1

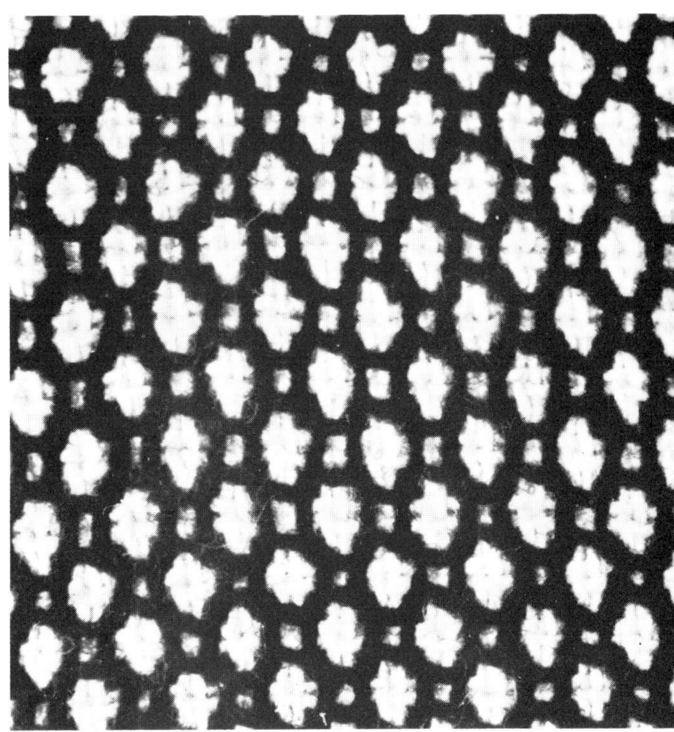

Fig 74 Birds eye dice weave colour and weave effect

Fig 75 Birds eye dice weave colour and weave effect

Fig 76 8-end barleycorn colour and weave effect

Fig 77 Dice weave colour and weave effect

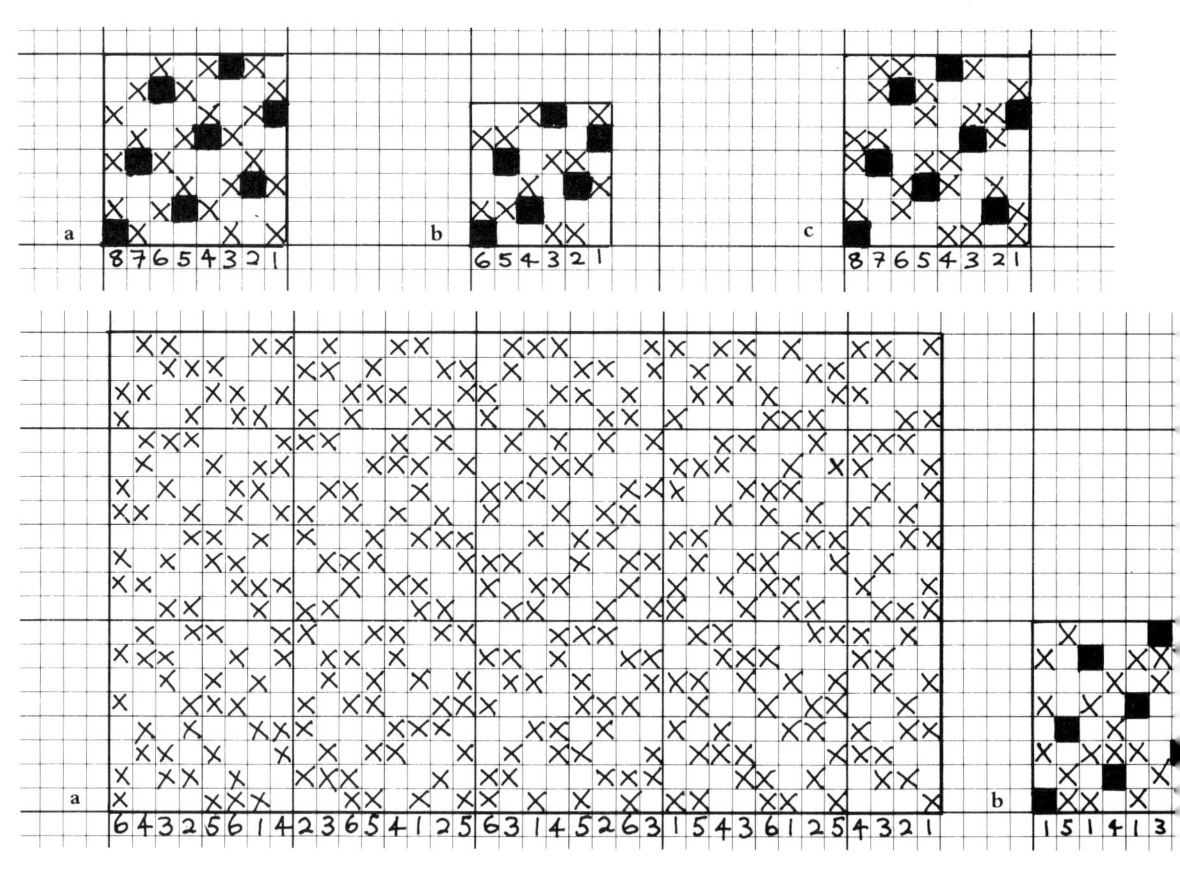

Diag 79 Crepe weaves (top)

Diag 80 Moss crepe weave and 5 shaft crepe weave

twill and 1/3 twill, they can all be combined to form striped and checked patterns.

Crepe Weaves

Crepe weaves are sometimes known as granite or oatmeal weaves. These names are given to weaves which have no prominent surface direction or pattern, but which give a cloth the effect of being covered in minute dots as well as a rough and irregular handle.

There are several methods of constructing crepe weaves. The simplest and perhaps most effective is a development of the sateen construction whereby additional floats are added to each end on a regular or irregular sateen base. The use of an irregular sateen base ensures that the crepe weave is also irregular and therefore produces a slightly better weave. The additional floats should follow the identical lifting sequence on each end above each base mark. The final weave should have an equal proportion of warp and weft showing on the surface. For example, a crepe weave repeating on

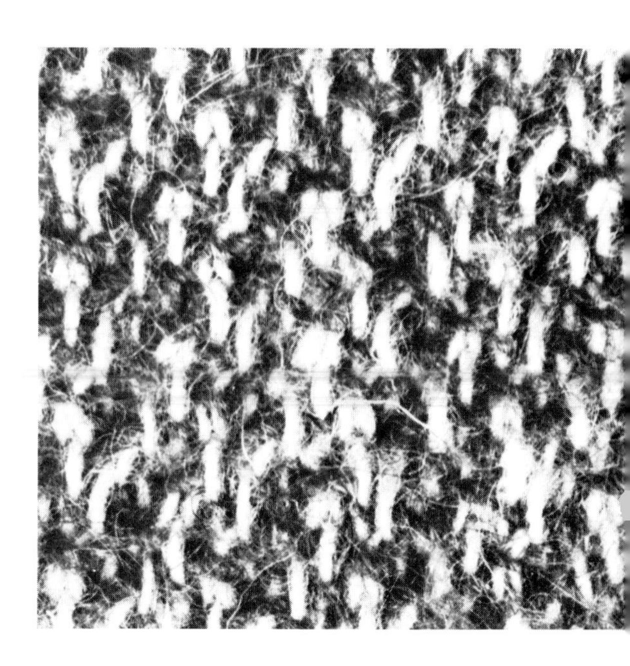

Fig 78 Crepe weave

eight ends and picks will need three extra warp-up marks per end of the sateen base, creating 4 marks and 4 blanks on each end and pick. At no point in the weave should any float be longer than 3 in any direction. Diagram 79 illustrates weaves constructed on the above principle. Diagram 80a shows a design known as moss crepe which can be woven on 6 shafts; it repeats on 36 ends and 20 picks. Diagram 80b illustrates an effective crepe weave which requires 5 shafts. Figure 78 shows this weave in a cloth.

The sett of crepe weaves should be square, and usually work out to be slightly higher than a basic 2/2 twill. The shrinkage of the crepe weave will also be greater than a twill cloth.

DESIGNING WITH CREPE WEAVES

Fine yarns and a self-coloured warp and weft will show the rough texture of a crepe weave to best effect. Combining a crepe weave with its satin or sateen partner in a stripe or check arrangement, would create a design with sharp contrasts in texture.

Corkscrew Weaves

Corkscrew weaves are twilled ribs, either warp-faced or weft-faced. The best corkscrews are constructed on an odd number of threads, but this is not an essential factor of the weave. They are all developed from a sateen base.

WARP CORKSCREW

A regular sateen base is run out on an odd number of ends and picks with a stitching step of 2 ends to the right to 1 pick upwards (Diagrams 81a and c). Additional warp-up marks are inserted in succession above each base mark until they cover one extra square per end than blanks (Diagrams 81b and d). Corkscrew weaves which involve long warp floats can be made more stable if the back floats are made to interlace in plain weave order with the picks (Diagram 81e).

Warp corkscrews that repeat on an even number of threads are constructed in a similar manner, except that the actual repeat size is on twice as many ends as picks. An initial sateen base line with a step of 2 outward to 1 upward is run out across the repeat and then another base line is inserted on all picks but on alternate ends, the first mark starting halfway up the repeat (Diagram 82a). Warp-up marks are now inserted above each base mark until there are two more marks per end than blanks (Diagram 82b).

WEFT CORKSCREW

Weft corkscrew weaves produce cloths which have a prominent twilled line made up of weft-faced ribs. They are constructed in a similar manner to the warp corkscrew. A sateen base line with a step of 2 upwards to 1 outward is inserted, either continuously if the design is on an odd number of threads (Diagram 83a), or comprising of two separate lines if the repeat size is an even number of threads with twice as many picks as ends (Diagram 83e).

Warp-up marks are inserted to the right of each base mark. On the odd-sized repeat there should be one extra blank square per pick than marks (Diagrams 83b and c), while on the even-sized repeats, each pick should contain two more blanks than marks (Diagram 83f). A more stable fabric will result if the back floats interlace in plain weave order with the ends (Diagram 83d).

Sett

The setting of these twilled ribs is similar in principle to the setting of ordinary plain weave ribs. That is, that there should be as many threads per cm/inch in the direction of the face floats as there are actual diameters per cm/inch of the yarn, while the sett of the crossing threads is found by the weave firmness formula. Shrinkage will be greater in the direction of the floating threads. As always, it is wise when designing these more complicated structures to weave a sample of the cloth to check sett and shrinkage before starting a major piece.

DESIGNING WITH CORKSCREW WEAVES

Usually the same counts of yarn are used in the warp and weft, but the crossing thread can be thicker than the face threads. Because of the close setting of the face threads, it is better that these threads should be smooth rather than textured, unless it is textured in colour only, or has only a slight surface interest. A self-coloured cloth will produce a very smart, quite deeply textured twilled surface.

Like ordinary plain weave ribs, a 1 and 1 colouring in the direction of the floating threads will produce alternate ribs in different colours. (Diagram 81f—*N.B.*: 'D' means dark coloured thread.) This idea is the simplest and most effective designing method with corkscrew weaves. A variation of this idea might involve a 1 light, 1 dark warp colouring plan changing to 1 dark, 1 light at regular or irregular intervals to produce a broken twill effect (Diagram 84). Figure 79 illustrates a cloth woven in this manner using the weave shown in Diagram 81b and Figure 80 shows the same cloth which is reversed in the weft with a point join after each repeat.

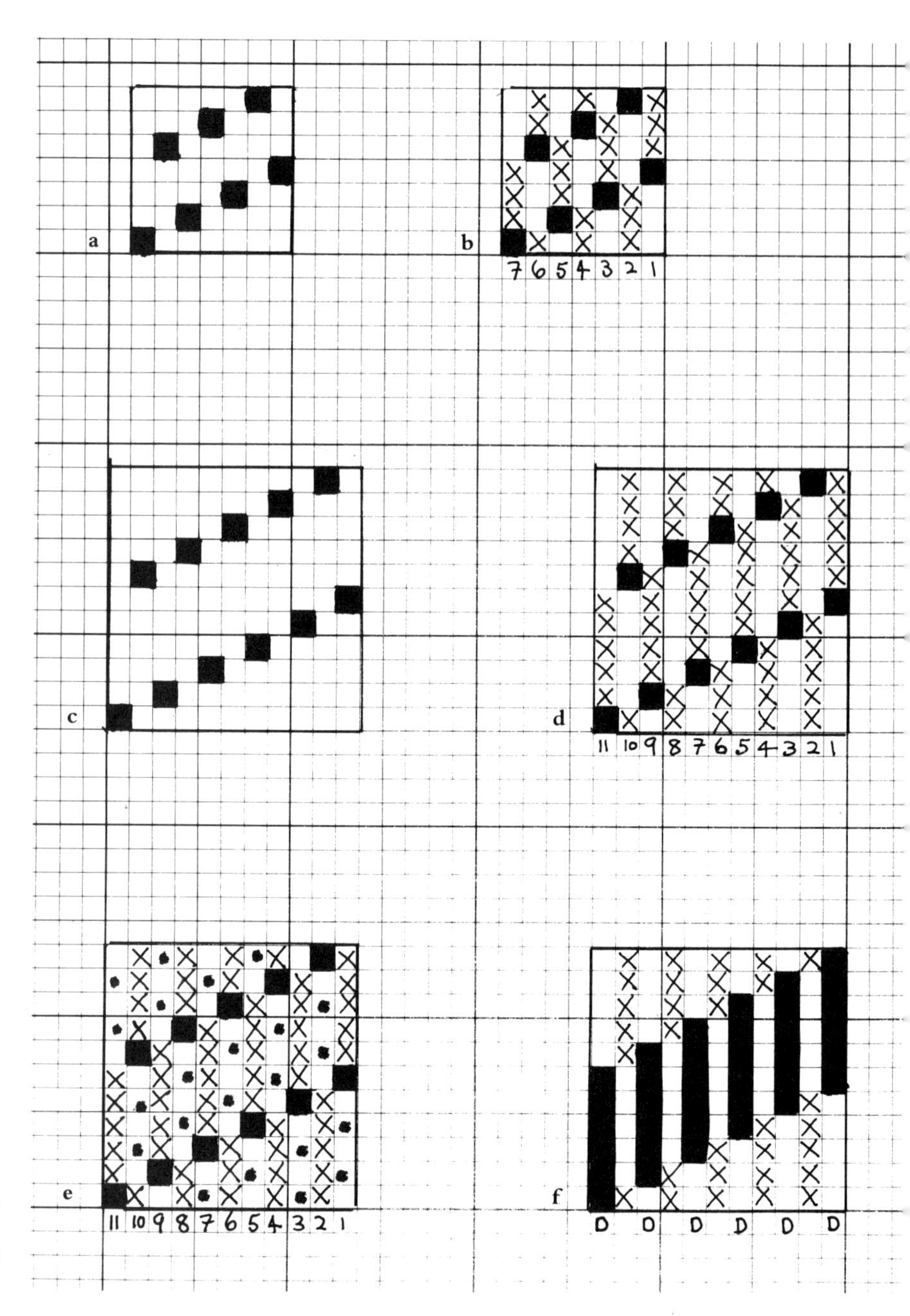

Diag 81 Warp corkscrews

Diag 82 Warp corkscrews on an even number of ends

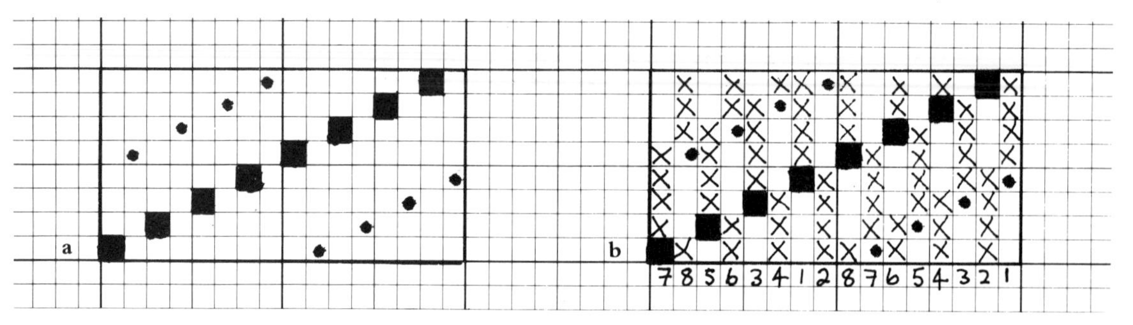

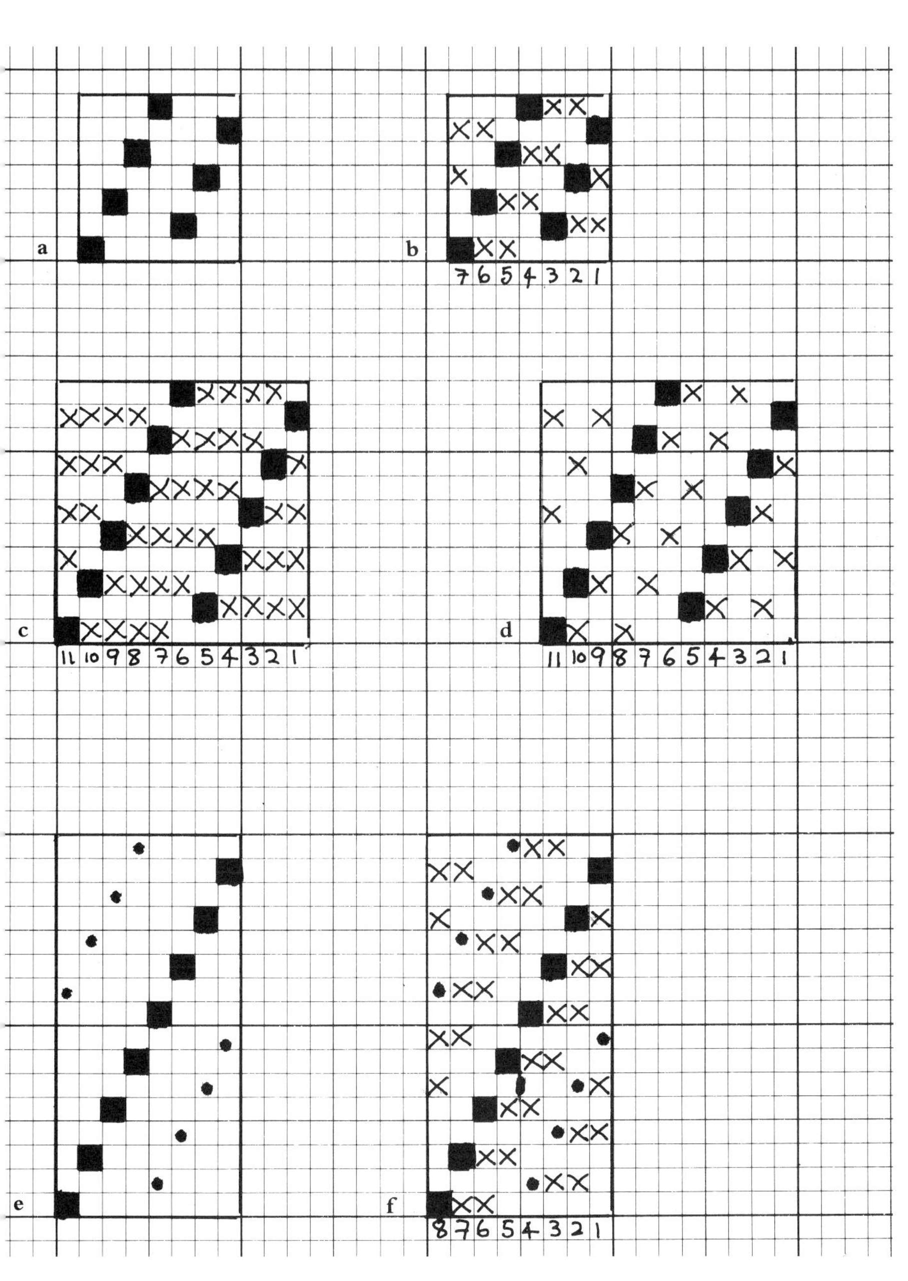

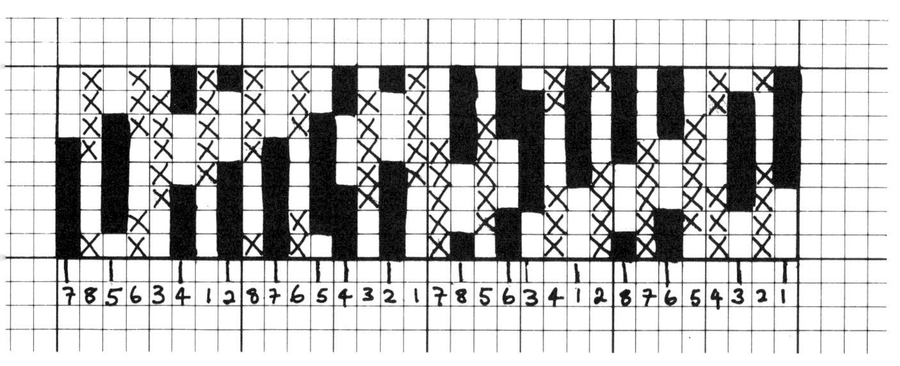

Diag 83 Weft corkscrews

Diag 84 Warp corkscrew with irregularly coloured warping plan in two colours

Fig 79 Warp corkscrew, broken twill effect

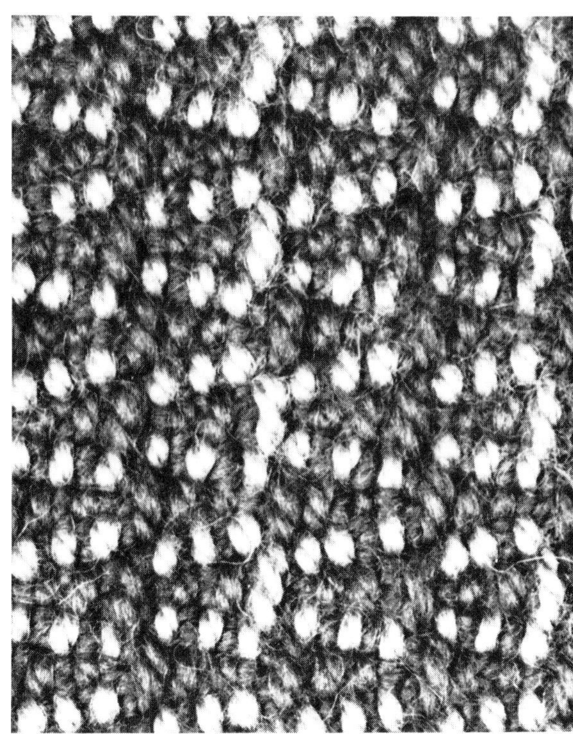

Fig 80 Reversed warp corkscrew

The basic corkscrew weaves can be reversed in either warp or weft or both using a point join. If these are combined with a 1 and 1 colouring, very bold zig-zag or diamond patterns in two colours will result (Diagram 85).

Figure 81 shows a cloth combining a weft corkscrew repeating on 8 ends and 16 picks which is reversed by a point join, and a 4/4 plain weave weft rib. A 1 and 1 coloured weft is inserted throughout resulting in bold coloured lines in three directions, twill to right, twill to left and vertical. Diagram 86 shows the weave diagram.

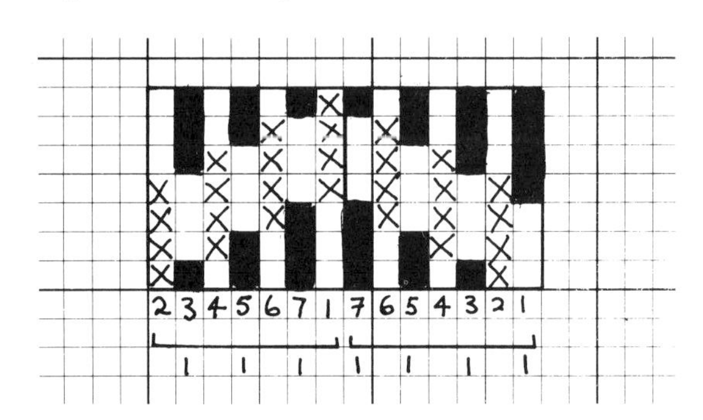

Diag 85 Reversed warp corkscrew with a 1 dark, 1 light warping plan

Honeycomb Weaves

These weaves combine areas of long floats with areas of plain weave. The long floats are in both a warp and weft direction and are diamond-shaped. Each diamond is surrounded by one or two rows of plain weave. After relaxation and shrinkage of the cloth, the floating threads rise to the surface, while the tightly interlacing plain weave areas take a much lower position, producing a cell-like effect resembling a honeycomb on both sides of the cloth.

The weave repeat can either be square or rectangular. A repeat size of 6 ends by 6 picks or 6 ends by 8 picks can be drafted onto four shafts. A larger repeat size gives a deeper and more textured fabric, but requires more shafts. The cell shapes are either square or rectangular.

CONSTRUCTION OF HONEYCOMB WEAVES

(Diagram 87)

1. Mark out a repeat size on even numbers.

2. Run a diagonal line of plain weave from bottom left to top right.

3. Cross this line by another diagonal running from right to left, starting one pick up on the right hand side. (Crosses in Diagram 87.)

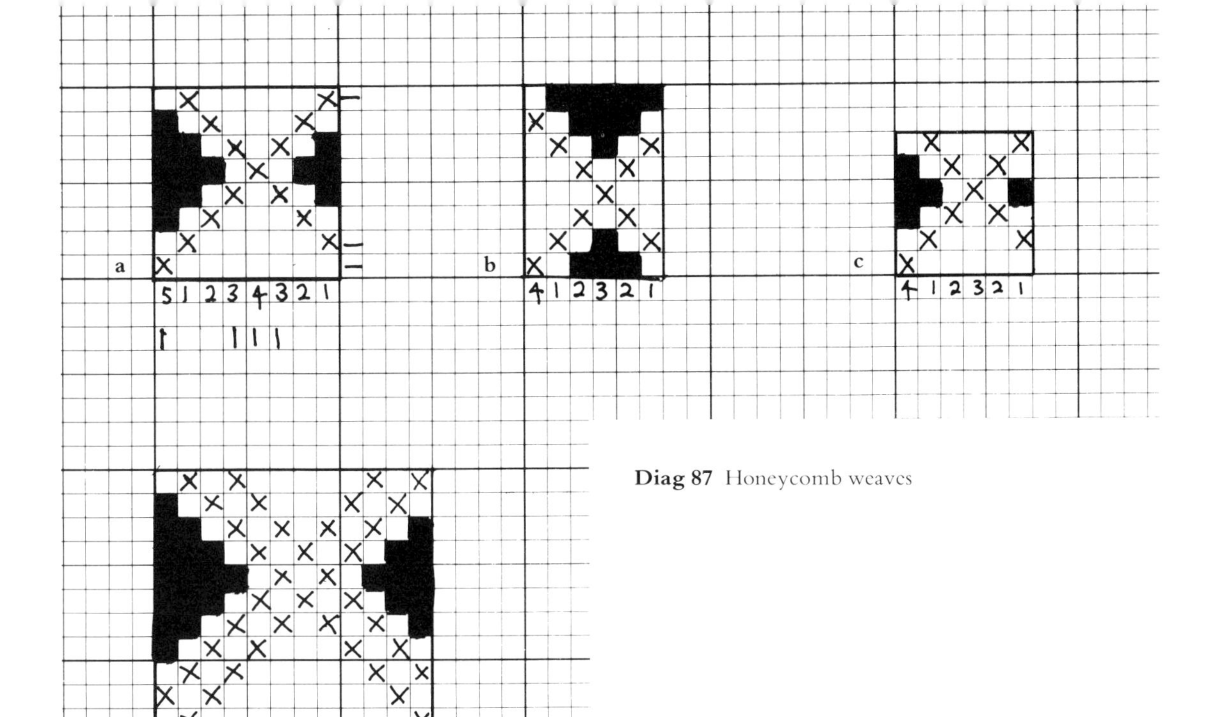

Diag 87 Honeycomb weaves

Fig 81 Weft corkscrew and 4/4 weft rib (below)

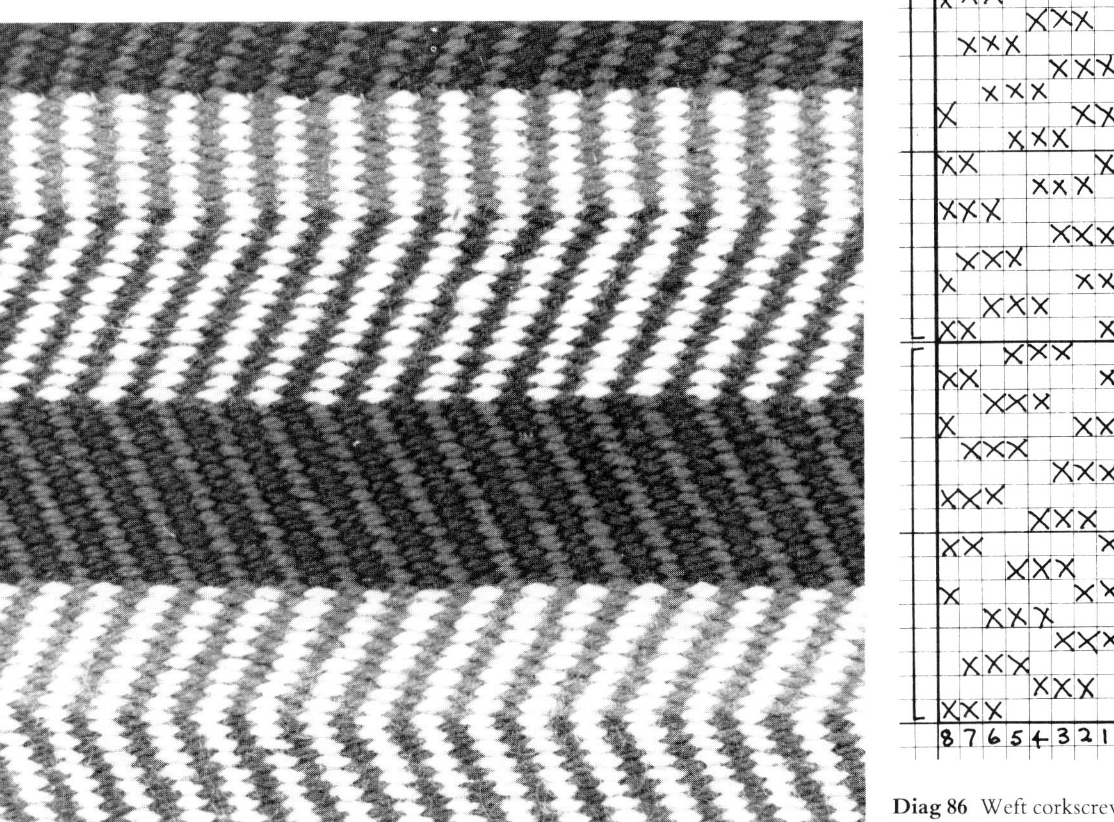

Diag 86 Weft corkscrew and 4/4 weft rib

4. Fill in a warp-faced diamond shape in two opposing sections, leaving a row of blanks between the diamond and the diagonal line. (Solid squares in Diagram 87.)

N.B. Once the repeat size goes above 12 ends × 12 picks, a double row of diagonal plain weave is necessary to give firmness to the structure (Diagram 87d).

Sett

The maximum square sett of honeycomb weave is approximately halfway between plain weave sett and actual diameters per cm/inch of a yarn. Shrinkage in both warp and weft is quite heavy.

A loosely sett 2/2 hopsack selvage will ensure a neat edge.

DESIGNING WITH HONEYCOMB WEAVES

The honeycomb structure produces so much interest and texture, it is better to use smooth yarns rather than textured ones. A warp and weft of the same colour allows the weave to show clearly. Yarns with a high degree of shrinkage such as woollen yarns emphasise the distortion. The cells increase the insulation properties of wool and therefore they are used traditionally for blankets. In cotton yarns, the cells create good moisture absorption properties and therefore can be used for towels. Honeycomb weaves can be used for clothing and soft furnishings as well.

The cells can be emphasised if some ends and picks are of a different colour to the main cloth. For example, if the ends and picks forming the central plain weave areas are coloured with a dark yarn, the depth of the cell is apparently increased. Alternatively, the ends and picks which form long warp and weft floats, will stand out and show as ridges if they are in a different colour to the main piece (Figure 82). The dashes below and by the side of Diagram 87a indicate the positioning of these contrasting threads.

Honeycomb weave will combine with plain weave to give a strong contrast in texture. Plate 6 shows a stripe of honeycomb and plain weave for a dress fabric. The plain weave stripe must be sett looser than the honeycomb weave. For example, if the plain weave stripes are sleyed 2 per dent in a reed, the honeycomb stripe will be sett 3 per dent. Ideally, the plain weave stripe should be run off a separate warp beam, to avoid distortion on relaxation of the cloth.

BRIGHTON HONEYCOMB WEAVE

Brighton honeycombs are a different construction to the ordinary honeycomb. They create a cloth

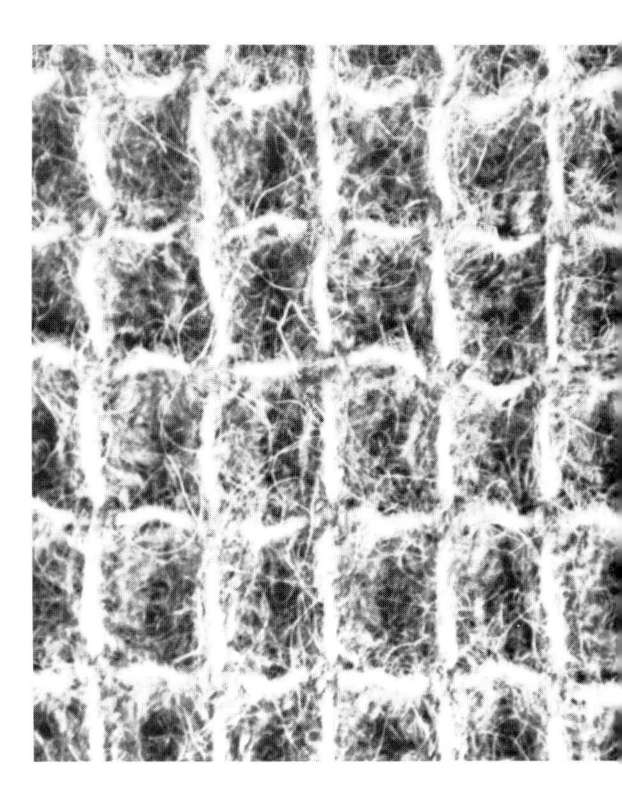

Fig 82 Honeycomb weave

Diag 88 Brighton honeycomb

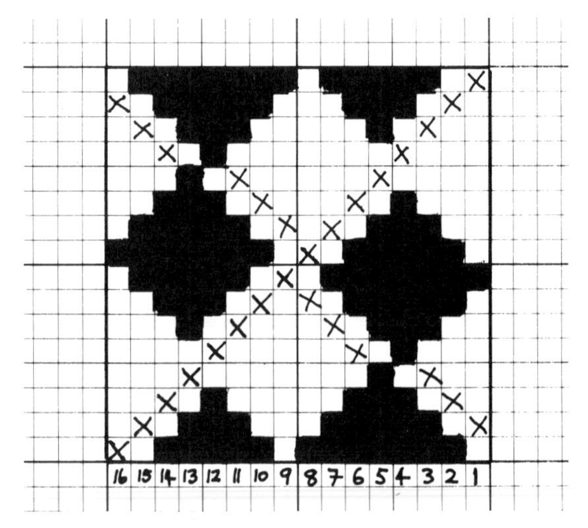

which has two sizes of cell showing on the face only. These cells are more circular in appearance, but slightly less deep than the ordinary honeycomb. The repeat size must be a multiple of 4, the most common being a repeat of 16 ends and picks (Diagram 88). Each end in the weave requires its own shaft. The sett should be the same as for ordinary honeycomb.

Huckaback Weaves

Huckaback weaves are designed to give a rough textured surface appearance and are constructed by combining areas of plain weave, and floating ends or picks, which distort on relaxation and shrinkage.

The weave repeat size is always twice an odd number, e.g. $5+5 = 10$, or $7+7 = 14$, or $5+9 = 14$. This arrangement allows two plain weave lifts to coincide at the join of each quarter in the weave.

CONSTRUCTION OF HUCKABACK WEAVES

1. Mark out repeat size on point paper, and divide into equal or unequal quarters.

2. Fill the whole area with plain weave (Diagram 89a).

3. Two opposing quarters remain as plain weave. The other two quarters are made into warp-faced floats by adding marks (Diagram 89b), or turned into weft-faced floats by removing marks from the plain weave diagram (Diagram 89c). These two quarters can either be identical or one can be warp-faced and the other weft-faced.

When sleying the reed, it is usual for the two adjacent ends, which are weaving plain weave throughout, to be sleyed in the same dent. This discourages the floating threads from pulling into groups. The appropriate sleying order is indicated with looped brackets under the weave diagrams.

Sett

A square sett should be employed which is equal to the normal plain weave sett of the yarn being used.

DESIGNING WITH HUCKABACK

The textured effect is quite effective in a plain colour. Figure 83 illustrates a cloth woven as Diagram 89b. Pattern can be combined with the texture by colouring the weft and/or the warp. Some possible designs are illustrated in Figure 84. The weave illustrated in Diagram 89b was used to

Fig 83 Huckaback weave

weave the patterns in Figure 84. The warp was white for all cloths. The wefting plan used to achieve the bottom pattern was

White	5
Black	5

The wefting plan used for the middle pattern was

White	1	1
Black	3	

and the wefting plan used for the top pattern was

Black	1	1
White	3	

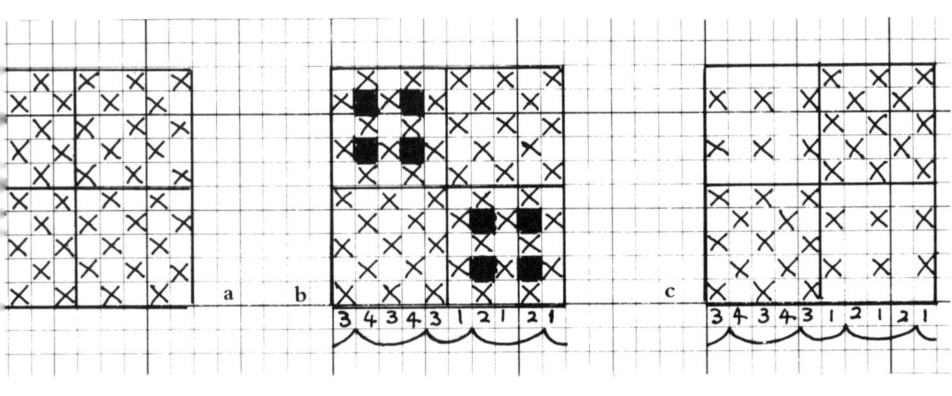

Diag 89 Construction of huckaback weaves

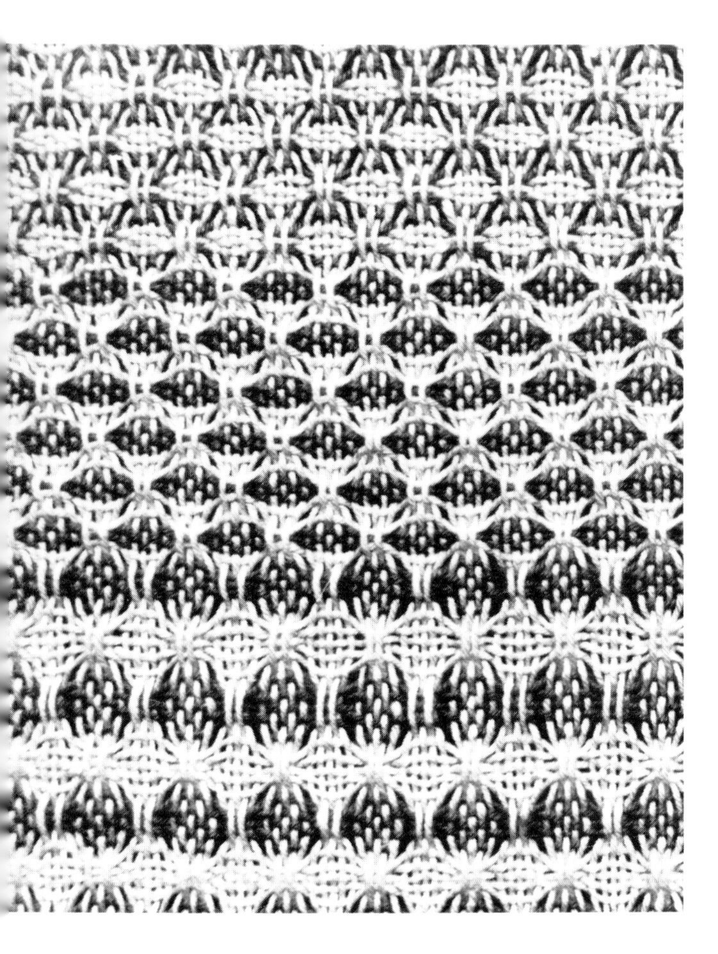

Fig 84 Colour and weave effects on huckaback weave

Fig 85 Colour and weave effects on mock leno weave

Huckaback combines well with plain weave for weave stripes and check patterns and these can be further enhanced by adding coloured stripes and overchecks.

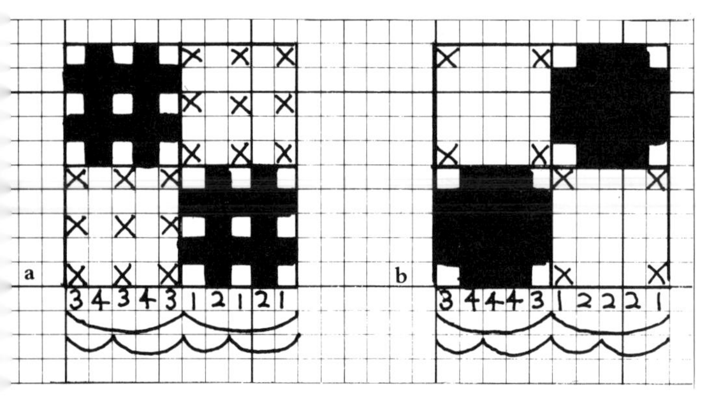

Diag 90 Mock leno weaves

Mock Leno Weaves

Mock leno weaves are an attempt to imitate the open work appearance of fabrics woven with the aid of doup mountings on the heddles, which enables ends to cross over each other.

CONSTRUCTION OF MOCK LENO WEAVES
(Diagram 90)

1. Mark out the repeat size on point paper. The weave repeats on the same number of ends as picks. The total repeat is then divided into quarters.

2. Fill in two opposite corners with a predominantly weft-faced motif.

3. The remaining quarters are filled in with the complete reverse of the first motif.

The perforated appearance of the cloth is created by sleying the reed properly. The two ends which are on either side of each quarter must be separated by a reed wire or even a space in the reed. Two appropriate sleyings for the weaves illustrated in Diagram 90, are indicated by the looped brackets underneath the diagram.

DESIGNING WITH MOCK LENO WEAVES

Traditionally, mock leno fabrics are used for embroidery canvas cloths, and are woven in cotton or linen. If smooth yarns and a self-coloured warp and weft are employed it is difficult to get away from the traditional look, so attractive yarns and an inspired imagination are needed to begin designing.

Colour and weave-effect combination can create unusual designs, and some to try are shown in Figure 85.

The weave illustrated in Diagram 90a was used to weave the patterns in Figure 85 and the warping plan was:

White	1	1	6
Black	1	1	

The wefting plan for the bottom pattern was:

White	1
Black	1

The wefting plan for the pattern above was:

Black	1
White	1

The wefting plan for the next pattern was:

Black	1	1	2	1	1
White	1	1	1	1	

The wefting plan for the top pattern was:

White	1	1	2	1	1
Black	1	1	1	1	

Mock leno weaves are particularly effective if combined with plain weave in either striped or checked arrangements. Plate 10 illustrates mock leno and plain weave used in linen table mats.

Distorted Thread Effect

Distorted thread effects are a group of weaves that again base their effect on the shrinkage differences between the tight interlacing of plain weave which shrinks little, compared to floating ends and picks lying over the ground cloth which shrink a great deal and are made to distort.

The ground fabric, being plain weave, is very stable, but care must be taken to ensure that the floating ends and picks are not too long in case they snag and break when in use. The distortion does not occur until after the fabric is relaxed off the loom. The distorting threads can be either in the warp or the weft.

Diagrams 91a and b illustrates a simple distorted thread effect weave in both warp and weft respectively. They are constructed by running out plain weave on an even number of ends and picks, leaving two evenly-spaced ends and picks free from marks. These blank ends and picks are the extra threads lying on top of the ground cloth. The way these extra threads interlace with each other and with the ground cloth, depends on whether a warp distort or a weft distort is required.

SIMPLE WARP DISTORT

The extra warp ends are of a contrasting colour, texture or thickness. The extra weft picks are usually the same yarn as the ground cloth.

The extra warp ends are floating completely over the ground cloth and therefore warp-up marks are inserted all the way up these ends (solid squares in Diagram 91a), except where they coincide with the extra weft picks which are going to hold them down. The extra pick has to draw the extra ends alternately towards and away from each other. This is achieved on point paper by indicating warp-up marks between the extra ends in opposing positions on alternate extra picks. (Dots in Diagram 91a.) The diverging and converging lines in the diagrams indicate the directions in which the distorting ends travel. This weave needs 6 shafts. Plate 9 illustrates a warp distort cloth incorporating many different yarns and colours as the distorting picks.

SIMPLE WEFT DISTORT

The same construction principles are employed in a simple weft distort as a simple warp distort. The weft yarn should now be the one that is of contrasting colour or texture and the extra warp the same yarn as the ground. The extra weft remains as blanks on the weave diagram, while the warp-up marks on the extra ends pull the picks alternately towards and away from each other in the manner illustrated by the fine lines in Diagram 91b. The weft distort can be woven on four shafts.

In either weave the distance between the extra ends and picks can be increased by bracketing up a repeat of the ground weave.

Sett

The sett is based on a normal plain weave sett with the distorting ends and picks regarded as extra threads and, therefore, sleyed as extras in the reed. On a long piece the extra ends should be wound onto a second warp beam as the take-up of these threads and the ground weave are different.

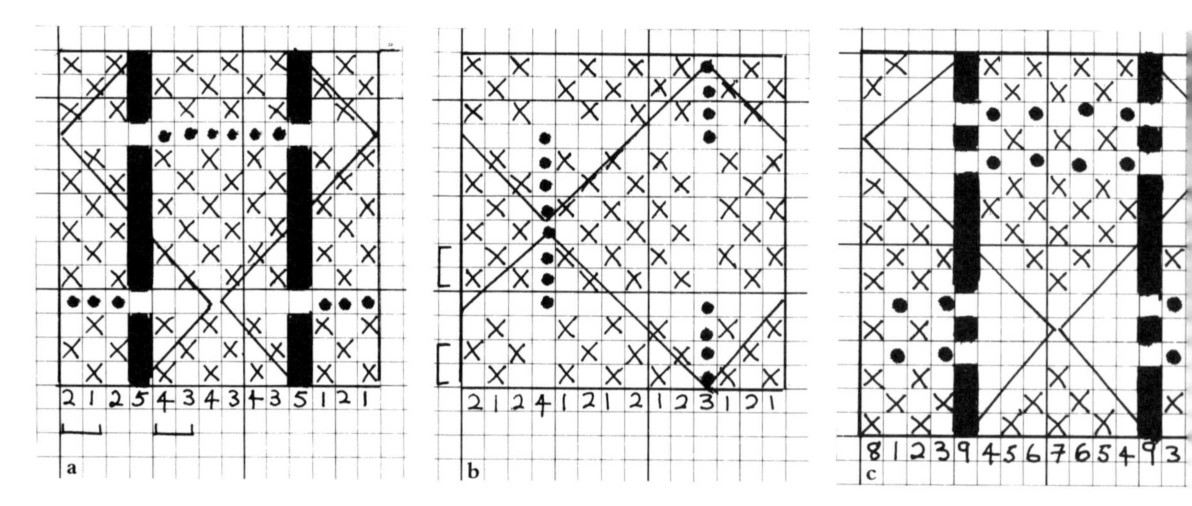

MORE WARP DISTORTED THREAD EFFECTS

The weave diagram in Diagram 91c produces a warp distorted fabric design which is much firmer than the previous example, although similar in appearance. The ground cloth is allowed to float loosely in alternating sections which causes the extra ends to bend more easily and the extra weft picks are allowed to interlace as plain weave with the ground cloth.

Diagram 91d illustrates the weave diagram for another distorted weave effect, and Plate 5 illustrates a fabric woven using the distortion as a stripe with a crepe weave. The two extra ends which are creating the distorted effect are indicated by solid squares in the diagram. These two ends are surrounded by 16 ends which are going to force them to converge and separate on relaxation and shrinkage, by combining areas of floating threads and areas of tightly interlacing threads. These 18 ends must be sleyed more closely together than the normal sett of a plain weave cloth using identical yarns. If a plain weave cloth would need 2 ends per dent the distorted strips would need 3 ends per dent.

DESIGNING WITH DISTORTED THREAD EFFECT

The main patterning effect is produced by the colour or texture of the extra threads that are distorting. But all these extra threads need not necessarily be the same colour or texture.

In its simplest form the ground cloth is usually self-coloured but again this is not essential. Stripes or checks can be incorporated into the ground cloth, although they should not conflict with the distorting ends or picks (Plate 9). If the ground cloth is plain weave, one of the simple colour and weave effects could make an interesting background pattern. Distorted thread effect weaves also combine well in striped designs using plain weave or any other simple weave as Plate 5 illustrates.

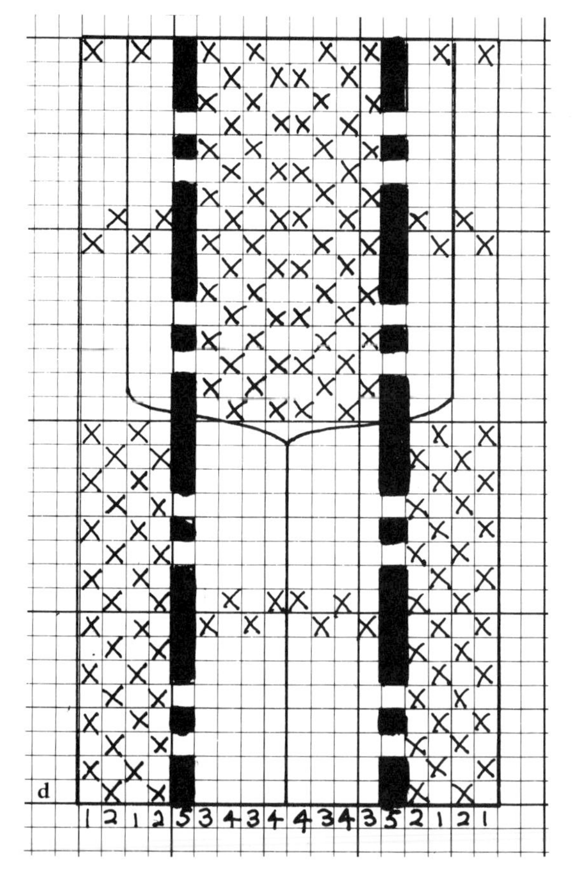

Diag 91 Distorted thread effects

The most important design consideration with these weaves is that they will be suitable for the end-purpose intended. The long floating ends and picks make this weave unsuitable for upholstery cloths or clothing fabrics in particular.

12 DESIGNING FROM A MOTIF, OR BLOCK DESIGNING

The concept of designing from a motif is an important approach to which several types of weave can be applied. The motif or pattern that is desired on the face of the fabric can be designed on point paper by a system which also considers the number of shafts that are required to weave it. It is a concept which looks at the motif or pattern in terms of blocks. One row of vertical squares of a motif sketched out on the point paper is one block. The shaft requirements to weave any one identically-intersecting block of the motif is dependent on the weave chosen to interpret it.

The weaves which can be applied to this idea are of two types: First, there are those which create contrasting textures or surface appearances. The motif is woven in one effect while the background shape is composed of the opposite effect. Weaves which combine to create this contrasting surface-interest in texture or colour, with the number of shafts required to weave each block, are listed below:

Warp-faced plain weave rib coloured 1/1 in warp and 1 fine, 1 thick in weft
— 2 shafts per block. (Chapter 6)

Summer-and-winter
— 1 shaft per block + 2 shafts for ground fabric. (Chapter 13)

1/3 and 3/1 twill
— 4 shafts per block. (Chapter 7)

Satin and sateen
— 4 shafts per block minimum. (Chapter 9)

2/2 twill to right and left, point join
— 2 shafts per block + 2 shafts. (Chapter 12)

Weft reversible
— 4 shafts per block. (Chapter 13)

Interchanging double plain
— 4 shafts per block. (Chapter 14)

Double plain + 2/2 twill
— 4 shafts per block. (Chapter 14)

Double plain + bold colour and weave effect
— 4 shafts per block. (Chapter 14)

Horizontal and vertical hairline on plain weave ground. Shadow weave
— 1 or 2 shafts per block. (Chapter 8)

In all the above cases the underside of the fabric is a complete reverse of the face.

Secondly, there are those weaves which allow extra ends or picks to float over the surface of a ground fabric to form the desired shapes and then float behind the ground fabric which now becomes the background or contrasting sections of the design. Weaves of this type with the number of shafts that each block requires are listed below:

Warp figuring
— 1 shaft per block + 2 shafts for plain weave ground fabric + 2 warp beams. (Chapter 13)

Weft figuring
— 1 or 2 shafts per block. (Chapter 13)

Ornamental repp
— 1 shaft per block + 1 shaft for ground fabric. (Chapter 6)

The Motif

Any motif, pattern or shape must be composed of a minimum of two blocks. All two block motifs are a development of a checkerboard and guard check arrangement. Diagram 92 illustrates the six basic 2-block patterns developed from these two forms. By extending and repeating the two blocks from each form, either horizontally and/or vertically, large attractive shapes can be designed (Diagram 93). Diagram 93 also show how a motif is visualised on point paper. A shape or pattern is built up by shading in different squares on point paper. The blank squares then represent the background or contrasting effect of the design. Each square of point paper within the motif represents one complete repeat of the actual weaves which will be used to create the shapes. It is important to draw out at least two repeats of your motif on point paper in both directions, to ensure that it will repeat attractively in

Diag 92 Basic two block motifs

Diag 93 Large two block motifs

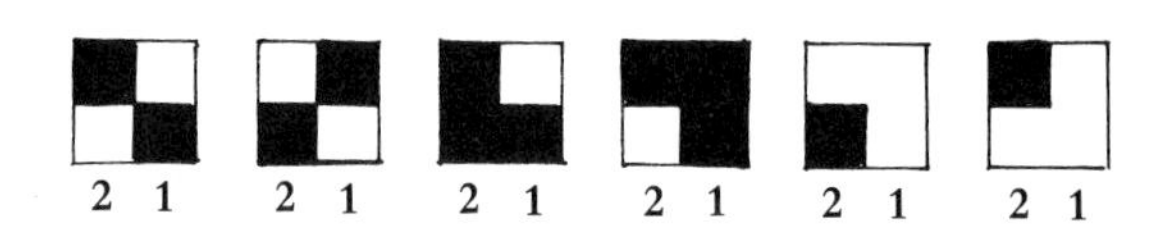

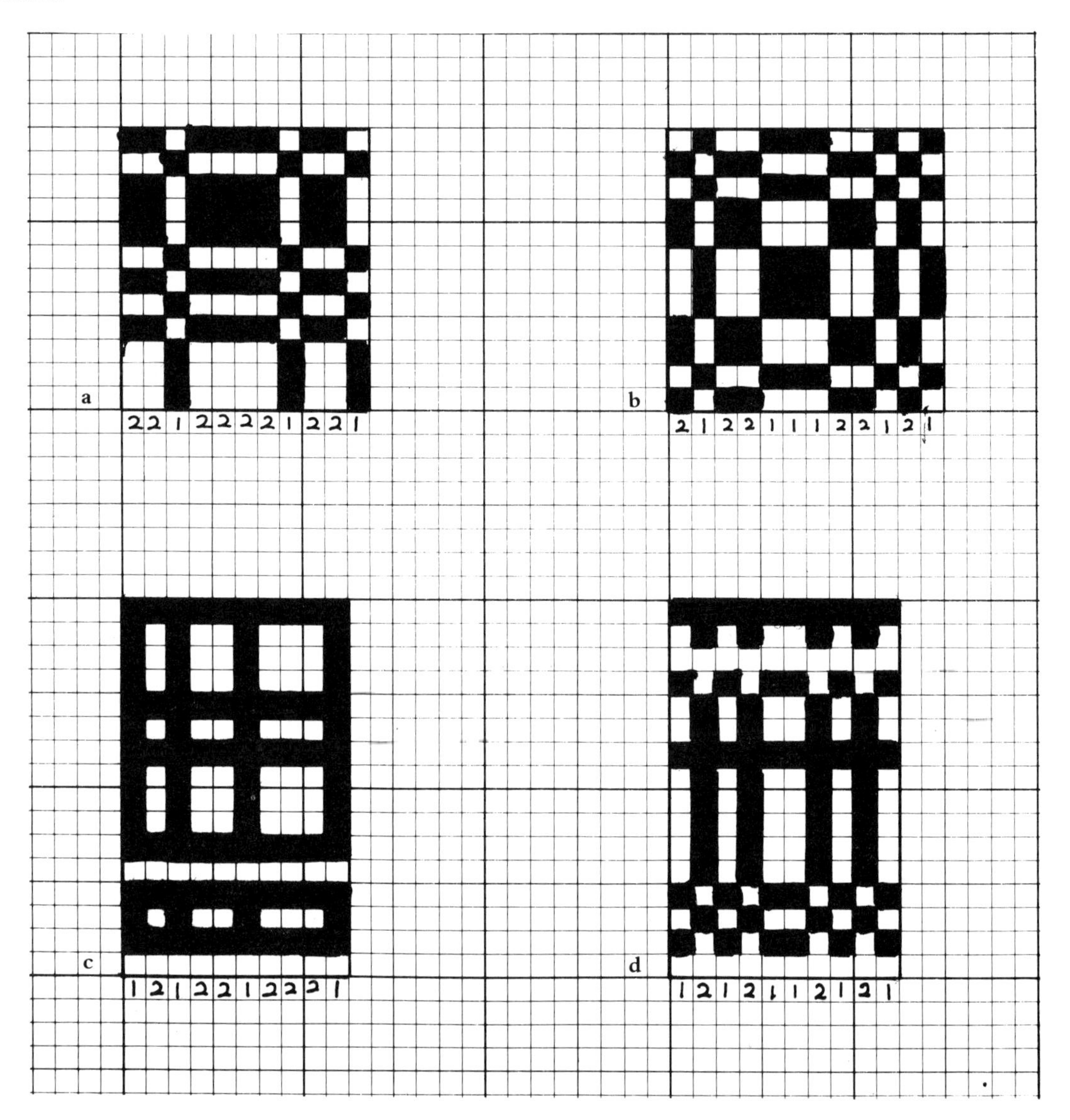

the cloth, and also that no additional blocks are required at the joins.

Once a repeating motif has been designed, it is possible to work out the number and the sequence of the different blocks in the pattern. This is established by the same process as drafting a weave. For example, write No. 1 under the first block on the right of the motif. Note how it is changing from shaded squares to blanks up the design. Write No. 1 under any other block which is following the identical route. Write 2 under the second block, and under any other identical interlacing block. Continue until each block has a number beneath it; the maximum number reached indicates the variety of independently working blocks in the motif. Owners of countermarche looms should do a similar thing with the horizontal blocks to ensure they have enough pedals to produce the lifting plan, remembering that each block may need up to 4 pedals to weave it.

The number of shafts required to weave each block is determined by the weaves to be used. In

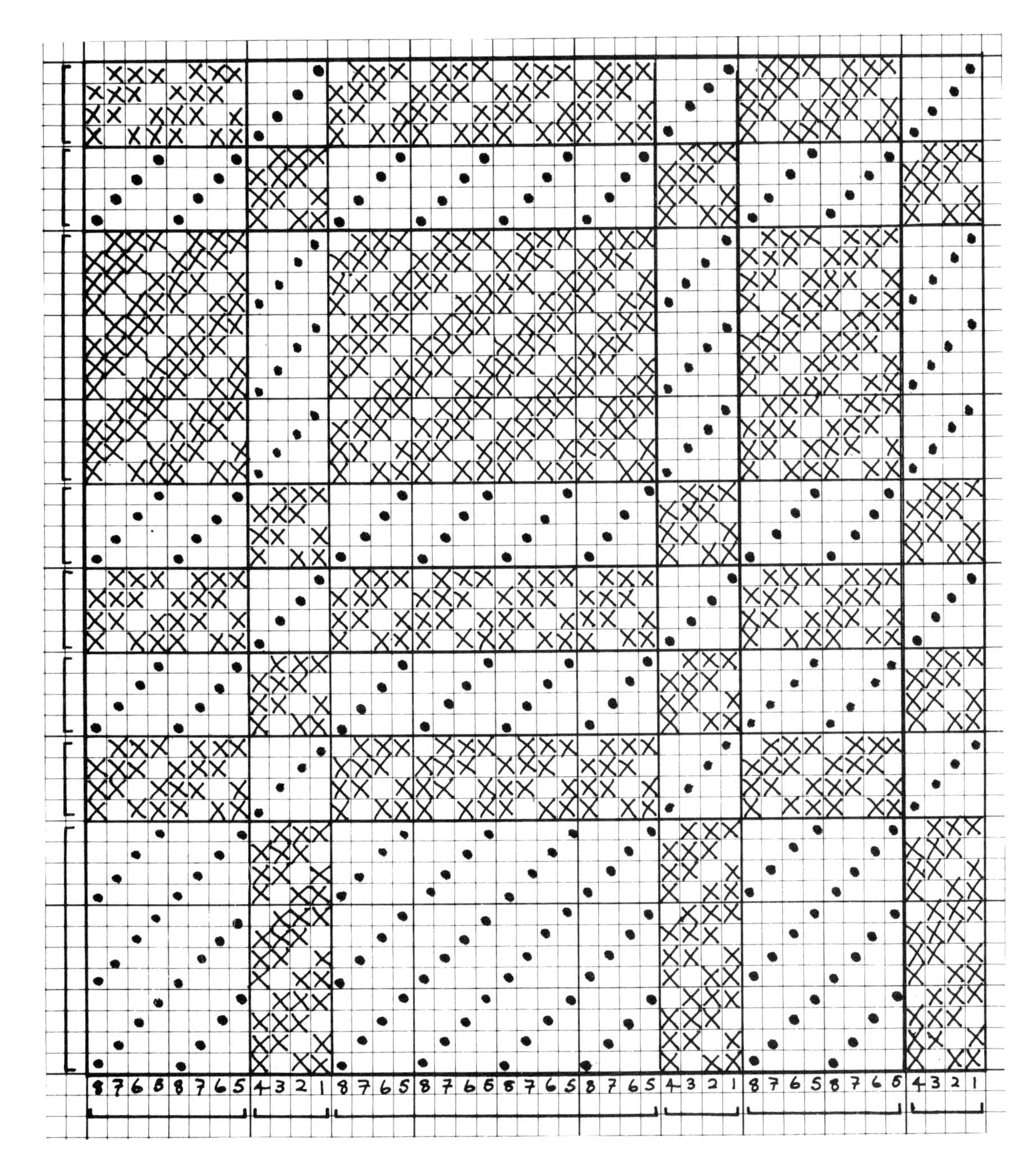

Diag 94 Motif design interpreted in 1/3 and 3/1 twill

most cases, 4 shafts are required per block resulting in a 2 block pattern needing 8 shafts. Summer and winter weave, however, will create a 2 block design on 4 shafts, and a 6 block design on 8 shafts, and warp rib weave only requires 2 shafts per block.

Once the motif is completed and the shaft requirements are available, it is necessary to transpose the design into a weave diagram from which a suitable draft and lifting plan can be determined in the normal manner.

METHOD OF TRANSPOSING A MOTIF INTO A WEAVE DIAGRAM, USING TWO WEAVES OF CONTRASTING TEXTURES (Diagram 94)

1. Choose the weaves to be used and note the minimum size of the basic weave repeat. (The motif shape in Diagram 93a is being interpreted by 1/3 and 3/1 twill weave. These weaves both have a

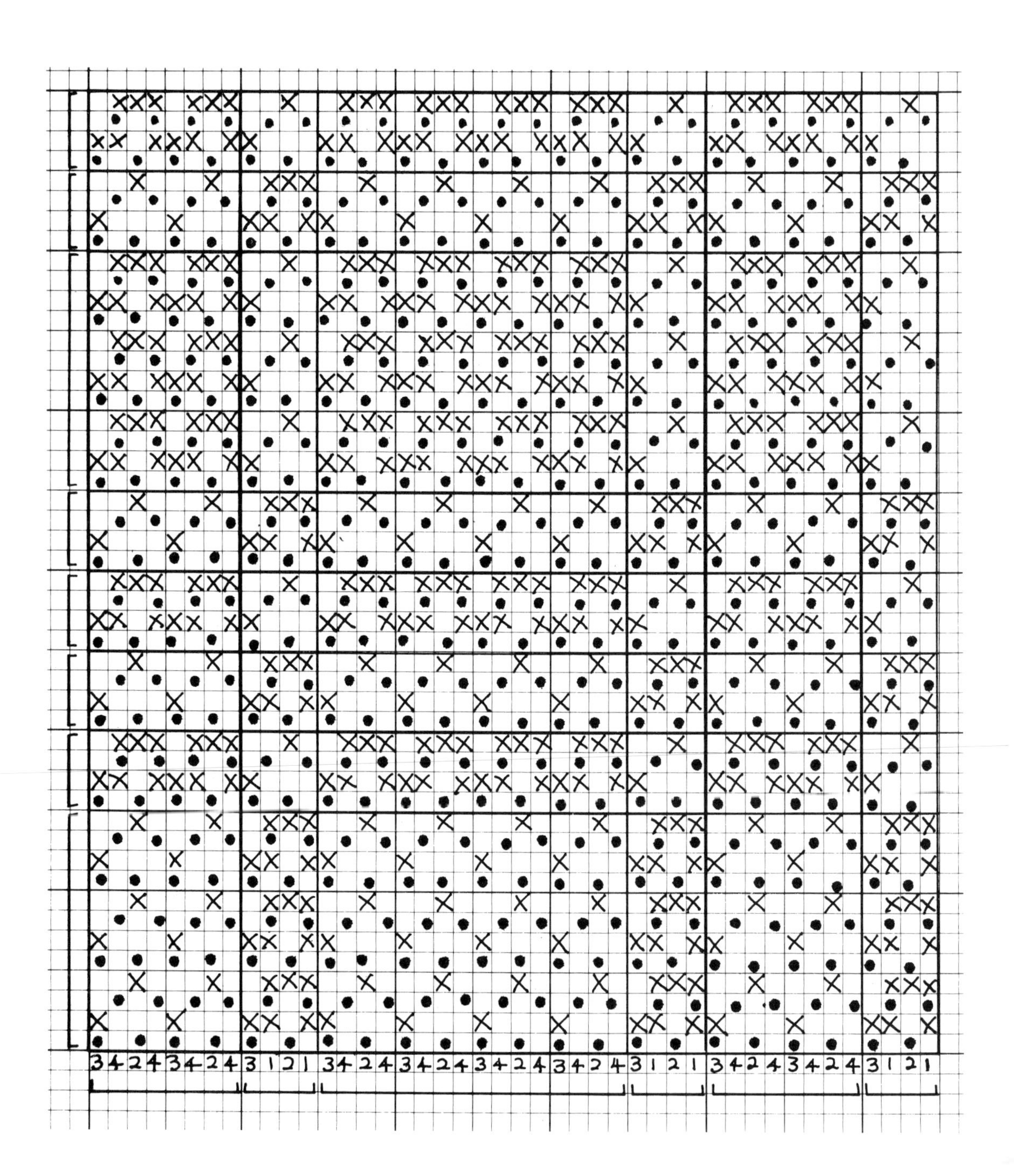
3 4 2 4 3 4 2 4 3 1 2 1 3 4 2 4 3 4 2 4 3 4 2 4 3 4 2 4 3 1 2 1 3 4 2 4 3 4 2 4 3 1 2 1

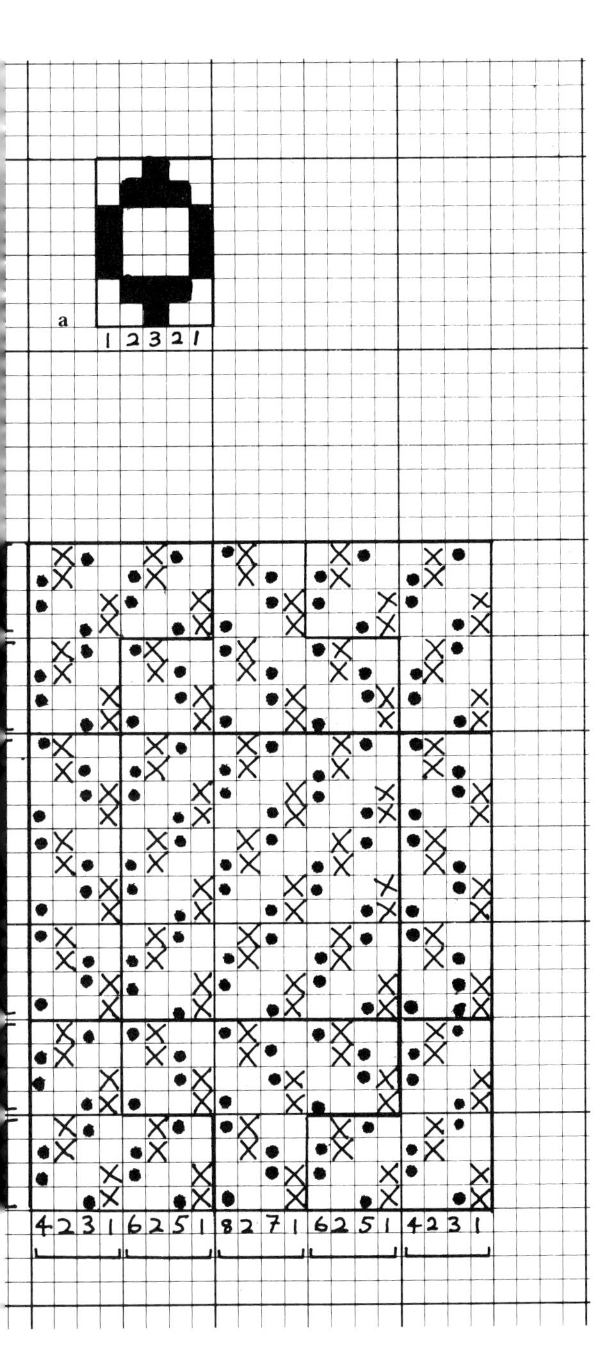

minimum repeat size of 4 ends and 4 picks.)

2. For each square in the motif, allocate on point paper an area equal to the minimum repeat size of the weaves chosen.

3. Lightly shade in the motif shape on this much larger scale.

4. Fill in the shaded areas with one of the weaves chosen, and the white areas with the contrasting weave.

5. Work out the exact drafting and lifting plans for the design in the normal manner. (In Diagram 94, 8 shafts will be required.)

6. Any or all of the blocks can be bracketed up in warp or weft to increase the size of the pattern. Diagram 95 illustrates the same motif being used as in Diagram 94 but this time summer-and-winter weave is interpreting it. Only 4 shafts are needed to weave this design.

The above method of designing offers enormous scope for producing innovating fabrics. The finished appearance of the cloth is closely aligned with the weaves that are used to interpret your design. For example, satin and sateens will produce a very smooth appearance. The motif will even show up if the cloth is completely self-coloured because of the reflection of light on the two surfaces. Interchanging double plain and weft reversible rely on colour for their contrast, as does summer and winter, which will also give a broken tweedy look compared to these other weaves. Warp rib gives a textured surface; 2/2 twill to right and left produces a fairly indistinct, subtle motif.

2/2 twill to right and left must be filled into a motif in the following manner to ensure that the shaft requirements are kept to a minimum of 2 shafts per block plus 2. Every second end should be inserted first, one lifting over 2 and under 2, while the alternate end lifts under 2, over 2. Diagram 96b shows crosses forming these marks on the motif shape of Diagram 96a. All other marks (dots) are then inserted in each 4×4 repeat around these previous marks, either twill to right or twill to left according to the motif requirements.

The method for transposing a motif into a weave using extra threads floating over a ground cloth is discussed in the next Chapter.

Diag 95 Motif design interpreted in summer-and-winter weave (opposite)

Diag 96 Motif and weave diagram interpreted in 2/2 twill to right and left

13 SPECIALISED WEAVES ASSOCIATED WITH DESIGNING FROM A MOTIF

Weft Figuring

Weft figuring allows extra weft picks to float over and under a stable ground fabric to form an all-over pattern, or a small repeating motif, in the process. Overshot is the traditional name for the same construction when applied to 4-shaft designs. Usually the ground fabric is plain weave, because it is the most stable and the most economical on shafts, but any of the simple weaves can be used as the ground fabric.

The order in which the extra picks interweave with the ground fabric depends on the shape of the pattern or motif desired on the face of the cloth. The shape must be sketched out on point paper in the same way as described in block designing (Chapter 12). A repeating unit must be established which can be woven on the number of shafts available on your loom. A weft figuring design on a plain weave ground needs 1 or 2 shafts for each identical block of the motif. Studying the weave constructions below should explain this discrepancy in shaft requirements.

Diagram 97a illustrates a motif to be woven on a cloth. The weave is constructed on point paper by running out plain weave on every end and on every other pick. (Crosses in Diagram 97b.) The alternate rows of blanks which result from this process are the extra picks floating over the surface of the ground cloth. Note that the weave diagram will repeat on the same number of ends, but on twice as many picks as the motif repeat.

The motif or pattern can now be transposed onto the weave diagram. It must be remembered that each vertical row of squares in the motif represents one end of the total warp, and each horizontal row represents every other pick. Look at the bottom row of squares of the motif and insert warp-up crosses on the first floating pick in the weave diagram in exactly the same positions as there are white squares on the motif. This causes the extra pick to float along the back of the ground fabric for these areas in the motif. The shaded squares of the motif are left as blanks on the weave diagram,

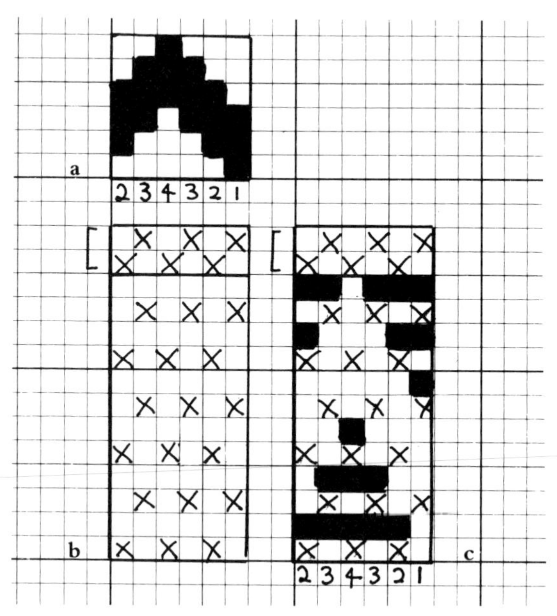

Diag 97 Construction of weft figuring weave diagram from a motif

which allows the extra pick to remain lying on the surface of the cloth at these places and thus form the desired shapes (Diagram 97c). The same process is done to each successive pick of the motif. Drafting and lifting plans can then be established in the normal manner.

In Diagram 97a it will be noted that there are four differently lifting blocks in the motif. When this motif is transferred onto the weave diagram and drafting is completed, it will be seen that four shafts are needed to weave this design. In other words each block of the motif requires one shaft.

The motif in Diagram 98a has the identical four blocks as the previous motif but expanded in the width. When this motif is transferred onto the weave diagram and drafting is completed, it is found that eight shafts are needed to weave this design. In other words, each block of the motif requires two shafts on the loom.

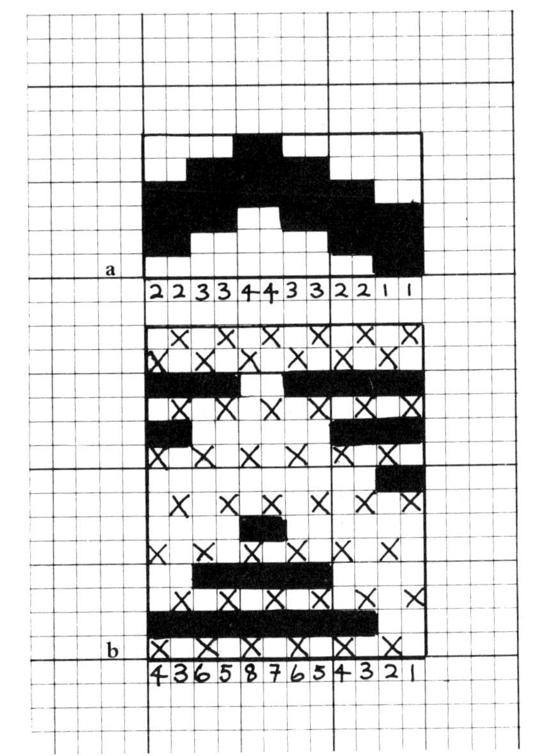

Fig 86 Weft figuring design (above)

Diag 98 Weft figuring design needing two shafts per block of the motif

Diag 99 Weft figuring design of a man motif (left)

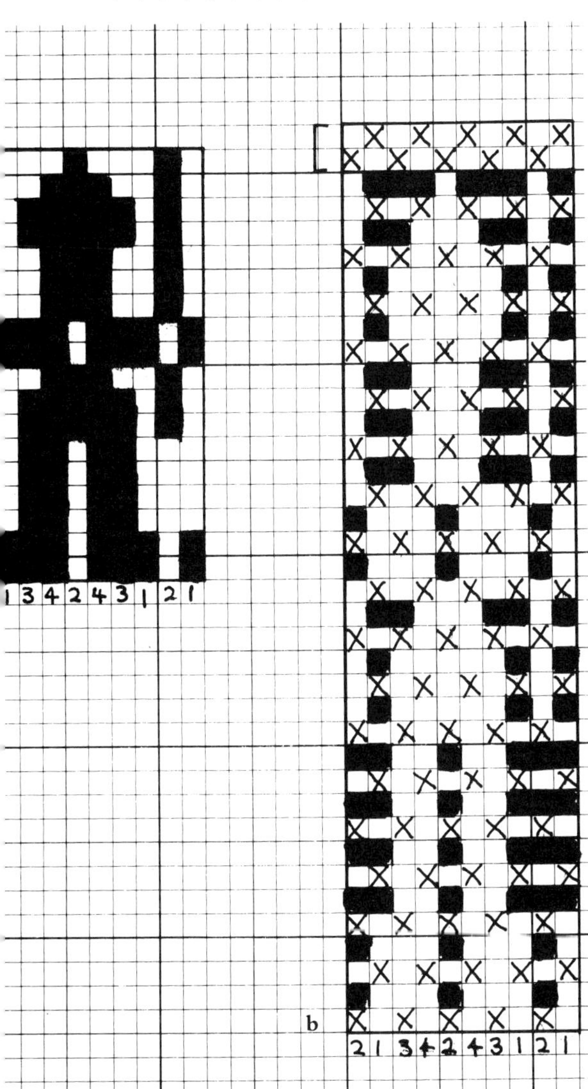

Two shafts are required instead of one for an identically lifting block, to allow for the two alternate lifts of the plain weave ground. It is therefore not possible to expand widthways any block of a motif and assume that it can be woven on the same number of shafts, although an expansion in height does not affect the shafts. A block repeated alternately with another, however, can be drafted onto the same shaft, as they will both coincide with the same plain weave lift of the ground fabric. Many of the large traditional four-shaft overshot patterns have only two blocks in the design to overcome this problem. There is still enormous scope for designing new patterns with two blocks. Diagram 99 illustrates a little man motif which can be woven on four shafts.

The motif is built up on the cloth during weaving when the extra picks are inserted. Usually these extra picks are of a slightly thicker count than the ground and can be either smooth or textured (Figure 86).

The cloth should be sett dependent on the ground weave and yarn, a basic square sett with the extra picks being regarded as extra in the weft sett. A floating selvage will be needed to catch the extra picks neatly.

Care needs to be taken to ensure that picks

floating over the surface forming the pattern are not so long that they hang loose, and are then liable to snag. A maximum of 2 cm (1 in) is long enough. If your design warrants much larger areas of floats on the surface, it will be necessary to tie the float down at regular intervals, perhaps every fourth end. This will increase the shaft requirements, however, and not give such a clear interpretation of the motif shape on the surface of the cloth.

Warp figuring

Warp figuring is similar in construction and appearance to weft figuring. It allows extra warp ends to float over a ground fabric and form a pattern. These extra warp ends will not interlace as frequently as the ground weave ends and, therefore, must be run off from a second back beam.

A motif is designed in the normal manner. This time every unique block will need an additional shaft, but any repetition of the blocks in any order will not increase the shaft requirements. Two additional shafts will be needed for the plain weave ground fabric.

The weave diagram is constructed by running out plain weave on every pick, but on alternate ends. The repeat size will be on the same number of picks and twice the number of ends as the motif (Diagram 100b). The motif (Diagram 100a) is transposed onto the blank ends of the weave diagram by inserting warp up marks in exactly the same positions as there are shaded squares in the motif. This brings the extra warp threads to the surface of the cloth where there are shaded sections in the motif. The blank areas of the motif remain as blanks on the weave diagram, thus causing the extra ends to hide behind the ground cloth at those points.

The sett is based on the square sett of the plain weave ground, and the extra ends are sleyed as extra in the reed.

Summer-and-winter Weave

Summer-and-winter is a weave which creates two distinctly opposite surface appearances, hence the name. The construction is a development of weft figuring whereby a plain weave fabric is woven and extra picks lie over and under this base cloth. Instead of floating loosely, however, the extra picks are tied down by every fourth end of the warp. This means that the problem of impractical long floats is overcome and huge areas of one colour or texture can be woven. Designing with summer-and-winter follows the block designing principle. (See Chapter 12.)

A motif is worked out on point paper. The ground fabric will require two shafts and each unique block in the motif requires one shaft. A four-shaft loom can, therefore, cope with a 2-block motif

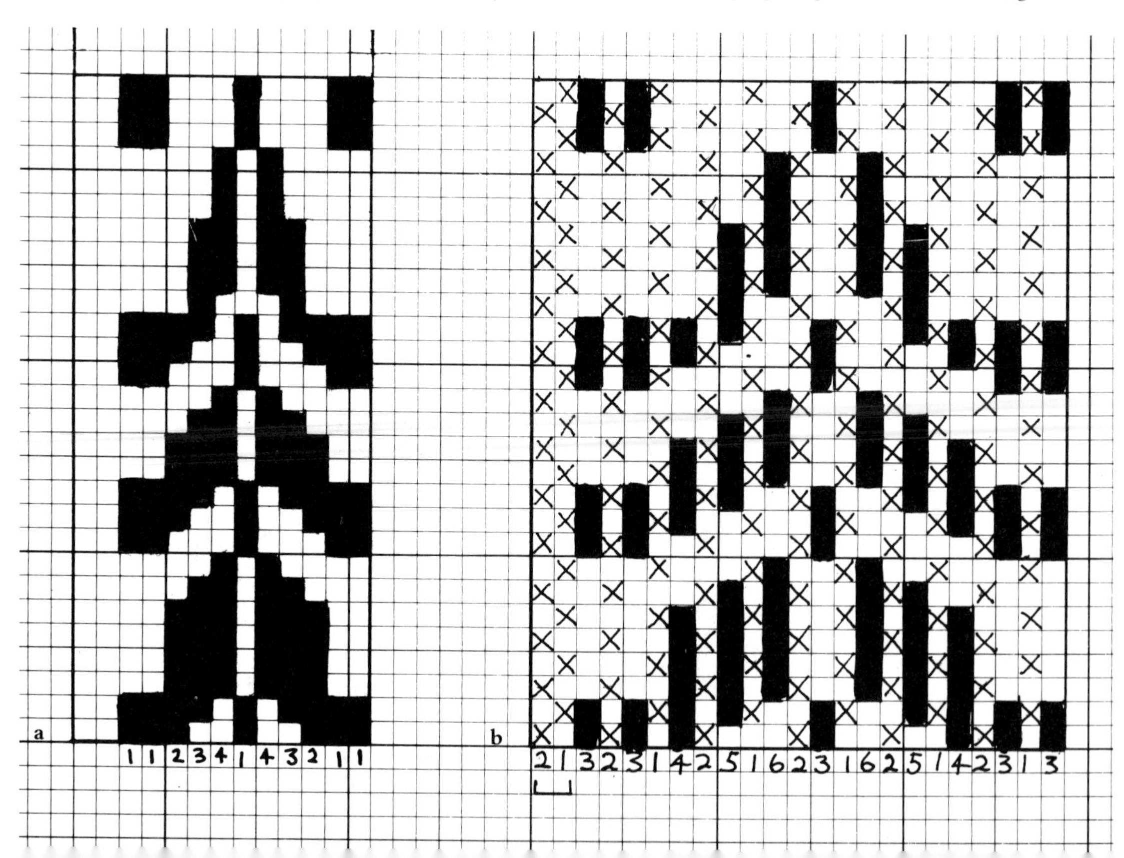

Diag 100 Warp figuring motif and weave diagram

while an eight-shaft loom can weave a 6-block design. Each block of the motif does not represent one end of the cloth but one repeat of the basic weave. Summer-and-winter has a basic repeat size of 4 ends and 4 picks. Any block in the motif can be extended in width or height without altering the shaft requirements on the loom.

The shaded areas of the motif represent where the extra weft lies on the surface and the blank areas where the extra weft lies along the back of the ground cloth.

Diagram 101 shows the construction of a summer-and-winter weave based on a two block guard check motif (Diagram 101a).

A 4 × 4 section of point paper is marked off for each square in the motif layout, and the appropriate areas are shaded in or left white to correspond with it. Plain weave is run out on every end and on every other pick (Diagram 101b). The row of blanks that result are the extra picks just lying on the surface. These extra picks are stitched down with warp-up marks on every fourth end. The stitching points are evenly staggered on alternate picks (Diagram 101c). The actual surface appearance of a cloth woven with the present construction would show the extra weft covering the whole area. The blank areas of the motif, however, must be made to show as ground fabric by making the extra pick float along the back of the cloth, under 3 out of every 4 ends. This is achieved by placing additional warp-up marks on either side of every stitching point, in the blank section of the weave diagram (Diagram 101d). Be careful to follow the repeat through from one side to the other. The weave diagram is now complete and drafting and lifting plans can be found.

The two opposite effects of the summer-and-winter weave are not clean alternatives. Small dots of extra weft are visible on the ground fabric areas, and dots of ground fabric are visible on the weft-faced areas. An attractive tweedy look results. Figure 87 illustrates these effects in a graduating checkerboard arrangement. The underside of the fabric is the exact reverse of the face. Designing with summer-and-winter can be very creative, especially with high shaft numbers. Fancy yarns can be sent across as the extra picks which produce additional texture, and these extra picks can be changed in colour and texture whenever the design warrants it. The ground fabric yarn should be smooth and the square sett is based on its diameter per cm/inch. All extra picks are considered as extra to the weft sett. Diagram 95 illustrates a large weave

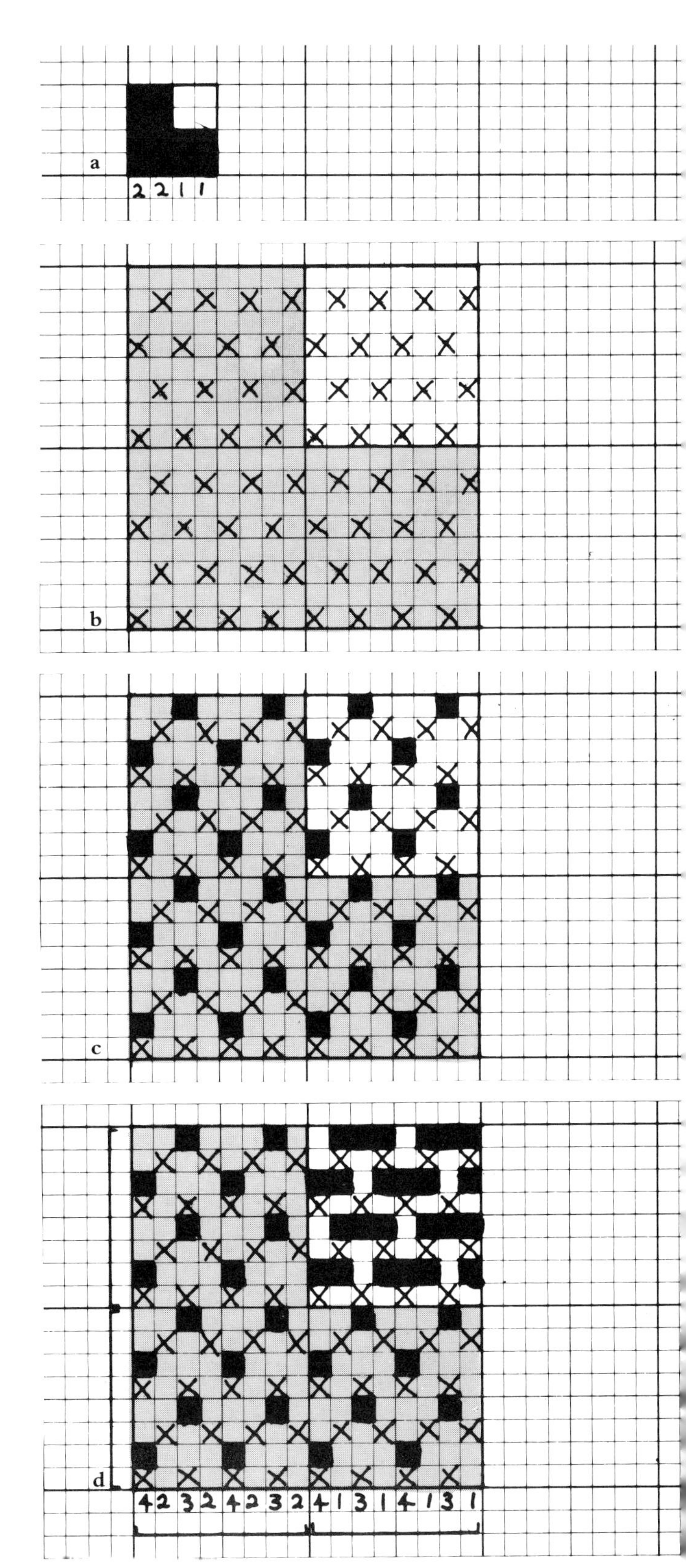

Diag 101 Construction of summer-and-winter weave from a motif

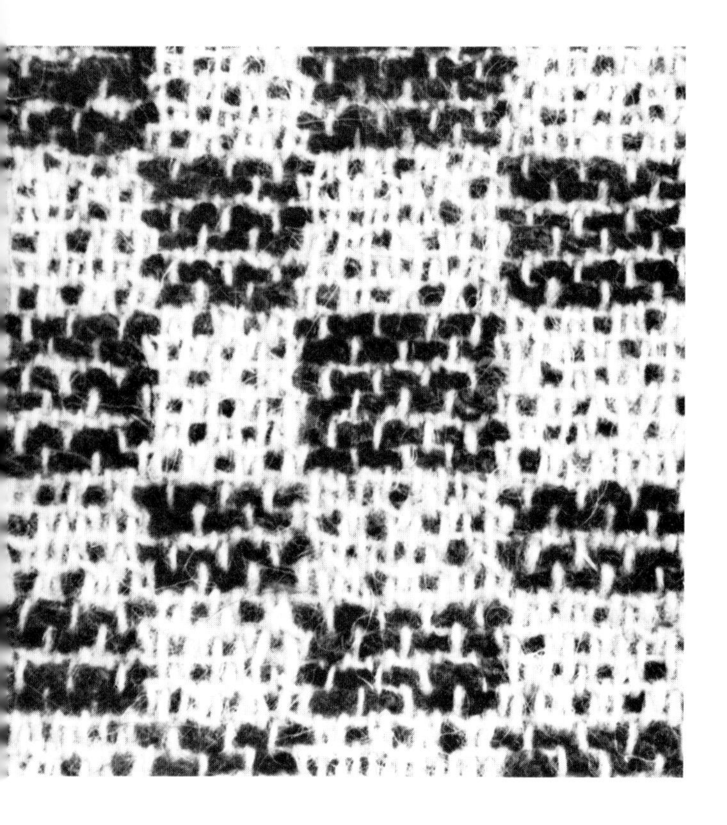

Fig 87 Summer-and-winter weave

diagram in summer-and-winter which can be woven on 4 shafts. Plate 7 illustrates a cloth woven in summer-and-winter weave using the motif of Diagram 93d. It needs 4 shafts.

Weft Reversible Weave

As the name implies, weft reversible weave creates a double-sided fabric made up of the colours and textures of the weft yarns used. The warp is considerably finer than the weft and is practically invisible on both sides, especially after milling during finishing.

Designing with weft reversible usually follows the block designing principle. (See Chapter 12.) A motif is designed on point paper in the normal manner, remembering that each unique vertical block will require 4 shafts, and each unique horizontal block will require 8 pedals (countermarche looms) to weave it. The two contrasting areas of the motif are created by alternate picks of different colour, showing either in one block or the other. Two picks are required to complete one weft of the design. The first pick showing sometimes on the face and sometimes on the back, and the second pick changing places, that is showing on the face where the previous pick was on the back and vice versa. The two basic weaves that achieve this colour interchange are either a combination of 1/3 and 3/1 twill or a combination of 4-end satin and sateen.

Diagram 102 illustrates how 1/3 and 3/1 twill are combined. Alternate picks from either weave are placed one above the other. Diagram 102a starts with the first pick from 1/3 twill while Diagram 102b starts with the first pick from 3/1 twill. If the weft colouring-plan is 1 black, 1 white, as indicated by dashes up the right hand side of each weave, it should be clear by studying the weft floats that the weave shown in Diagram 102a will have a black face and a white underside, while the weave shown in Diagram 102b will have a white face and a black back.

Diagrams 103a and b illustrates a similar combination of 4-end satin and sateen, achieving a similar interchange of colour, but losing the distinct twill line on both sides of the cloth. Note also that the repeat size of the basic weaves in both combinations is 4 ends and 8 picks.

A weft reversible block design weave diagram can now be constructed. Diagram 104 shows the construction of a weave based on a two-block checkerboard motif (Diagram 104a). The shaded squares are to be formed by black yarn and the blank squares are to be formed by white yarn. The two weaves chosen to create this contrast is the combination of 4-end satin and sateen.

Allocate a point paper area of 4 ends and 8 picks for each square of the motif. Shade the appropriate areas to correspond with the motif. Indicate the weft colouring-plan up the right-hand edge of the repeat in the same order as shown on the basic weaves. Fill in the weave shown in Diagram 103a in the shaded areas and the weave shown in Diagram 103b in the blank areas. Drafting and lifting plans can now be determined. Any individual block can be increased in width or height by repeating its section of the draft or lifting plan respectively.

Horizontal stripes can be woven by constructing a weave diagram with the two contrasting weaves, placed one above the other (Diagram 105). This weave can be woven with four shafts. The stripes can be of varying widths and colours depending on the order that colours are sent across as weft. The striped pattern on the back of the cloth need not be the same in proportion or colour, and can even be self-coloured if desired, which can make an attractive reversible effect for a coat or blanket fabric.

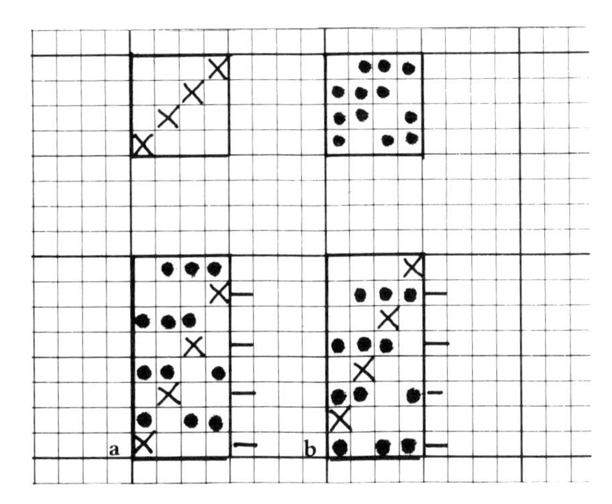

Diag 102 Weft reversible weave combining 1/3 and 3/1 twill

Diag 103 Weft reversible weave combining 4-end satin and sateen

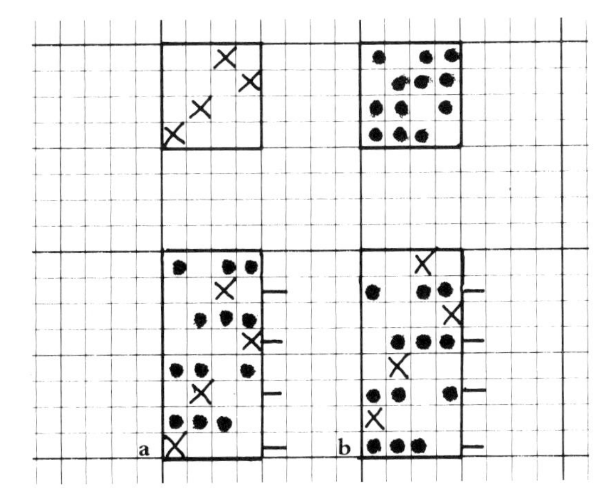

Sett

The sett of weft figuring cloths is quite difficult to determine, and a sample should always be woven to check the sett and shrinkage of a cloth before starting a main piece.

As a guide, the warp yarn should be about 1/3rd finer in count than the weft. For example, if 125 Tex (20c Gala) is to be used in the weft, then 40 Tex (2/42 wrst or 2/30 Ctn) should be used in the warp. The warp is sett at about $\frac{1}{4}$ of its diameters per cm/inch, while the weft is sett at $\frac{2}{3}$ of its diameters per cm/inch doubled. For example:

Warp = 40 Tex (2/30) Ctn
$\therefore$ diameters = 60/cm (148 per inch)

Warp sett = $\frac{1}{4}$ of 60 (148)
= 15/cm (37 per inch)

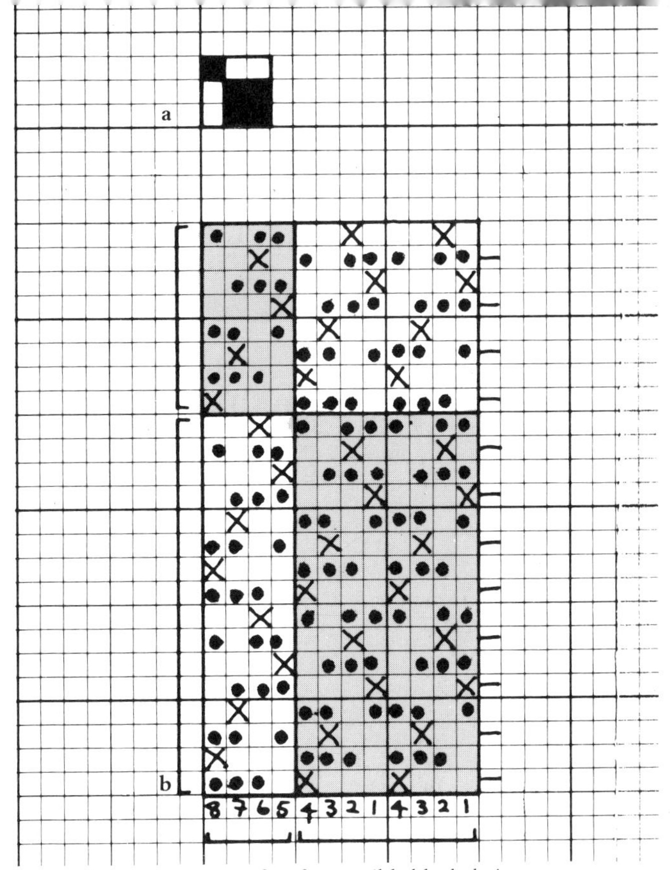

Diag 104 Construction of weft reversible block design

Diag 105 Horizontal stripe in weft reversible weave

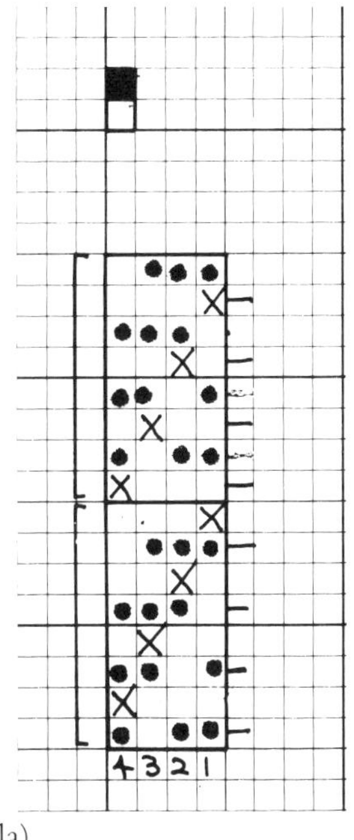

Weft = 135 Tex (20c Gala)
$\therefore$ diameters = 21/cm (54 per inch)

Weft sett = $\frac{2}{3}$ of 21 (54)
= 14/cm (36 per inch)

Weft sett doubled
$14 \times 2 = 28$/cm ($36 \times 2 = 72$/inch)

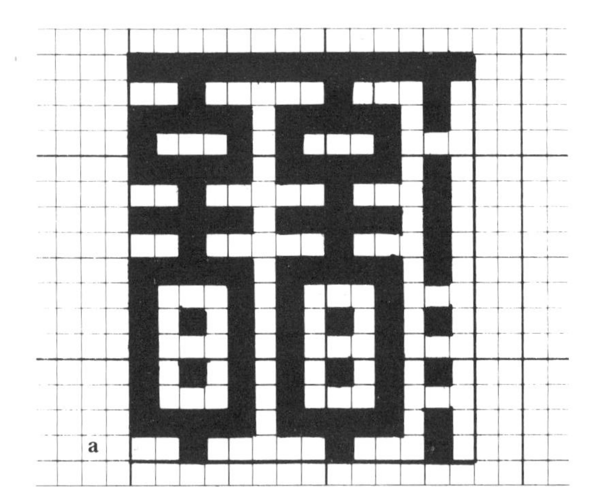

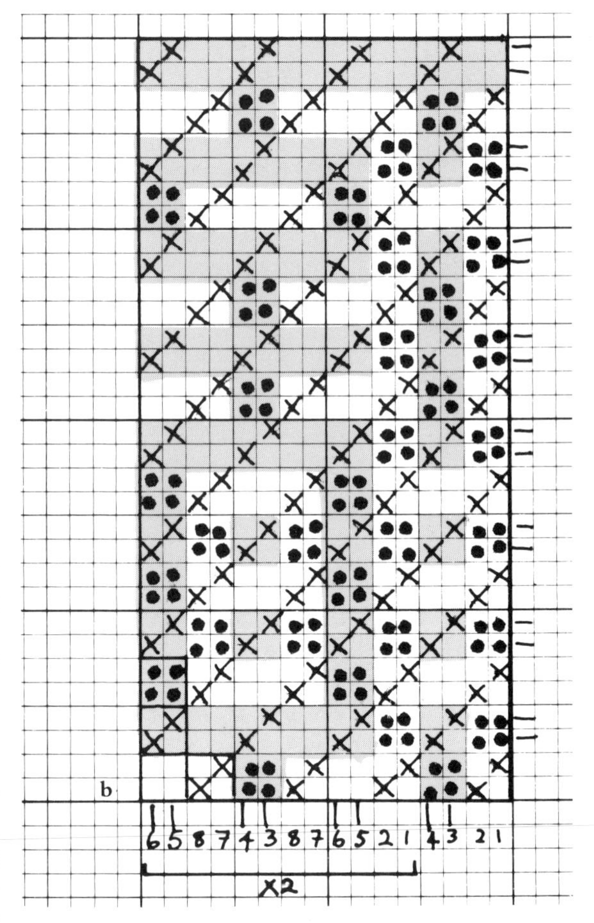

Diag 106 Construction of bold colour and weave effect from a motif

Wool is an excellent fibre for the weft as it covers the warp well initially and can be milled during finishing to obtain complete cover so that the warp yarn is invisible. A strong, fine worsted or cotton yarn is ideal for the warp.

Bold Colour and Weave Effect Patterns

Bold patterns made up of horizontal and vertical lines in two colours can be constructed by careful study of an appropriate motif in conjunction with 2 and 2 coloured warping and wefting plans, by noticing which of the two colours must show on the surface at any time.

It is the exact opposite in construction to a normal colour and weave effect design, when the weave is known but the warping and wefting plans must be worked out to suit the pattern. In the following idea, the colouring plans are known and an appropriate weave that will create the motif must be established.

CONSTRUCTION OF WEAVE DIAGRAM

(Diagram 106b)

1. A motif is designed on point paper made up alternate horizontal and vertical lines in two colours, ensuring that it will repeat correctly in all directions. On point paper each vertical and horizontal row of squares will represent two ends and picks. Two shafts and two pedals (countermarche looms only) will be required for each vertical and horizontal block of the motif respectively. The motif in Diagram 106a will therefore need 8 shafts and 10 pedals.

2. The motif is transferred onto a full weave diagram repeat, on point paper. Two ends and two picks are allocated for each line in the motif (Diagram 106b).

3. A 2 dark, 2 light warping and wefting plan is indicated on the bottom and up the right-hand side of the weave diagram. The 2 dark ends and picks should coincide where possible with the dark horizontal and vertical lines in the motif. Likewise the light ends and picks should coincide with the light lines.

4. The appropriate lifting marks can now be inserted by carefully studying the colour of 2 ends and 2 picks which meet, and must interlace, at any point. Two dark ends and 2 light ends are studied alternately starting from the left hand side.

a) Look at the four point paper squares in the bottom left hand corner of the weave diagram. In Diagram 106b they are light coloured. The two ends which will form that square are dark, but the two picks are light. These four points must therefore show as weft-up blanks to ensure that a light area will form on the surface of the cloth at that point.

b) Look at the four point paper squares above. They are shaded in dark in Diagram 106b. The two warp ends and two weft picks which meet at that point are both dark, therefore any arrangement of warp-up or weft blanks inserted in these four squares will result in dark showing on the surface of the cloth. When this indifferent situation occurs, plain weave is inserted in this area. (Crosses in Diagram.)

c) Look at the four point paper squares above. They are shaded dark in Diagram 106b. The two warp ends are dark at that point, but the weft picks are light. Warp-up marks must be inserted in the four squares to ensure that the dark colour will dominate the surface at that point. (Dots in Diagram.)

d) Continue in the above manner, considering each four point paper squares in turn. Fill in warp marks if the warp colour is to dominate, or weft blanks if the colour of the picks is to dominate, or plain weave if both colours are identical at the intersection. It may be necessary occasionally to alter the motif slightly to accommodate the colouring plan.

e) Drafting and lifting plans can now be worked out. Figure 88 illustrates a cloth woven with this design.

Fig 88 Bold colour and weave effect (below)

Fig 89 Stripes with bold colour and weave effect

Designing with Bold Horizontal and Vertical Lines

Quite unusual and intricate patterns can be designed by this method, but the larger the design the more shafts will be required. The two colours involved should be of quite a strong contrast for the pattern to show clearly. Figure 89 illustrates a simple stripe of bold horizontal and vertical lines which can be woven on 4 shafts. Diagram 107 shows the weave diagram. The maximum sett of this construction is identical to 2/2 twill, that is $\frac{2}{3}$ of the diameters per cm/inch. A square sett is employed.

The sett is also identical to interchanging double plain. Interesting designs can, therefore, be woven combining these two constructions as discussed in Chapter 14.

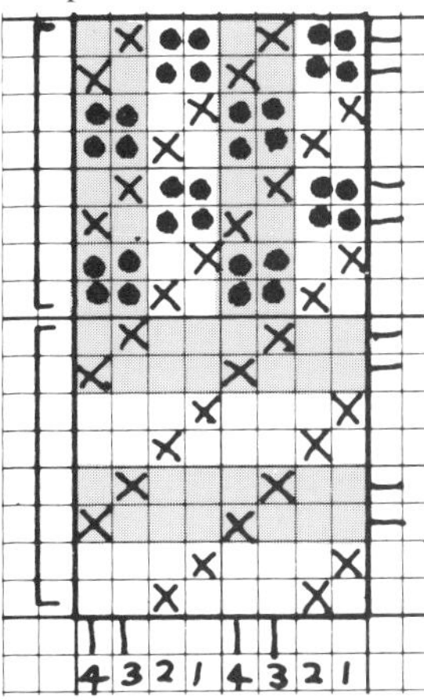

Diag 107 Stripe pattern in bold colour and weave effect

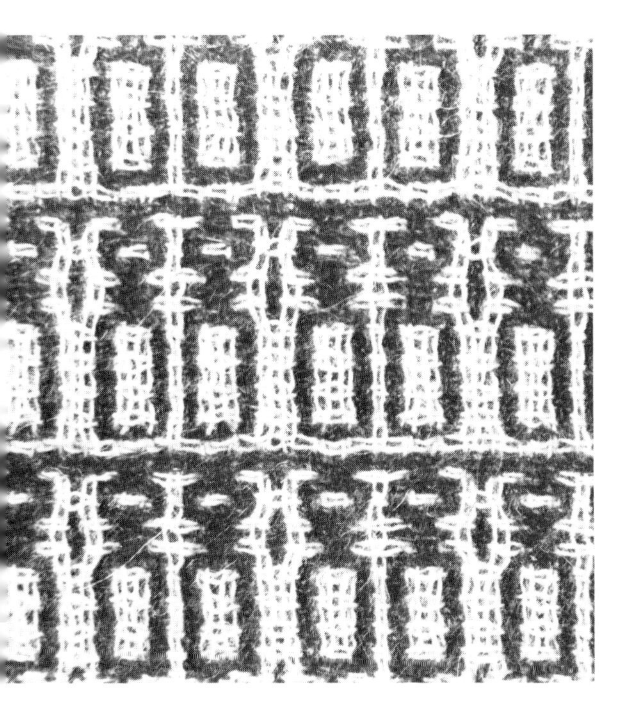

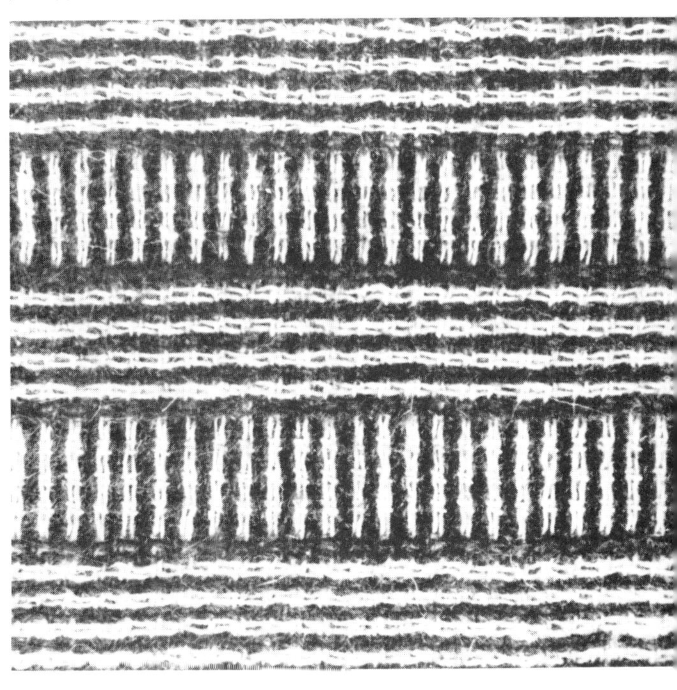

DOUBLE CLOTHS

All double cloths are composed of two single cloths which are woven simultaneously one above the other and stitched or tied together during weaving so that they form a composite fabric. It is important to realise when constructing and weaving double cloths that you are dealing with two sets of warp threads, one for the face and one for the back, which usually run off the same warp beam and are drafted through the same set of shafts. Two wefts are also employed, one for the face and one for the back, and these are combined into one lifting plan and wefting plan.

There are three constructions of double cloth, each defined by the method that they are bound together:

1. The self-stitched double cloth, whereby an end or pick from the bottom cloth is made to catch periodically either a pick or an end from the top cloth (Diagram 108a).

2. The centre-stitched double cloth, which has a third warp catching alternately a pick from both cloths (Diagram 108b).

3. Interchanging double cloth, allows two single cloths to alternate between showing on the face or the back of the composite cloth, binding the two together at the change over points (Diagram 108c).

The double cloth construction that should be used at any time, is dependent on the desired effect and the end use of the finished cloth.

A self-stitched or centre-stitched construction enables a heavy cloth to be woven which has a fine appearance on the face. It also enables a completely reversible fabric to be made with either side being totally different in colour, yarn, weave or pattern. The self-stitched construction is also used if a cloth is to be dominated by the use of thick fancy yarns. A single cloth woven with fancy yarns in both warp and weft would be extremely heavy, spongy to handle and expensive in yarn. A 1-face to 3-back ratio of ends and picks in a self-stitched construction would produce a similar appearance to the single cloth, but be lighter, less expensive and have a better and more attractive handle.

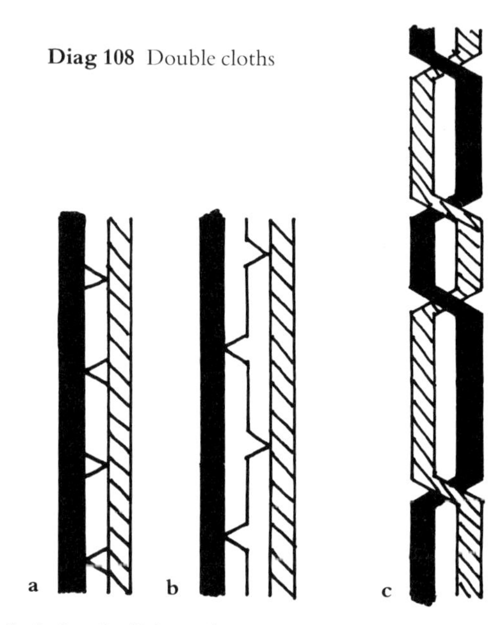

Diag 108 Double cloths

The interchanging double plain construction is very versatile for designing. In its simplest form it can create horizontal or vertical stripes and checks in two colours, which can be wadded to create additional interest. Tubular fabrics can be woven, as can single cloths of double width if the interchange occurs on one side only. Block designing principles can be applied to produce very exciting and effective patterns.

The three weave constructions are described in detail in the following sections, with additional design possibilities suggested.

Self-stitched Double Cloth

Three factors need to be taken into consideration before a self-stitched double cloth can be constructed: First, the two weaves to be employed on the face and back; secondly, the yarns and sett of each cloth; and thirdly, the ratio of face ends and picks to back ends and picks.

The 1-face to 1-back ratio in warp and weft is the most common arrangement. This is used when the two weaves chosen have similar setts and take-up, and the yarns to be used are similar in count. Maximum sett should be calculated for each cloth, the numbers combined and the total reduced by 20% to 30%.

The 2-face to 1-back ratio in warp and weft is employed if the back yarn is twice as thick as the face yarn. It will produce a fabric with a very fine surface appearance, but heavier reverse. The back weave should have a tighter interlacing than the face, for example, a 2/2 twill face and a plain weave back. Again, the combined maximum sett of both cloths should be reduced by about 30%, otherwise a very stiff, almost boardy fabric will result.

The 1-face to 3-back ratio is used in particular for constructing fabrics with thick fancy yarns on the face. The back yarn should be very fine and strong and is designed to give support and stability to the face cloth without contributing much to the design or weight of the fabric. Invariably the back cloth is plain weave, while the face is 2/2 twill, satin or any of the simple constructions. The cloth has a very open sett. The face may have about 2 to 3 ends per cm (6–8 ends per inch), making a combined sett of 8 to 12 ends and picks per cm (24–32 ends and picks per inch).

CONSTRUCTIONS OF SELF-STITCHED DOUBLE CLOTHS

Diagram 109. a–f is 1 face to 1 back ratio.
Diagram 110. a–f is 2 face to 1 back ratio.
Diagram 111. a–f is 1 face to 3 back ratio.

a. Write down the two weaves that are to be used for the face and back cloths.

b. Indicate the ratio of face (F) to back (B) ends and picks along the bottom and side of the combined repeat unit. (A complete repeat of the face weave must coincide with a complete repeat of the back weave. This may involve, especially on the 2-face 1-back or 1-face 3-back ratios, repeating one of the weaves two or three times to coincide with one repeat of the other weave).

c. Separate the face ends and picks, making them lie above the back ends and picks. This is achieved by indicating 'lifting' marks ⧄ on the face ends in the positions suggested by the following mnemonic:

When a back pick goes in, face ends lift.

d. The face weave is inserted on face ends and picks. ■

e. The back weave is inserted on back ends and picks. ⊡

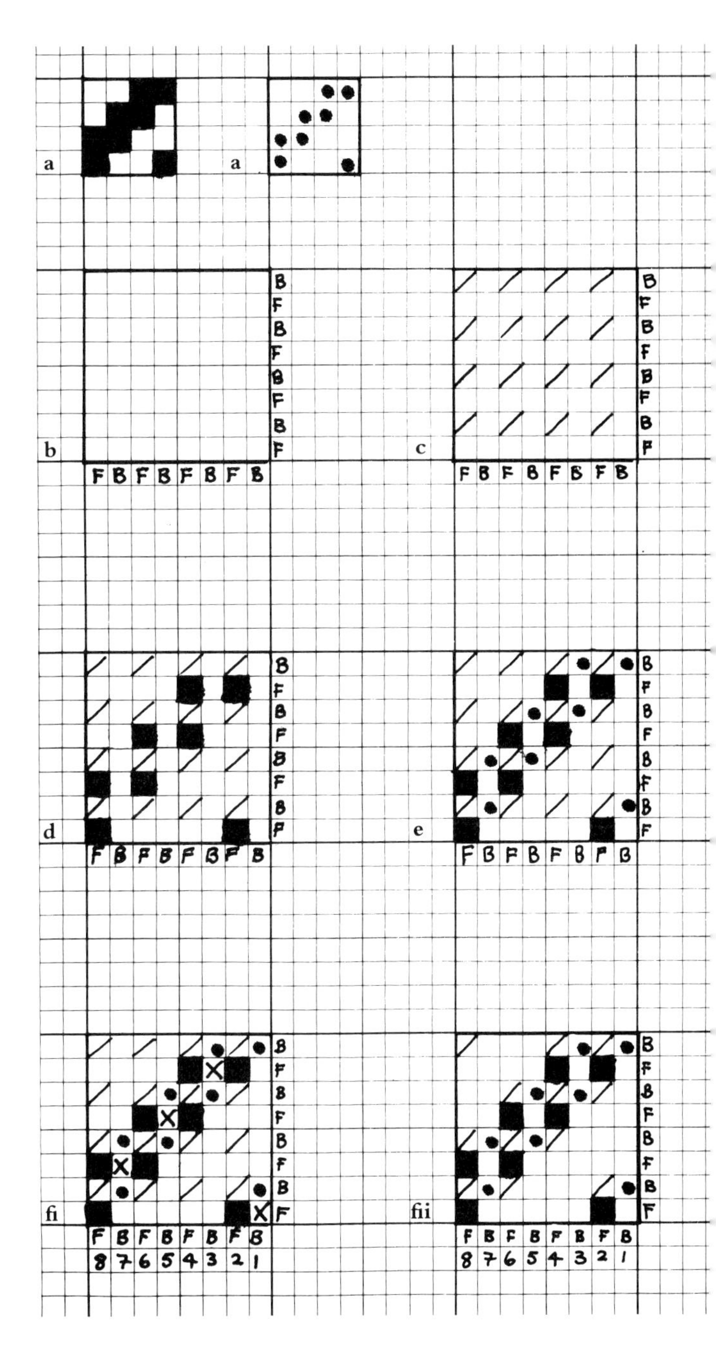

Diag 109 Construction of 1 face : 1 back self-stitched double cloth

f. The two cloths are stitched together by either:

i. Warp stitching ☒ which lifts an end of the back weave over a pick of the face weave, or

ii. Weft stitching which lifts a pick of the back weave over an end of the face weave. (In practice this involves removing a lifting mark from the diagram.)

It is very important that no stitching point should be visible on the face of the cloth. This is achieved where possible by inserting a warp stitch between two warp-up marks of the face weave and a weft stitch between two weft floats of the face weave.

It is usually only necessary to bind the cloths together by either warp stitching or weft stitching, not both, but the stitching points must be evenly distributed around the cloth. *N.B.* By using weft stitching only in Diagram 111fii the weave can be drafted onto six shafts as compared to 10 shafts when warp and weft stitching is used (Diagram 111fi).

Drafting and lifting plans can now be determined in the normal manner.

Designing with Self-stitched Double Cloth

Designing with self-stitched double cloth relies mainly on the individual patterns on the face and back cloths. As these are usually simple weaves, such as plain weave or twills, any of the design possibilities of these can be incorporated into the double cloth construction. Coloured stripes and checks and colour and weave effects are an obvious starting point. Care needs to be taken when constructing the warping and wefting plans that stripe and check patterns will coincide correctly with the weave diagram and create two different patterns on either side of the cloth. Alternatively, the two sides can simply be different in colour, yarn, fibre or finishing.

With the 1-face to 3-back arrangement, it is best to let the thick textured yarns show off themselves in the cloth design. Simple stripes and checks can be incorporated if desired. The back cloth should not influence the surface pattern of the fabric (Figure 90).

Centre-stitched Double Cloth

The centre-stitched double cloth construction produces a fabric which is practically identical to the self-stitched construction. The difference between the two lies only in the method of binding the two cloths together, which in the case of the centre stitched cloth involves the making of a second warp which lies between the two cloths and alternately catches picks on the face or back cloths. The stitching warp needs to be run off from a second back beam. This construction is used in preference to the self-stitched, only when it seems impossible to stitch invisibly and neatly the self-stitched cloth because of the wide contrast in colour, yarn or weave of the two sides.

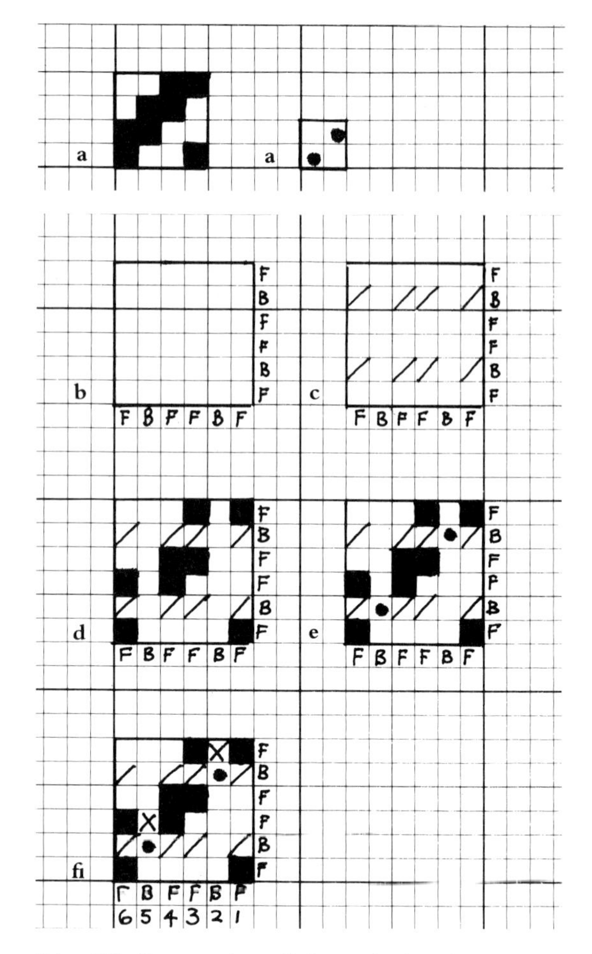

Diag 110 Construction of 2 face : 1 back self-stitched double cloth

Diag 111 Construction of 1 face : 3 back self-stitched double cloth (right)

The stitching warp should be of a neutral colour which will tone in with either cloth, as well as being fine and strong. A worsted thread is ideal for the job.

The actual construction of the weave diagram follows a similar formula to the self-stitched. The two weaves that are to be used for face and back and the ratio of face ends and picks to back ends and picks, must be decided (Diagrams 112a and b). Either one or two extra ends per repeat must be allocated in the weave diagram to accommodate the stitching ends. Two additional ends will create a tighter bound cloth than one stitching end per repeat. The lifting marks are inserted with the mnemonic now reading. *When a back pick goes in, face and stitching ends lift.* The face and back weaves are then inserted in the normal manner. Each stitching

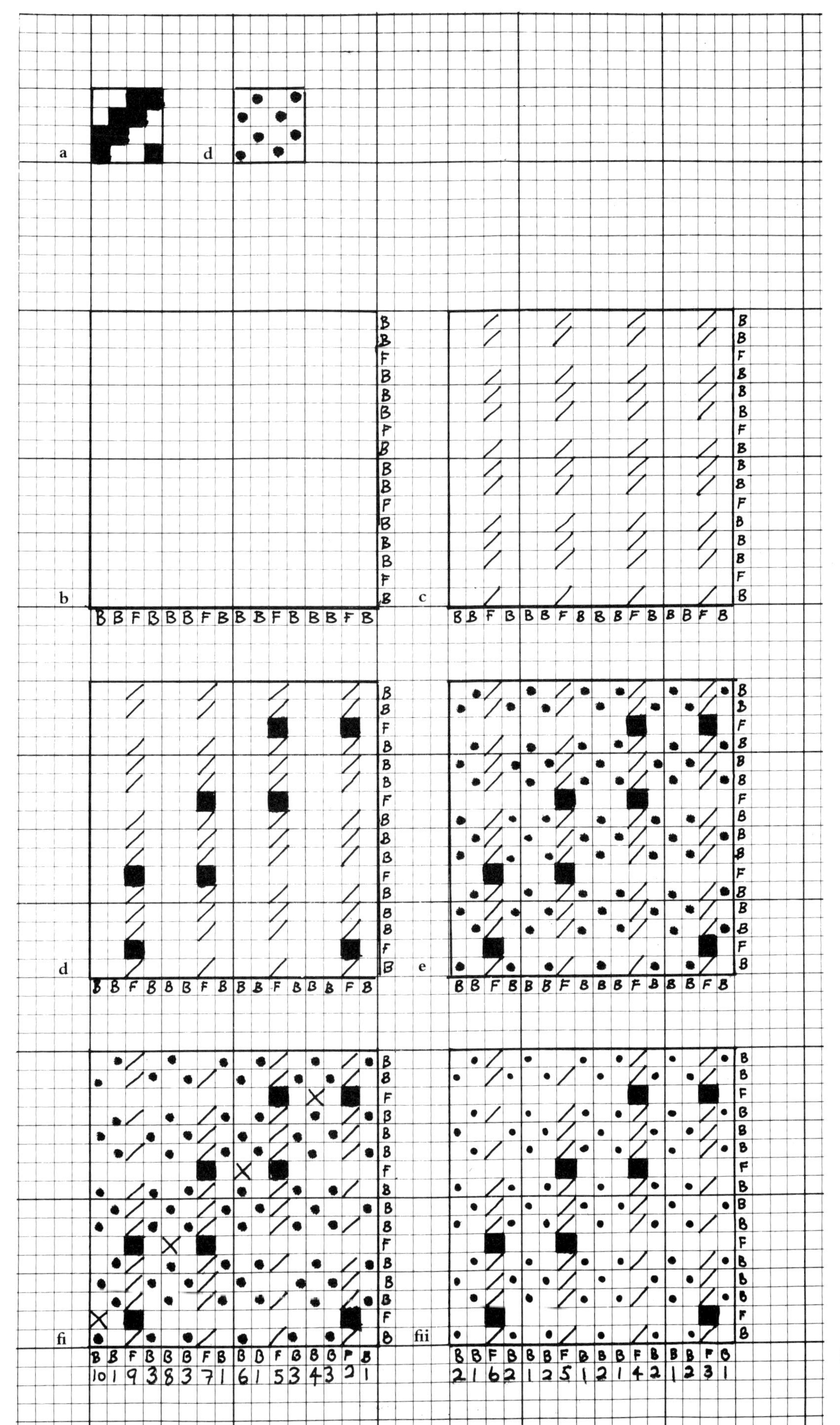

a
d
b
c
B B F B B B F B B B F B B B F B
d
e
fi
fii
B B F B B B F B B B F B B B F B
10 1 9 3 8 3 7 1 6 1 5 3 4 3 2 1
2 1 6 2 1 2 5 1 2 1 4 2 1 2 3 1

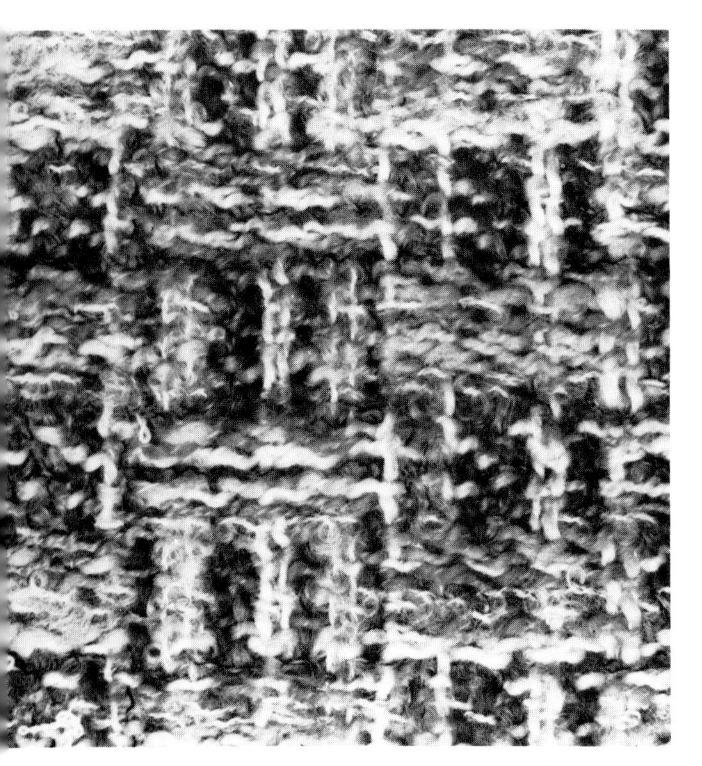

Fig 90 1 face : 3 back self-stitched double cloth

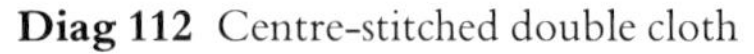

Diag 112 Centre-stitched double cloth

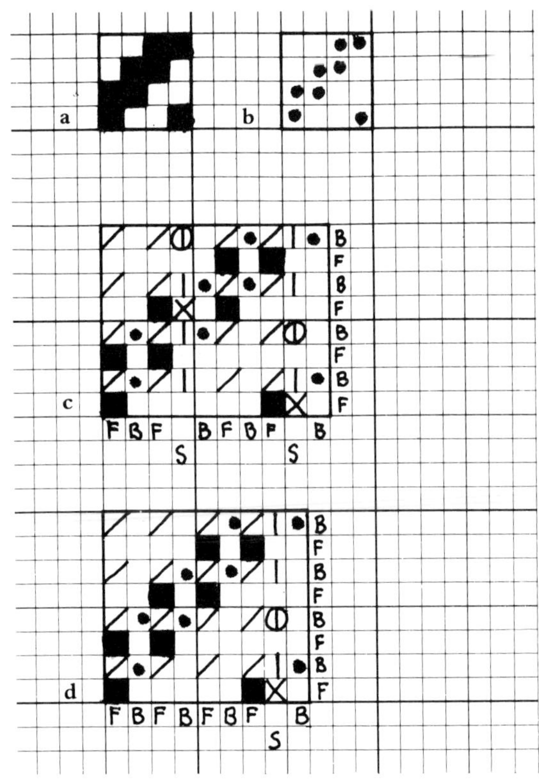

end must be made to pass alternately from catching a back floating pick from the top cloth ⊠ to lifting up an inside floating pick of the bottom cloth, i.e. removing a lifting mark.

Diagram 112c illustrates a 1 face to 1 back centre-stitched double cloth, with 2/2 twill on face and back with two stitching ends in the total repeat. Diagram 112d illustrates the same cloth with only one stitching end per repeat.

The sett of the cloth is determined in the same manner as the self-stitched cloth with the stitching ends being sleyed as extra in the reed.

Interchanging Double Cloth

The interchanging double cloth joins two single cloths together by allowing the bottom cloth to periodically come up onto the surface, while simultaneously the top cloth moves down onto the back (Diagram 108c). In other words they change positions.

The two cloths should be dissimilar in some way, either in colour, yarn, fibre or weave, as it is this contrast which is used to create pattern and design.

The proportion of ends and picks in one cloth in relation to the other is normally 1:1. In these cases, the two weaves are usually identical, or if different, their setts are equal and the yarns in both cloths similar in count, the contrast being achieved with colour or fibre. A 2:1 ratio would be used, either if the count of yarn in one cloth was twice as thick as the other, but the weaves were identical, or if the sett of one cloth was much lower than the other, due perhaps to different weaves in each single cloth.

The interchange can take place in the weft only which produces horizontal striped patterns, or in the warp only which produces vertical striped patterns. An interchange in both directions simultaneously will form squares, rectangles or any other irregular shape that may be desired, given that your loom has enough shafts to accommodate a complicated motif. At least four shafts are needed for each unique block of a motif design. (See Chapter 12.) A motif pattern on the face will be crisp and detailed due to the decisive interchanging action of the weave, and will be completely reversed on the back of the cloth. The more frequently the two cloths are interchanged in warp or weft, the more the stability of the composite cloth is increased.

Interchanging Double Plain

Interchanging double plain is the simplest, most common and versatile of the interchanging constructions. Two plain weave cloths change positions. Two shafts are required for each single cloth so the composite cloth with a weft only interchange can be woven on four shafts. Any uniquely working block of a motif design will need its own four shafts.

The following discussion, with examples, illustrates the construction of the double plain cloth. The procedure for other weave combinations is identical, no matter what the ratio of face ends and picks to back ends and picks. The crucial factor in any interchanging weave construction is the positioning of the initial lifting marks, which determine which ends and picks show on the surface and which show on the back in any section. Once these are correct, any face and back weave can be inserted, in the same way as for other types of double cloth, and then the weave diagram is complete.

CONSTRUCTION OF INTERCHANGING DOUBLE PLAIN IN WEFT ONLY (Diagram 113)

A ratio of 1:1 is being used. The counts of yarn in each cloth are identical and the contrast between the two fabrics will be created by colour. One cloth will be white and the other grey. The motif for the weft interchange is sketched in Diagram 113a, a horizontal stripe, alternately grey and white.

1. The minimum weave repeat unit for each square of the motif is marked out on point paper. A double plain with a 1:1 ratio repeats on four ends and four picks.

(An interchanging double twill using 2/2 twill weave in each cloth and a 1:1 ratio will repeat on 8 ends and 8 picks—4 for each cloth. An interchanging double plain with a ratio of 2:1 will need 6 ends and picks per repeat as will a 2:1 ratio design with 2/2 twill in one cloth and plain weave in the other.)

2. Shade in lightly the grey areas of the motif onto the weave diagram repeat. The white areas remain clear (Diagram 113b).

3. Below and up the right hand side of the diagram indicate the warping and wefting plans, which are usually identical. Diagram 113c illustrates the 1:1 ratio of grey (G) to white (W).

4. Insert lifting marks by following this mnemonic: *When a back pick goes in, face ends lift.*

a) In the white section, white ends and picks will form the face cloth. The mnemonic is, therefore, interpreted as, *When a grey pick goes in, white ends lift* (Diagram 113c ⧅).

b) In the grey stripe, the grey ends and picks will form the face cloth. The mnemonic is interpreted as,

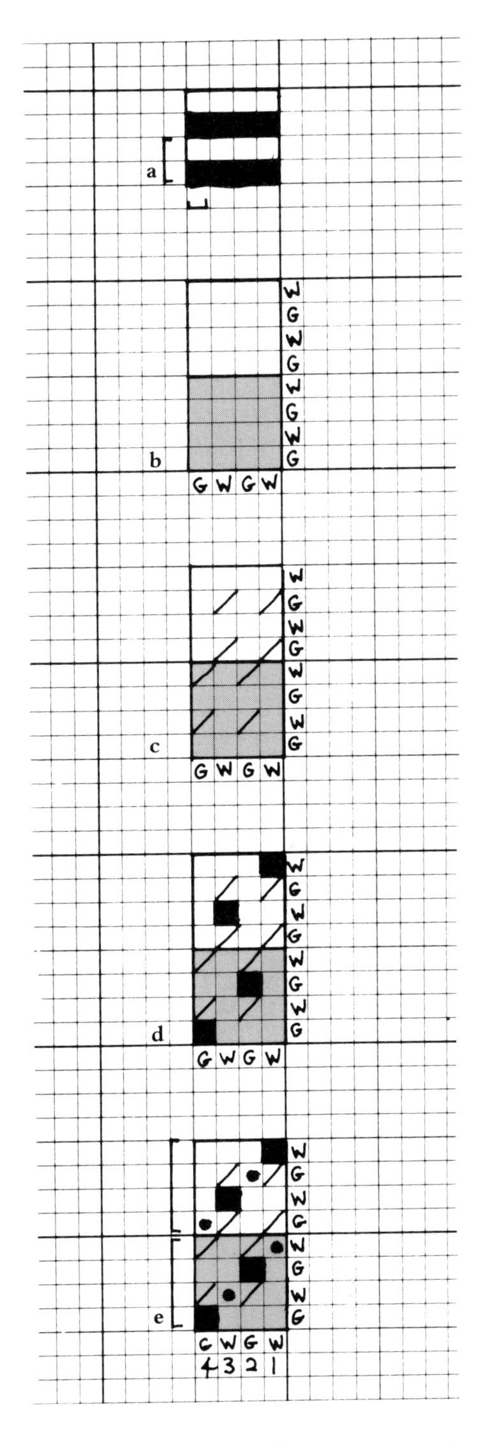

Diag 113 Construction of interchanging double plain with a horizontal stripe motif

When a white pick goes in, grey ends lift (Diagram 113c ☒).

5. Insert plain weave on face ends and picks in both sections (Diagram 113d ■).

6. Insert plain weave on back ends and picks in both sections (Diagram 113e ⊡).

7. Drafting and lifting plans can now be determined.

N.B. It should be noted by studying the weave diagram that the combined plain weave marks in both cloths form a fine diagonal line to the right, lifting over every fourth pick like a 1/3 twill. This fact enables double plain fabrics with a 1:1 ratio to be constructed very easily and quickly, and at the same time checks the correct positioning of the lifting marks.

Lifting marks are inserted in both sections in the normal manner. The first plain weave lift on face ends and picks in the bottom left hand repeat is marked (Diagram 114c). This mark is called the starting mark. The 1/3 twilled lifting diagonal is continued from this mark, and inserted over the whole weave diagram ensuring that it repeats continuously from side to side as well as from top to bottom.

If any of the 1/3 twill marks coincides with a lifting mark, the lifting mark must be in the wrong place.

This quick method should only be used when constructing double plain with a 1:1 ratio.

INTERCHANGING DOUBLE PLAIN IN WARP ONLY

The motif for a warp only interchange is illustrated in Diagram 114a, a vertical stripe of alternately different colours, fibres or yarns. The construction procedure is exactly the same as the weft-only interchange above. The finished weave diagram is illustrated in Diagram 114b. Diagram 114c shows the same weave constructed by the quick method described above.

INTERCHANGING DOUBLE PLAIN IN WARP AND WEFT SIMULTANEOUSLY

Diagrams 115 and 116 illustrate the construction of a 1:1 ratio and a 2:1 ratio. Figure 91 illustrates a fabric woven as Diagram 115b. A motif is designed in the normal manner remembering that four shafts will be needed for each uniquely interlacing block of the motif. The construction procedure is followed in the same manner as the weft only interchange above. The minimum repeat unit for the 1:1 ratio is four ends and picks, but six ends and picks for the 2:1 ratio. (In Diagram 116 (T) and (F)

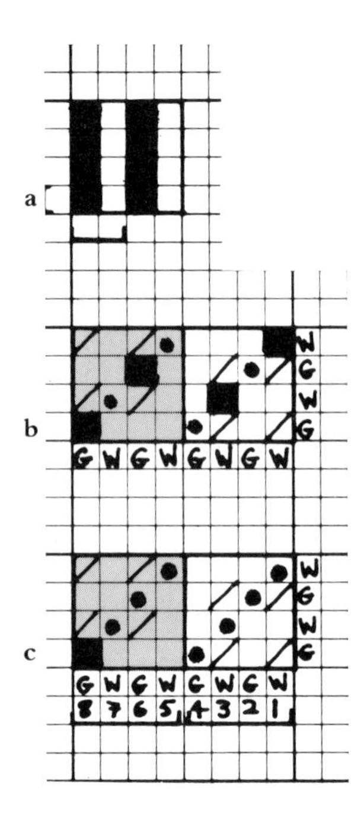

Diag 114 Construction of interchanging double plain with a vertical stripe motif

Diag 115 Interchanging double plain with checkerboard motif

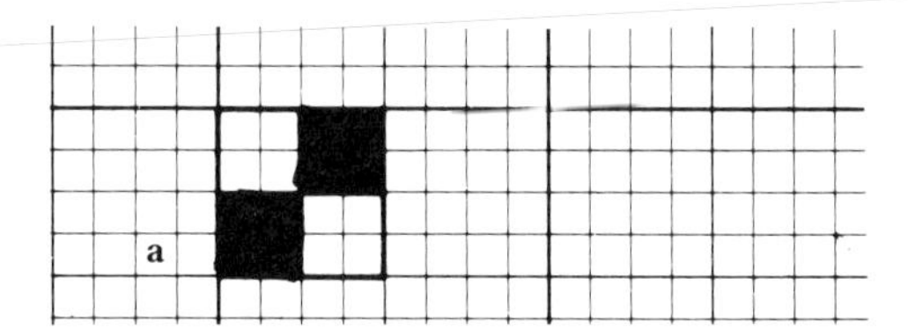

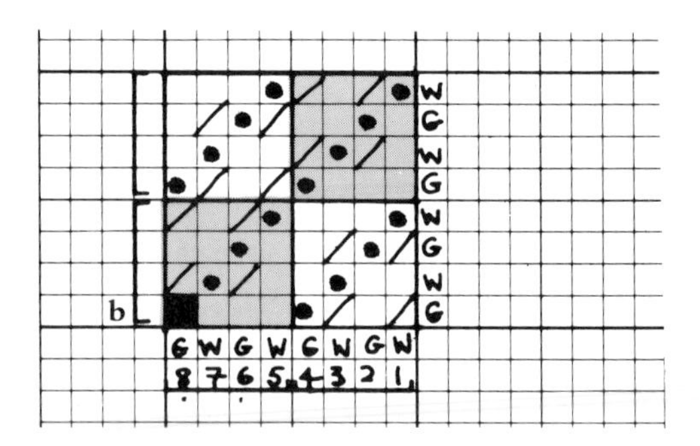

stand for thick and fine threads.) A faint but large F and T are notating the appropriate face cloth areas in the weave diagram, so that lifting marks can be easily inserted.

Maximum sett

The sett of a 1:1 ratio double plain cloth equals $\frac{2}{3}$ of the diameter per cm/inch of the yarn being used.

Designing with Double Plain

A 1 and 1 colouring in warp and weft is the most usual arrangement with double plain weave and results in a contrast in colour, yarn or fibre after each interchange (Figure 92). Any repeat unit in warp or weft in the weave diagram can be bracketed up to increase its width or height, so that in the warp only or weft only interchange, varying widths of vertical and horizontal stripes respectively are possible. These stripes will be clear and distinct in appearance, quite unlike a normal plain-weave, single-cloth stripe pattern. The stripes will be of alternate pure colours, if the same shades are sent across the warp as weft, although the 1 and 1 colouring can involve any two colours in either direction so that mottled stripes can be introduced for additional interest. Plate 2 illustrates a checkerboard motif design using several different colours in warp and weft. It produces a design made up of squares of pure colour and squares of mixed colours.

A horizontal stripe can be stuffed with wadding materials before each interchange to turn a flat stripe into a large rib. The wadding is inserted by raising the two shafts which are carrying the face ends of the stripe to be stuffed. (Normally shafts 1+3 or shafts 2+4.) This will separate the two single cloths and enable the wadding to be laid in easily.

Because both cloths have a simple plain weave face, any colour and weave effect possible on the single cloth can be introduced onto one or both of the striped or rectangular areas. A weave diagram (Diagram 117e) is constructed in the normal manner from a motif (Diagram 117a). A model weave diagram plan of the chosen colour and weave effect is worked out for reference (Diagrams 117c, d), and the correct warping and wefting plans for this design is superimposed onto all the white ends and picks in the double plain diagram (Diagram 117e). This will result in the chosen colour and weave effect emerging on the white areas of the design, while the black areas remain self-coloured.

Fig 91 Interchanging double plain in warp and weft

Diag 116 Interchanging double plain with a 1:2 ratio of ends and picks (below)

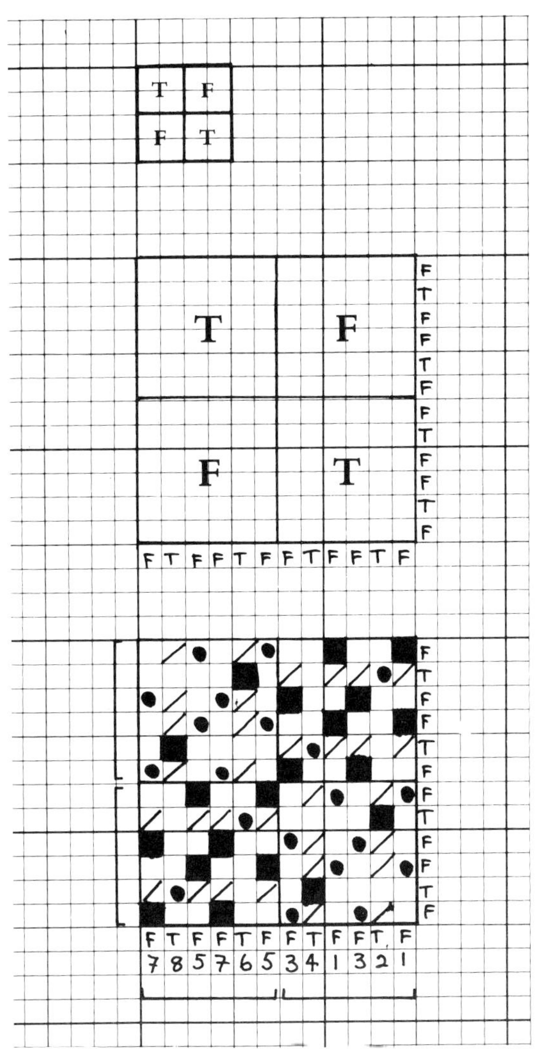

The now very irregular warping and wefting plans of the double cloth must be followed carefully to ensure that they coincide accurately with the drafting and lifting plans as designed.

FRINGES

If on one of the weft-only interchanges the back plain weave cloth is constructed in the normal manner, but the face picks of the top cloth are removed, the ends of the top cloth will be lying straight and loose. This manipulation of double plain has limited use, but can be attractive for certain end uses such as curtains. If desired, these long ends can be cut to create fringes across the fabric. The cut can occur in the middle of the float or at one side. Diagram 118 illustrates the motif and construction of this weave in a weft only interchange. Figure 93 illustrates fringed sections separated by 2/2 twill instead of double plain weave. (See Diagram 120.)

TUBULAR AND DOUBLE-WIDTH CLOTHS

When a plain coloured warp and weft is employed and a single repeat unit is woven with no interchange in warp or weft, two self-coloured plain weave cloths are woven simultaneously. If the warp is made with an uneven number of ends and a single shuttle used, a tubular fabric will be constructed with the joins at both sides following through the plain weave repeat (Diagram 119a).

A double-width fabric can be woven in a similar manner, by joining the two cloths on one side only, so that it will open out into a single cloth when taken off the loom. The weave diagram must be rearranged, but a single shuttle is still employed to travel across the back cloth round the edge and across the face, turn back across the face in the opposite shed and continue back along the bottom cloth. Diagrams 119b and c illustrates the weave diagrams with the direction in which the shuttle should traverse in order to obtain a join either on the right or left hand edge.

COMBINING DOUBLE PLAIN WITH 2/2 TWILL

Double plain with identical counts in warp and weft in both cloths and a 1:1 ratio has a sett which is similar to 2/2 twill. The two weaves, therefore, combine well together. 2/2 twill coloured 1 and 1 in warp and weft produce step-effect colour and weave pattern. A completely different characteristic to the double-plain cloth is, therefore, available to use when designing. The 2/2 twill areas can be introduced in warp and weft stripes or as a third texture in a block design. Diagram 120a illustrates a simple motif and Diagram 120b its weave diagram.

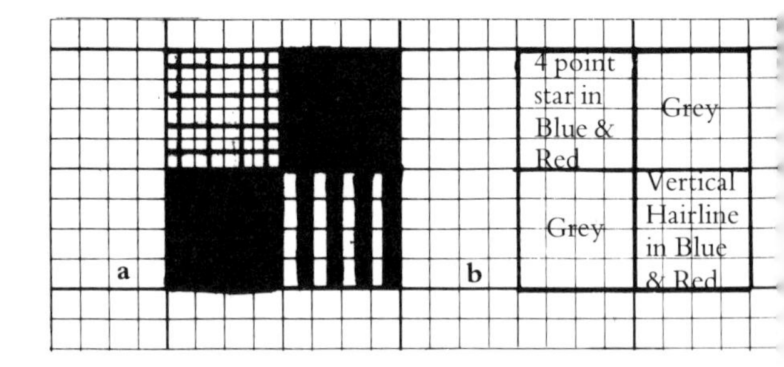

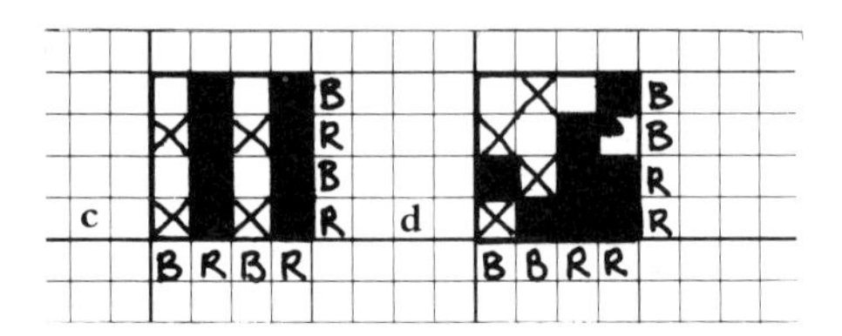

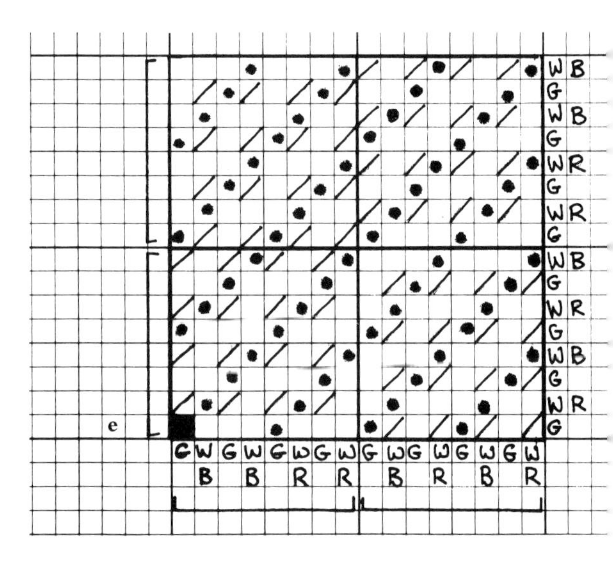

Diag 117 Double plain with colour and weave effect

Diag 118 Double plain and fringes

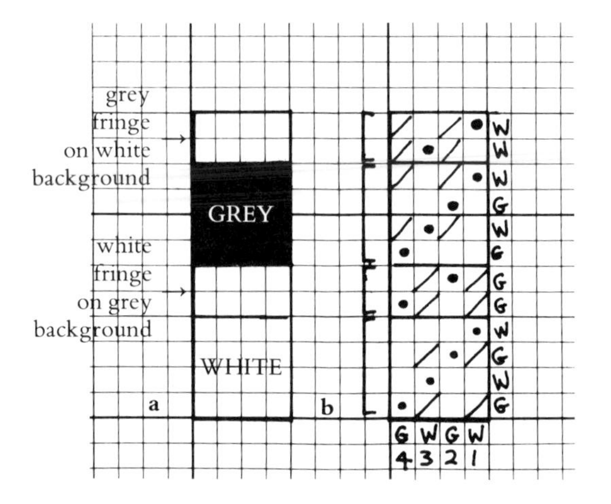

Fig 92 Interchanging double plain

Fig 93 2/2 twill and double plain fringes

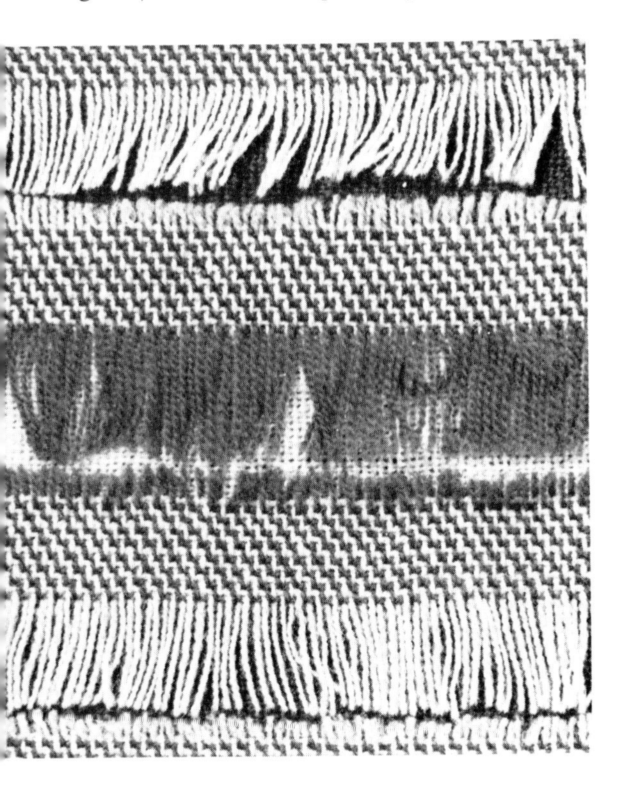

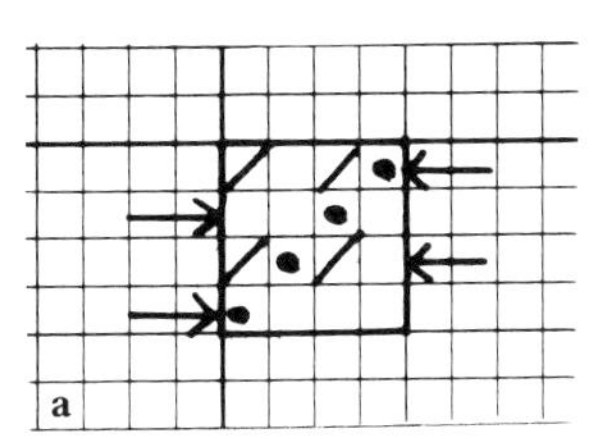

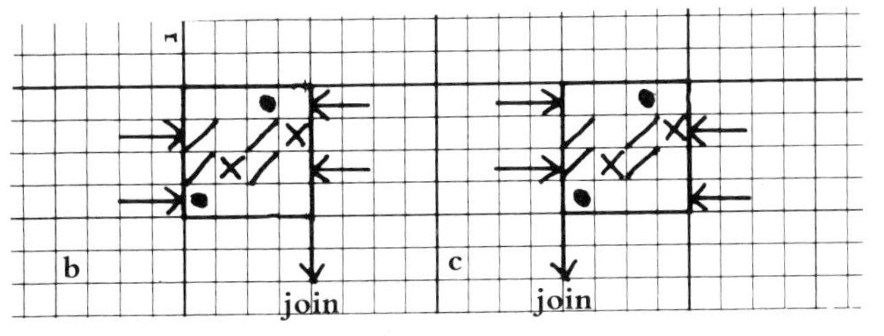

Diag 119 Tubular and double width weaves

Diag 120 Double plain and 2/2 twill

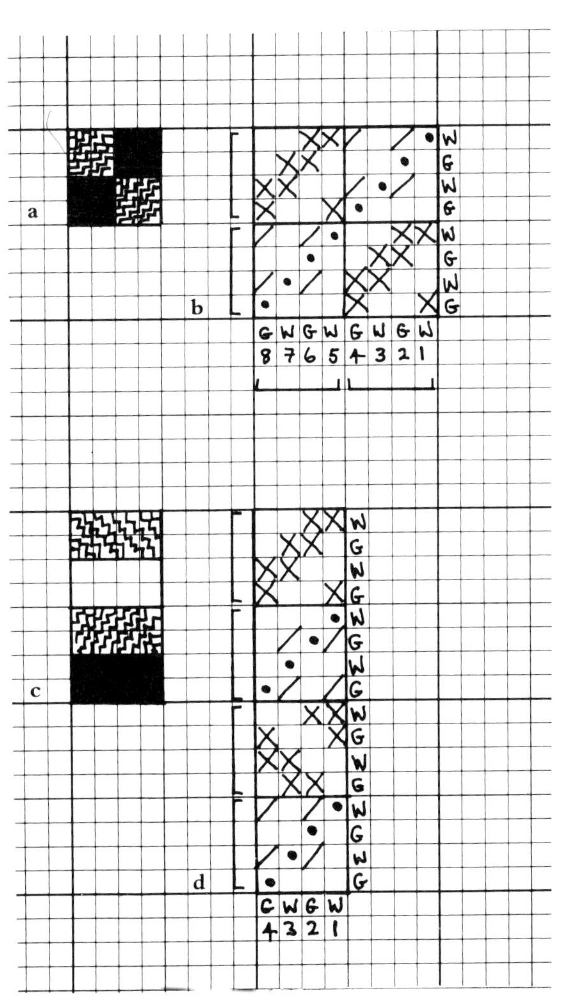

Figure 94 illustrates a cloth woven in this manner. Step effect can travel to the right or left depending on the direction of the original twill weave (Diagram 120d).

DOUBLE PLAIN COMBINED WITH PLAIN WEAVE

Plain weave has a tighter interlacing than double plain. If areas of plain weave are surrounded by areas of double plain, on relaxation and shrinkage off the loom the plain weave areas will swell out into circular or oval shapes while the double plain areas will converge and buckle. A quilted effect is possible. Figure 95 illustrates this combination of weaves in a checkerboard arrangement, and Diagram 121 shows the weave diagram. The plain weave areas appear as fine vertical or horizontal hairlines because of the colour and weave effect produced with the 1/1 warp and weft colouring plans. The sett of the total cloth should be based on a firm plain weave sett.

Diagram 122 and Plate 3 illustrate a fabric combining a 2-face to 4-back interchanging double plain and plain weave in a checkerboard arrangement. The thick face threads are textured yarns.

DOUBLE PLAIN COMBINED WITH BOLD HORIZONTAL AND VERTICAL HAIRLINE

Chapter 13 discusses the construction of bold colour and weave effect patterns using 2 and 2 coloured warping and wefting plans. These cloths have the same sett as double plain and therefore combine well together.

One repeat of either a simple vertical or horizontal hairline, repeats on four ends and picks, which is the same unit size as the basic double plain. Block motif patterns can, therefore, be easily designed combining four different effects, two areas of solid colour plus areas of vertical or horizontal lines. The minimum requirements of four shafts per vertical block of a motif is maintained.

Diagram 123a illustrates a two block motif incorporating areas of dark and areas of vertical and horizontal hairline. The weave diagram for this motif is shown in Diagram 123b. Each part of the weave construction is completed individually. The double plain areas follow the normal construction rules, but are rearranged to accommodate the 2 and 2 colouring plans in warp and weft. The vertical and horizontal hairlines are built up section by section in the normal manner, to coincide with the warping and wefting plans. Figure 96 shows a cloth woven in this manner. Plate 11 illustrates a suit fabric with a 2 block design.

Fig 94 Double plain and 2/2 twill

Fig 95 Double plain and plain weave

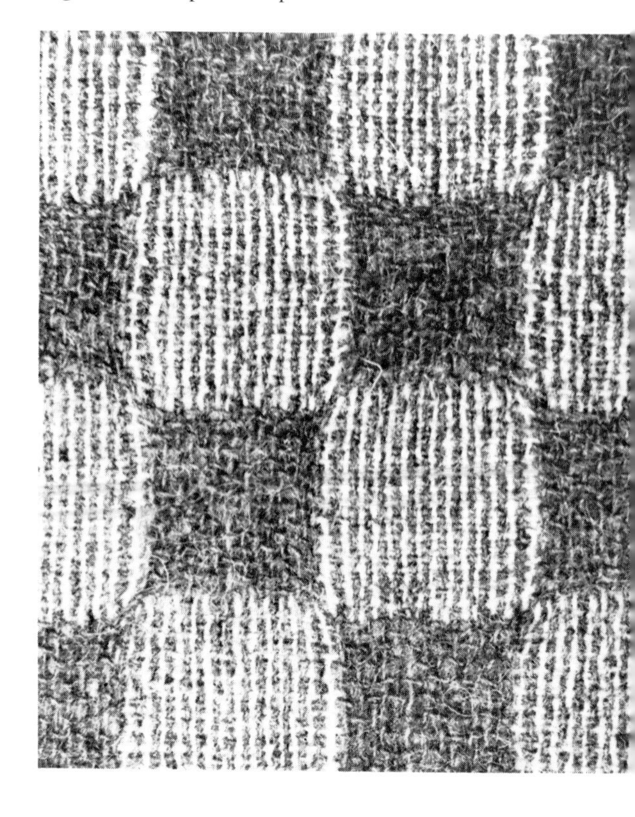

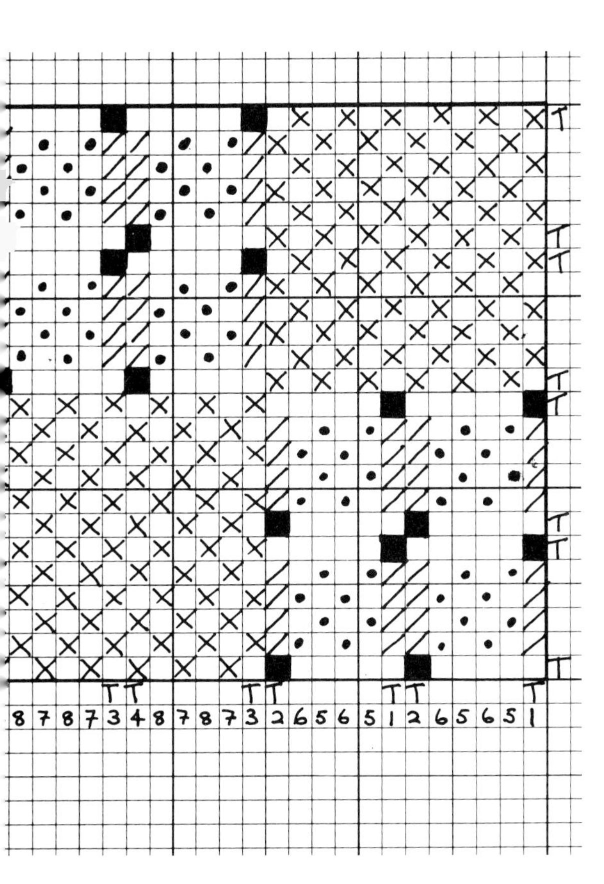

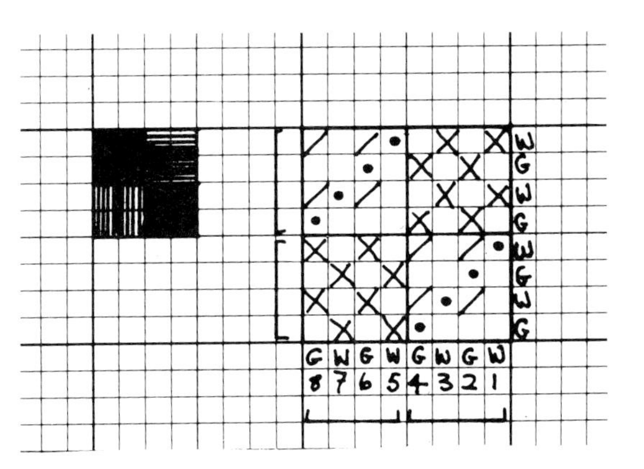

Diag 121 Double plain and plain weave

Diag 122 2 face : 4 back double plain and plain weave

Fig 96 Double plain and bold colour and weave effect

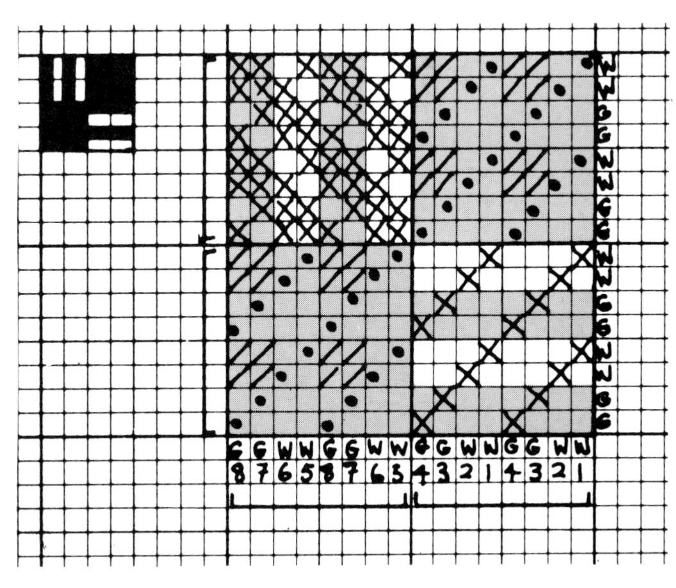

Diag 123 Double plain and bold colour and weave effect

15 CLOTH FINISHING

All cloths, after they are woven and taken off the loom need some form of finishing before they can be put to the use for which they are intended. The finishing processes must ensure that the cloth is free from surface faults, that it is clean, pre-shrunk and stable, and that the fibres, yarns or weave are shown off to their best advantage. In addition, finishing techniques can be applied, which will completely change the appearance and character of the original piece, and therefore finishing can be used as a means of designing. Careful finishing will considerably improve the appearance, handle and wearing qualities of a loom state cloth. Faulty finishing, however, can often not be rectified, spoiling a length completely.

It is a subject that is often overlooked by many handweavers. This is probably due to the fact that a number of the traditional finishing techniques, especially those associated with woollen cloths, are difficult to accomplish in a small studio or home. For this reason, a few commercial firms will undertake to finish handwoven pieces. Unfortunately, this usually involves simply washing and pressing a fabric, and since several lengths have to be treated simultaneously in order that the large industrial machines can operate, no careful individual finishing can be given to your particular cloth. It is better, if possible, to finish your own cloths.

I propose to go through the main finishing processes that can be accomplished by a handweaver in the home. Those which should be applied to all cloths and those specifically given to fabrics woven with various fibres.

MENDING (BURLING)

All fabrics should be meticulously inspected after they are taken off the loom to find any weaving faults, knots or broken ends which need mending. A weaving fault resulting in a long weft float, must have the floating section cut in half, a new thread darned in to replace it, overlapping the original pick by about 1 cm ($\frac{1}{2}''$) on each side. A long warp float is treated in a similar manner. Broken ends also need to be repaired by darning them into the cloth following the interlacings of the weave. Knots must be untied before being darned in to overlap each other. All protruding ends produced during mending or during weaving when joining weft picks, need to be trimmed flush to the surface of the cloth.

It is remarkable how the appearance of a piece is improved once this tidying up process has been done.

FINISHING OF FABRICS WOVEN WITH COTTON, LINEN, MAN-MADE FIBRES AND SILK

Cloths woven from cotton, linen or man-made fibres should be lightly washed, preferably by hand in warm soapy water, followed by a thorough rinsing, to remove any soiling that may have occurred during weaving, and to pre-shrink the fabrics before they are made into garments. Cotton and linen fabrics can be starched if desired to make them crisp. They then need to be ironed. Cotton fabrics need a strong heat, and ironed on the wrong side to avert unnecessary shiny marks on the face. Linen, on the other hand, benefits from being pressed on the face with a hot iron, as its natural sheen increases after the fibres are flattened. Careful ironing from side to side over a damp cloth increases the lustre even more. Man-made fibres generally need the iron set cooler. The handle of all cloths will be softened by this pressing.

Silk fabrics woven from spun silk yarns also need to be pre-shrunk, by hand washing in warm soapy water, followed by several rinses and a very light press on the wrong side with an iron set at a medium heat.

Undyed silk filament yarns may well have the natural sericin still present, making the woven fabric stiff and hard, like organza. The gum can be removed by a process called boiling off. The fabric must be totally immersed and gently agitated in a soapy solution for $1\frac{1}{2}$ hrs, at just below the boil, followed by several rinses to remove all trace of soap. It is then squeezed gently and dried away from direct heat before being ironed with a warm heat. Silk filament fabrics have no noticeable shrinkage.

FINISHING OF FABRICS WOVEN IN WORSTED YARNS OR OIL-FREE WOOL

Fabrics which are woven with worsted, or oil-free wool yarns, do not necessarily need to be washed before they can be used. They do, however, need to have the warp and weft threads 'set' or locked together to prevent thread slippage and bagging of the cloth once it is put into use. This setting process is known as crabbing and it has the effect of maintaining the loom-state appearance of the cloth, with the weave structure and texture clearly visible.

Crabbing is achieved in industry by winding a cloth, at full width, and under tension, around a cotton-covered perforated roller and rotating this for about 10 minutes half immersed in a trough of hot or even boiling water. This process is repeated after the cloth has been re-wound onto another roller. Alternatively, a wet cloth is wound onto a perforated metal roller and steam is blown through until it is dry. It is then cooled by sucking air through, before the process is repeated after the cloth is wound onto another roller. This re-winding is done in both methods to ensure that both ends of the fabric are processed evenly. Both these procedures are difficult to perform easily by a handweaver at home.

An adequate crabbing, however, can be achieved at home by placing the fabric between two damp cloths and pressing it with a very hot iron, leaving the iron in position until all the steam has risen. It is important to lift the iron clear of the cloth before placing it in the next position, rather than sliding the iron across the surface. In order to maintain the warp and weft at right angles to each other, the cloth should be held out taut by pins inserted regularly up either selvage and attached to the ironing board base cloth. If the correct finished width of the cloth is marked on the ironing board, the cloth can be stretched to fit the space each time it is moved forward over the board, thus producing straight edges.

As long as any subsequent washing that may be needed to remove soiling does not subject the cloth to a greater heat than given during crabbing, the crisp, clear appearance will always be maintained.

Washing should be done preferably by hand in warm soft water which has a good soap powder dissolved in it. Agitation should be kept to a minimum. Rinsing must be very thorough in several changes of water which are gradually cooling down in temperature. A spin dryer will remove any excess moisture before the final drying is done on a drying roller, as described under woollen finishing below.

FINISHING OF FABRICS WOVEN FROM WOOLLEN YARNS

The object in finishing a woollen cloth is, first, to remove the oil that has been added to the fibres prior to carding, and secondly, to allow the loom state cloth to close up and shrink quite considerably as a means of giving the cloth more bulk and a softer handle. These objectives are achieved by the two processes of scouring and milling respectively, and most woollen cloths will be given both treatments.

Sometimes, however, the openness of the weave structure of a cloth needs to be maintained, or it is important to prevent irregular distortions that may occur during shrinkage. In these cases a woollen fabric should be crabbed prior to scouring, as described in the section on worsted finishing, after which no milling needs to take place. Quite often it is advisable to subject a plain weave cloth to a crabbing process as this can prevent a cloth from producing an unattractive irregular pattern known as crazing or crow's foot, which sometimes occurs during finishing (Figure 97).

Alternatively, a woollen fabric should be scoured first. A bath is filled with warm water into which is dissolved a scouring agent of pure soap or a soap and soda ash (sodium carbonate) mixture. The length of cloth is submerged and given only very gentle agitation. Dirty cloths can be allowed to soak for about half an hour in the bath. No rough squeezing or rubbing must be done and if the suds subside before the cloth is clean, the fabric must be taken out of the bath and then scoured again in fresh soapy water. The cloth is then rinsed thoroughly in several changes of water which should all be at the same temperature as the now cooled water of the original bath.

Fig 97 Crazing or crows foot

MILLING

The milling or fulling process can bring about a considerable change in the appearance and handle of a woollen cloth. The cloth is consolidated and softened and the weave structure is concealed by varying degrees depending on the amount of milling given. It also makes the cloth more stable and hardwearing. There is a decrease in the length and width of a piece and simultaneously an increase in the weight per square metre/yard. A cloth must have been woven at a looser sett and a wider width to allow for the shrinkage that will occur.

The consolidation is achieved by the movement and friction of the individual fibres. When a wool fibre is wet, it swells out making its overlapping scales stick out. Agitation and a soapy lather causes the fibres to move in the direction of the fibres' root end. After continual movement the scales close up, holding the entangled fibres permanently together. Fine fibres with smaller scales generally felt up more easily than coarser fibres, as do yarns which have only been lightly twisted. Weaves which interlace frequently, such as plain weave, are more difficult to mill than looser constructions such as 2/2 twill.

Milling can be accomplished in the home by folding a damp length of cloth in layers in a bath which is already holding enough warm water with a soapy lather that will just cover the piece. Less soap is needed for the milling process than scouring. The fabric is then trampled under foot, or pummelled with a household sink plunger to create the movement. The water temperature and the lather should be maintained, which may necessitate the bath being refilled. The cloth should be refolded frequently to ensure even milling and inspected often to determine when enough felting has taken place. Over milling is a fault that cannot be rectified. A light milling may only require a few minutes trampling, while a very heavy mill could take an hour.

After milling, the piece must be thoroughly rinsed in several changes of water, ensuring that the now cool water temperature is maintained.

DRYING

Excess moisture can be removed by spin drying, or by wrapping a piece in a towel and patting gently. The final drying in industry is done on a tentering machine. This machine holds the cloth exactly square, and stretches it wide between tiny pins called tenterhooks, while passing it across several steam-heated pipes and hot-air fans.

The essential features of holding the cloth square, straight and wide can be recreated at home with the use of a slatted drying roller (Figure 98). This roller, with a minimum diameter of 15 cm (6 inches), must be about 25 cm (12 inches) wider than the widest piece that you can weave. A clean cotton sheet is wound tightly around the roller. The woven piece, with its face inwards, is then sewn centrally and loosely to the last few centimetres of the cotton cloth. After laying the roller across a table, the piece can be carefully rolled onto the dryer, while simultaneously stretching it sideways by gently stroking it with the palms of the hand. Once the whole piece is rolled on, a straight stick can be used to hold the end in place, binding it down with cotton tapes. The roller is then allowed to stand on its end, away from direct sunlight or radiant heat. It should be turned over onto its opposite end periodically to ensure even drying, and on a long length, the whole piece may need to be unwound, and then rewound starting with the end that was outermost before, for the same reason.

Alternatively, if space is available, the whole piece can be laid out flat on a length of chipboard which is covered with a clean cotton or polythene sheet to prevent staining. Strong drawing pins placed every 2.5 cm (1 inch) along either selvage can be used to hold the cloth straight and even, while it is left to dry on the board away from direct sunlight. This may take several days.

RAISING

If required, the fibrous nature of the milled woollen fabric can be increased by brushing the surface with a stiff bristle brush. The dry fabric is laid flat on a table, held firmly down with heavy weights. The brush is dampened by dipping it in water before being used to brush the cloth systematically in one direction (e.g. to the right), along its length. The brush must be re-dampened frequently. Once the total area has been completed, the process must be repeated, but this time the brushing action is in the opposite direction (to the left), in order to produce an even texture.

Fig 98 Cloth drying roller

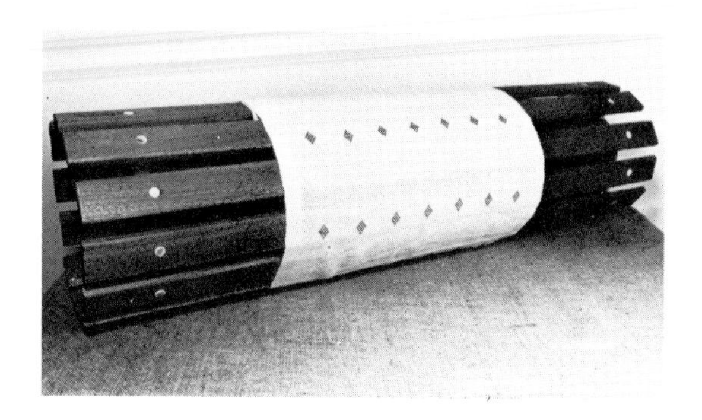

YARN AND EQUIPMENT SUPPLIERS

UK

Yarns and cloth finishing service
Craftsman's Mark Ltd
Tone Dale Mill
Wellington
Somerset TA21 0AW

Yarns
J. Hyslop Bathgate & Co
Victoria Works
Galashiels
Scotland

Wool yarns and cloth finishing service
T. M. Hunter
Brora
Sutherland KW9 6NA
Scotland

Yarns
William Hall & Co
(Monsall) Ltd
177 Stanley Road
Cheadle Hulme
Cheadle
Cheshire SK8 F6R

Yarns
Texere Yarns
College Mill
Barkerend Road
Bradford
West Yorkshire BD3 9AQ

Silk yarns
The Glemsford Silk
Mills Ltd
Mr & Mrs J. Piper
'Silverlea'
Flax Lane
Glemsford
Suffolk CO10 7RS

Silk yarns
H. T. Gaddum & Co Ltd
3 Jordongate
Macclesfield
Cheshire SK10 1EF

Yarns and books
Yarncraft
112A Westbourne Grove
London W2 5RU

Yarns and equipment
The Handweavers
Studio and Gallery
29 Haroldstone Road
London E17 7AN

Equipment
Frank Herring & Sons
27 High West Street
Dorchester
Dorset DT1 1UP

Equipment
Harris Looms
Emmerich (Berlon) Ltd
Wotton Road
Ashford
Kent

Books
K. R. Drummond
30 Hart Grove
London W5

Association of Guilds of
Weavers, Spinners &
Dyers
BCM 963
London WC1N 3XX

Crafts Advisory Committee
28 Haymarket
London SW1Y 45U

Crafts Council
8 Waterloo Place
London SW1

USA and Canada

Yarns
Scotts Woollen Mill
Dept 130
Elmdale Road
Uxbridge
Mass 01569

Yarns and equipment
Harrisville Designs
Box 51A
Harrisville
NH 03450

Yarns and equipment
School Product Co Inc
1201 Broadway
New York
NY 10001

Yarns
Belding Lily Co
PO Box 88
Shelby
NC 28150

Yarns
Stanley Berroco Inc
140 Mendon Street
Uxbridge
Mass 01569

Yarns and equipment
Frederick J. Fawcett Inc
129 South Street
Boston
Mass 02111

Yarns and equipment
Robin & Russ
533 N Adams St
McMinnville
Oregon
97128

Yarns
Oregon Worsted Co
PO Box 02098
Portland
Oregon 97202

Yarns
The Yarn Depot
545 Sutter St
San Francisco
California 94102

Yarns and equipment
Greentree Ranch
163 N Carter Lake Road
Loveland
Colorado 80537

Yarns
William Condon & Sons Ltd
PO Box 129
Charlottetown
Prince Edward Island
Canada C1A 7K3

Yarns and equipment
Northwest Handcrafts House Ltd
110 West Esplanade
North Vancouver
BC Canada

Publishers of Shuttle, Spindle and Dyepot *magazine*
The Handweavers
Guild of America Inc
PO Box 7–374
65 La Salle Road
West Hartford
Conn 06107

Publishers of Handwoven *magazine*
Interweave Press Inc
306 North Washington Avenue
Loveland
Colorado 80537

Australia and New Zealand

Druva Handweaving
373–375 Camberwell Road
Camberwell
Victoria 3124

Loom & Yarn Depot
I. R. Stephens Pty Ltd
24 Whiting Street
Artarmon
NSW 2064

Wondoflex Yarn Craft Centre
1353 Malvern Road
Malvern
Victoria 3144

Village Weaver
29 Sterling Highway
Nedlands
WA 6009

Palm Beach Towel Co
Baden Terrace
O'Sullivan Beach
SA 5166

Australian Thread Pty Ltd
390 St Kilda Road
Melbourne
Victoria

Mohair Farm
PO Box 145
Kangaroo Flat
Victoria 3555

Cambridge Wools Ltd
16–22 Anzac Avenue
PO Box 2572
Auckland
New Zealand

Equipment
Ashford Handicrafts Ltd
Box 180
Ashburton
New Zealand

The Australian Forum for Textile Arts
PO Box 77
University of Queensland
St Lucia
Brisbane
Qld 4067

The Craft Council of Australia
100 George Street
The Rocks
Sydney
NSW 2000

BIBLIOGRAPHY

ALBERS, Anni *On Weaving* (Studio Vista, London) 1974

ALBERS, Anni *On Designing* (Wesleyan University Press, Middletown, Connecticut) 1961

BAINES, Patricia *Spinning Wheels: Spinners and Spinning* (B. T. Batsford, London) 1977

BREARLEY, Alan *The Woollen Industry* (Pitman & Sons Ltd, London) 1965

BREARLEY, Alan *The Worsted Industry* (Pitman & Sons Ltd, London) 1964

BROWN, Rachel *The Spinning Weaving and Dyeing Book* (Routledge and Kegan Paul, London and Henley-on-Thames) 1979

CHADWICK, Eileen *The Craft of Hand Spinning* (B. T. Batsford, London) (Van Nostrand Reinhold, Australia) 1980

FANNIN, Allen A. *Handloom Weaving Technology* (Van Nostrand Reinhold, New York, Cincinnati, Toronto, Melbourne, London) 1979

GADDUM, H. T. & Company Ltd *Silk* (H. T. Gaddum & Company Ltd, 3 Jordongage, Macclesfield, Cheshire) 1979

HALSEY, Mike and YOUNGMARK, Lore *Foundations of Weaving* (David and Charles, Newton Abbott, London, Vancouver) 1975

MILLER, Edward *Textiles, Properties and Behaviour* (B. T. Batsford, London) 1976

MOORMAN, Theo *Weaving as an Art Form, A Personal Statement* (Van Nostrand Reinhold, New York, Cincinnati, Toronto, London, Melbourne) 1975

MORTON, W. E. and WRAY, G. R. *An Introduction to the Study of Spinning* (Longman, London) 1962

POWELL, Marian *1000 (+) Patterns in 4, 6 and 8 Harness Shadow Weaves* (Robin and Russ Handweavers, Oregon) 1976

ROBINSON, A. T. C. and MARKS, R. *Woven Cloth Construction* (The Textile Institute & Butterworths, Manchester and London) 1973 (Plainfield N. J., Textile Book Service) 1973

STRAUB, Marianne *Handweaving and Cloth Design* (Pelham Books, London) 1977

TEXTILE INSTITUTE, The *Identification of Textile Materials* (Fifth Edition) (The Textile Institute, Manchester) 1965

TOVEY, John *The Technique of Weaving* (B. T. Batsford, London) 1975

TOVEY, John *Weaves and Pattern Drafting* (B. T. Batsford, London) 1978

WATSON, William *Textile Design and Colour* (Newnes-Butterworth, London) 1975 (Plainfield N. J., Textile Book Service) 1975

WATSON, William *Advanced Textile Design* (Longman, Green & Co, London) 1965 (Plainfield N. J., Textile Book Service) 1975

WHYTE, Kathleen *Design in Embroidery* (B. T. Batsford, London) (Charles T. Branford, Massachusetts) 1969

WOOL TEXTILE DELEGATION, The *The Tex System* (The Wool Textile Delegation, Bradford, Yorks) 1966

INDEX